KW-479-816

CONTENTS

GLOBALIZATION DEMYSTIFIED:

AFRICA's POSSIBLE DEVELOPMENT FUTURES

7 Day

DAR ES SALAAM UNIVERSITY PRESS LTD.

Published by
Dar es Salaam University Press Ltd.
P.O. Box 35182
Dar es Salaam
TANZANIA

ISBN 9976 60 416 5
ISBN-13: 978-9976-60-416-0

LIST OF ABBREVIATIONS

AAPS	African Association of Political Science
AC	Andean Community
ACP	Africa, Caribbean and Pacific
ACP-EU	Africa, Caribbean and Pacific-European Union
ACRI	African Crisis Response Initiative
ADB	African Development Bank
AIDS	Acquired Immune Deficiency Syndrome
AEC	African Economic Community
AGOA	African Growth and Opportunity Act
AMU	Arab Maghreb Union
APFTA	Asian Pacific Free Trade Area
ASARECA	Association for Strengthening Agricultural Research in Eastern and Central Africa
ASEAN	Association of Southern Asian Nations
AU	African Unity
CACM	Central American Common Market
CAP	Common Agricultural Policy
CARICOM	Caribbean Economic Community
CEAO	West African Economic Community
CEMAC	Central African Economic and Monetary Community
CMA	Common Monetary Area
COMESA	Common Market for Eastern and Southern Africa
CPI	Corruption Perception Index
CSSDCA	Conference on Security, Stability, Development and Cooperation
DAC	Development Assistance Committee (of OECD)
EAC	East African Community
ECA	Economic Commission for Africa
ECCAS	Economic Community of Central African States
ECOMOG	ECOWAS Monitoring Group
ECOWAS	Economic Community of West African States

EEC	European Economic Community
EO	Executive Outcome
EPA	Economic Partnership Agreements
EU	European Union
FDI	Foreign Direct Investment
FTA	Free Trade Area
G7	Group of Seven: USA, UK, Germany, France, Canada, Japan, and Italy
GATS	General Agreement on Trade in Service
GATT	General Agreement on Tariffs and Trade
GDP	Gross Domestic Product
GNP	Gross National Product
GSP	Generalized System of Preference
HIPCs	Heavily Indebted Poor Countries
IDC	International Data Corporation
IGAD	Intergovernmental Authority on Development
IMF	International Monetary Fund
KANU	Kenya African National Union
LAFTA	Latin American Free Trade Area
LAIA	Latin American Integration Association
LDC	Least Developed Country
MAI	Multilateral Agreements on Investment
MERCOSUR	Southern Cone Common Market
MIGA	Multilateral Investment Guarantee Agency
MULPOCs	Multinational Programming and Operational Centers
NAFTA	North American Free Trade Area
NAM	Non-Aligned Movement
NATO	North Atlantic Treaty Organization
NEPAD	New Partnership for Africa's Development
NICs	Newly Industrialized Countries
OAU	Organization of African Unity
ODA	Official Development Assistance
OECD	Organization for Economic Cooperation and Development
PAMSCAD	Program of Action to Mitigate the Social Costs of Adjustment
PMC	Private Military Companies
PSC	Private Security Companies
REC	Regional Economic Community

RPT	Rassemblement Populaire Togolais
SAARC	South Asia Association for Regional Cooperation
SACU	Southern African Customs Union
SADC	Southern African Development Community
SAPs	Structural Adjustment Programs
SSA	Sub-Saharan Africa
STABEX	Commodity Export Stabilization Program
TANU	Tanganyika African National Union
TC	Trilateral Commission
TNBs	Transnational Banks
TNCs	Transnational Corporations
TRIMs	Trade Related Investment Measures
TRIPs	Trade Related Intellectual Property Rights
UDI	Unilateral Declaration of Independence
UNAIDS	Joint United Nations Program on HIV/AIDS
UNCED	United Nations Conference on the Environment and Development
UNCTAD	United Nations Conference on Trade and Development
UNDP	United Nations Development Program
UNESCO	United Nations Educational, Scientific and Cultural Organization
UNICEF	United Nations Children's Fund
UNIDO	United Nations Industrial Development Organization
UPC	Uganda People's Congress
WAIPA	World Association of Investment Promotion Agencies
WEF	World Economic Forum
WMD	Weapons of Mass Destruction
WTO	World Trade Organization

PREFACE
AND
ACKNOWLEDGEMENTS

We live in the era of globalization. Media pundits, corporate elites, academics, civil society activists and policy makers variously cite globalization as the central challenge they face today. Since the early 1990s, the concept has become the stock in trade of every opinion maker. Surprisingly, for a concept of such wide currency, there is considerable debate about what constitutes globalization: its historical origins, geographical spread, intensity and impact, driving force, direction, or its future. In short, there is no consensus definition of globalization. This is a source of confusion and a cause for controversy. But, for all its imprecision, it has acquired the mantle of a new paradigm that seeks to account for the so-called "new world order" at the beginning of the 21st century.

In very general terms, globalization is understood as the widening, deepening, and spreading of worldwide interconnections among all aspects of contemporary social life, from the cultural to the criminal, from the financial, trade, investment, or technological to the spiritual. Central to this conceptualization is a claim that a global economy has emerged or is in the process of emerging, in which distinct national economies and, therefore, domestic strategies of national economic and societal management are becoming irrelevant. The claim is that it is unbridled market forces rather than states that are increasingly and effectively governing almost every social and economic transaction. As a normative prescription, it is claimed that with the triumph of capitalism over communism, there is thus no alternative to capitalism and liberal democracy. It is claimed that globalization will provide the foundations for a dynamic world economic system characterized by free trade, unrestricted capital mobility, open markets and harmonized institutions. This dispensation, it is claimed, promises prosperity for countries that join the system but economic deprivation for those that do not.

These claims are, to say the least, sweeping and false exaggerations. On the one hand, rich countries in the North that have managed to become post-industrial information societies and users of new technology seem to offer ever more favorable conditions to openness and good governance, democracy and human rights. On the other hand, there is a considerable disquiet in many countries in the South concerning the impact of unregulated capitalism on their economies and societies. This was convincingly stated in the United Nations Millennium Declaration of September, 2000: "For while globalization offers great opportunities, at present its benefits are very unevenly shared, while its costs are unevenly distributed." The worldwide anti-globalization campaigns are not only a testimony against neo-liberalism and the New Right, but most importantly, they are a broad movement for the social emancipation of all mankind. The thesis of the present work is to demonstrate that, left unmitigated, the ultimate logic of capitalism and imperialism is the accumulation of wealth and power by the few at the expense of the rest in a given society and in the world as a whole.

This study has four specific objectives. First, we seek to demystify neo-liberal claims that globalization has ushered in a 'new world order,' or a 'new economy' that represents a fundamental departure from the past and is driven by a different systemic logic. Unquestionably, capitalism has undergone profound changes in its national and global forms of development in the post-World War II period. However, this study argues that the internal logic of capitalism has remained essentially the same: production for profits, alienation and exploitation of labor, tendency of capital toward concentration, centralization and outward expansion, and exploitation and domination of weak regions, economies and societies. In our view, the globalization process should be understood primarily as an ideological construct, a convenient myth that helps to justify and legitimize the neo-liberal global project of the transnational capitalist class that seeks to impose unrestrained market capitalism. As a socio-economic process, global capitalism is not entirely driven by the invisible hand of market forces, but rather by the deliberate political, economic and security interests of great powers.

Second, we argue that Africa's marginalization is not a function of limited or insufficient integration into the world economy. The continent has been fully but asymmetrically integrated into the world economy throughout modern history. The study seeks to unmask the injustices and power relations built into the prevailing global order and thereby contribute to the emancipation of the excluded. Whether in the trans-Atlantic slave trade, the colonial conquest and partition, during the Cold War ideological competition between the communist East and the capitalist West, or under the current wave of capitalist globalization, Africa has simply been a victim of exploitation, domination and humiliation by multilateral institutions, transnational corporations and great powers. For the last five hundred years and longer, Africa has not enjoyed the right to develop on its own terms. It is a history of never-ending adjustments to the interests of external forces over which it had marginal influence. The nature and character of the continent's integration into the Europe-based world capitalist system, and the resulting power relationship between these two unequal communities, has largely defined and continues to define the uneven distribution of opportunities, constraints and vulnerabilities for Africa. We argue that this is a manifestly imperialist relationship, characterized by exploitatation and oppression.

Third, we argue that the African continent offers a classic case of two paradoxical and contradictory tendencies - of integration into and marginalization within the global capitalist system. The deeper it integrates, the more it becomes structurally weakened and marginalized. The more it liberalizes its economies and polities, the more it becomes structurally excluded from the dynamics of global investment flows, expanded trade, information technology and vibrant security arrangements. Arguably, the perverse nature of Africa's initial and continued integration into the world economy has engendered an unenviable position in the international division of labor and power across class, gender, ethnicity, sexuality and age. The solution to this socio-economic predicament, it is argued, is not to blindly seek further integration into the world economy, but rather to reconstitute the inchoate, post-colonial states, and change the balance of social forces internally that privilege the popular masses and consolidates their position as the *premium mobile* of social change and transformation.

Fourth, this study argues that the unmitigated forces of globalization and democratization have undermined Africa's institutional and organizational capacity to redefine alternative and emancipatory development strategies. Notwithstanding the miserable record of structural adjustment policies, the 'end of history' diatribes that have been paraded to justify the notion that we now have a world without an alternative, all of these have enormously influenced recently crafted development visions in Africa. It is hardly surprising that the NEPAD vision and the Abuja Treaty for an Economic Community for Africa neither challenge the asymmetrical global governance structures nor defy the received neo-liberal economic orthodoxy.

Prescriptively, this study builds on the work of a number of national and transnational social movements that have over the years pursued collective self-determination. It seeks to stimulate a genuine dialogue on the implications of blind integration into the world economy for the development of Africa. Both the externally imposed policies and home-grown, top-down elitist visions should be studied, interrogated and widely debated before arriving at people-based, democratically negotiated and emancipatory policies and strategies of development for Africa. Innovative development perspectives are only possible if the established patterns are challenged and alternative ideas are developed by social groups and alliances previously excluded from decision-making. This challenge calls for new modes of politics and economic organization that transcend liberal democracy and economics. It is therefore argued that in order to transform the current situation, governance at all levels must be reconstructed by democratic strategies that help to redistribute power and resources, empower the under-represented sections of society and reduce systemic inequalities.

The writing of this book has benefited from the generous intellectual support, encouragement and criticism of many individuals. I am greatly indebted particulary to Professors Julius Nyang'oro of the University of North Carolina at Chapel Hill, Tim Shaw of the University of London and Professor Miti Katabaro of Vista University, South Africa who, at short notice, set aside their work and provided helpful comments on the earlier drafts. Among others who read and offered criticisms on some of the chapters, I must mention Dr. Musa Abutudu, Program Officer at the African Association of Political Science, Pretoria, Dr. John Tesha of the International Migration Office, Pretoria, and the 1997 African Studies Association panel on globalization. I also wish to acknowledge the editorial criticisms I received from Dr. Azaveli Lwaitama who belongs both to the Department of Foreign Languages and Linguistics as well as the Philosophy Unit at the University of Dar es Salaam. To all of them I owe a considerable debt. While this book could not have been produced without the assistance of those mentioned above, I am solely responsible for the opinions and any errors of fact or judgment which remain.

The overall argument of this book has never appeared in print before, although some of the core ideas in chapters 3, 4 and 5 appeared in my previous papers: "Globalization and Africa's Futures: Toward Structural Stability, Integration and Sustainable Development" (*AAPS Occasional Paper Series* 5 (2) 2001), and "Globalization, Liberalization and Africa's Marginalization" (*AAPS Occasional Paper Series* 4 (1) 1999). It is further acknowledged that some sections of Chapter 3 were published in "Africa's Debt Bondage: A Case for Total Cancellation" (*Eastern and Southern African Research Review* 17 (1) 2001); in "Globalization and Marginalization in Euro-African Relations in the Twenty-first Century" (in Ikubolajeh Logan, B. (Ed). *Globalization, the Third World State and Poverty Alleviation*. Aldershot: Ashgate, 2002:31-46); and as "New Partnership Agreement between ACP and EU: Unresolved Issues" (in *Cooperation South* #2 2000). All the same, the book was written in its entire present form in Harare, Zimbabwe and in Pretoria, South Africa during 2001-2003, while I served as Executive Secretary of the African Association of Political Science (AAPS). This is partly why I would also like to express my gratitude to the University of Dar es Salaam for granting me the relevant extended leave of absence from my regular teaching duties.

When all is said and done, however, my greatest debt is to my wife Frieda and our children Afrika, Dan, Samora, Happiness and Muta who shared the discomforts of both my long absence from home, and while at home, my inattention to the practical aspects of our family life. I dedicate this book to them with gratitude and love.

CHAPTER 1

AFRICA's DEVELOPMENT FUTURES:
THEORETICAL QUESTION MARKS

Introduction: Africa and the Emerging World Order

....The need for constantly expanding the market of its products chases the bourgeoisie over the whole surface of the globe. It must nestle everywhere, settle everywhere, and establish connections everywhere. The bourgeoisie has, through its exploitation of the world market, given a cosmopolitan character to production and consumption in every country. To the great chagrin of reactionaries, it has drawn from under the feet of industry the national ground on which it stood (Marx and Engels, 1970:56).

As the opening statement from the *Communist Manifesto* aptly sums it all, Karl Marx and Friedrich Engels emphasized the intrinsic logic of capitalism as an exploitative, oppressive and global system from its early beginnings. Despite epochal surface change manifestations, the fundamental logic of capitalism and capitalist relations has essentially remained unchanged. At the turn of the twentieth century, John Hobson (1905:94) in his book, *Imperialism: A Study,* highlighted the use of the state machinery by private capital interests to secure economic gains outside their countries. He noted that in the process of its growth and expansion, capitalism exploits, dominates and controls other relatively weaker classes, peoples and nations in its trail. Thus, for the last five hundred years and longer, the historical record of Africa's participation in the ever-expanding world capitalist system has been disappointing.

The nature and character of Africa's integration into the modern world system, and the resulting asymmetrical power relationships between Europe and Africa, has largely been defined and continues to be defined by its uneven share of opportunities, constraints and vulnerabilities. Whether in the trans-Atlantic slave trade, the colonial conquest and partition, during the Cold War ideological competition between the West and East, or under the current wave of capitalist globalization, Africans have been pawns in the political chess game of great powers. Regardless of the epochal dynamics, the continent's changing roles were essentially structured by unequal, exploitative and oppressive relationships with relatively more powerful actors from outside the continent. It is a history of perpetual adjustment to the interests of external forces. Africa's peoples have largely become victims of contradictions not of their own making. In typical Thucydidesian terms, "…. The strong did what they could and the weak suffered what they must" (Thucydides, 1951:331). In other words, for the last four centuries, Africa has never enjoyed the right to develop on its own terms.[1] The contemporary focus by neo-liberal intellectuals on globalization as a new phenomenon may seem like too much ado about nothing.

However, some unprecedented developments in the last two decades of the twentieth century have tended to have some interesting impacts. These developments have included: the demise of the Soviet Union as a nation and superpower, the collapse of the Warsaw Pact and communism in the Eastern Bloc, the unification of Germany, the new and expanded role of NATO, the emergence of the United States as the hegemonic military power in the world,[2] the further rise of the East Asian economies, the emergence of information and communication technology, and expansion of international economic as well as political integration under the banner of neo-liberalism. All of these developments have created temporary false hopes that these happenings would usher in new and progressive dynamics in the conduct of international politics and the management of the world economy.

Under the apparently new political dispensation, it was widely hoped, particularly in the South that the post-Cold War geopolitics would give rise to a surge of worldwide enthusiasm for a safer, cleaner, friendlier and more empathetic world.[3] It was also hoped that the end of the Cold War would allow for a significant portion of the emerging 'peace-dividend' to finance sustainable and democratic development and eliminate the scourge of poverty and underdevelopment throughout the world. Above all, it was envisaged that, with the apparently increased possibilities for consensus in the Security Council, the United Nations system (U.N.) would play an enhanced role in international life, in keeping the peace, promoting democratic global governance, regulating the world economy, furthering development, or protecting the environment. The U.N. began an encouraging series of world conferences dealing with some of the greatest development issues of our age: poverty, population, children, gender, cities and the environment.

It is important to put these major global changes in perspective. Indeed, there is little doubt that the end of the Cold War has signaled a new configuration of global power, more complex international structures, a changed world agenda and actors, and new contradictions. The bipolar system of managing global affairs has vanished. Although the United States continues to assert its unquestioned military power as the world's police, its economic leadership and legitimacy is increasingly questionable.[4] Moreover, while the East-West conflict is over, the North-South divide has only widened further, giving rise to bloody inter-ethnic conflicts, chaotic disintegration of states, growing organized crime, insecurity linked to the proliferation of nuclear weapons, mass migration, the spread of deadly diseases and the widening of North-South inequality gaps, along with a corresponding weakening of sovereignty and of the states' capacity for social control and economic management.

At the same time, the global neo-liberal order has emerged as the dominant mode of economic regulation and ideology. It has imposed new notions of societal, political and economic organization throughout the world, which are based on certain assumptions about the state, market and society. The collapse of communism in Europe in 1989-90 was a turning point. It added to the world capitalist economy an additional 30 former communist countries with a combined population of about 400 million people. Capitalist blind belief in free trade, deregulation and privatization has become the credo of economic orthodoxy for the entire world. The so-called 'globalization process,' is manifested by the increased mobility of capital and production facilities across borders and the growing liberalization of trade, the restructuring of the European welfare states, dramatic progress in communication technology, and a considerable enhancement of the role of multilateral institutions. In the major industrialized economies of the North, there is a vehement political attack on big government as being incompetent, oppressive, and even undesirable. This was apparently vindicated by the claimed failure of centralized planning in the former Soviet Union and other communist countries in the 1980s.

The above contradictory developments in the global political economy were interpreted by some influential observers in the North as harbingers of a new and qualitatively different stage of global capitalism. More poignantly, they prompted former President George Bush (senior) of the United States to declare a 'new world order' in 1991 at the beginning of the Gulf War. With the Cold War competition over, the United States' leadership hoped to consolidate its hegemonic role and establish cohesion and stability in the world system in order to promote and enhance its vital national interests. In fact, the President's position had earlier been embellished with a quasi-religious intellectual status by Francis Fukuyama who claimed that – "what we may be witnessing is – the end of history as such: that is, the end point of mankind's ideological evolution and the universalization of Western liberal democracy as the final form of human government." He further claimed that "there is no other alternative" and, therefore, all other peoples of the world must adapt to the rationality and efficiency requirements of the markets (Fukuyama, 1989:4).

To be sure, the Soviet model has been thoroughly discredited, not only as an ideology of development but equally, and perhaps more seriously, as an ideology of nation-building for countries in the South. Viewed retrospectively, the new century and millennium were perceived to have signaled the beginning of a new world order because neo-liberal economics, bourgeois democracy and Western social values were claimed to have triumphed over all other social systems, particularly communism. To hard-core neo-liberal ideologues, Western values were to be accepted globally, not only as universal and natural but, most disturbingly, as synonymous with development and civilization. Whatever the scale and magnitude of suffering some sections of society were to endure, it was perceived as but the necessary price for a better future.

Similar wildly optimistic beliefs held sway in the South. On the African continent, where economic stagnation, military and civilian dictatorships, and violent conflict had long been the defining realities, the appearance of profound political changes in the international system was greeted with unquestioning optimism. For some observers, the globalization of markets would progressively reduce inequalities within and between states and increase cooperation through economic interdependence. International institutions would be strengthened and democratized, since states would increasingly perceive that their interests would be better served through cooperation rather than competition. For others, the new international political dispensation held the potential for the inauguration of the 'second liberation.' In the words of Crawford Young, "at the beginning of the 1990s, Africa faced a common conjuncture, the imperative of democratization, broadly defined. Battered by economic decline and weakened by political decay, the African state faced narrow choices: the political opening was no longer an option but an obligation" (Young, 1994:230). Since then, the rhetoric of democracy has moved to the center of political discourse and debates throughout Africa.

Ruling parties and governments in various countries on the continent have begun to move in the direction of establishing at least some aspects of a democratic political system and have publicly pledged themselves to the values of democracy. Even where incumbent regimes have managed and manipulated democratization to preserve their power, some parameters of politics have changed. Indeed, there is a discernible change in the political agenda on the African continent.

The above epoch-making developments notwithstanding, and despite Africa's near total integration into the world economy, the continent remains poor, marginal, powerless and vulnerable to almost every one of the major global trends. Africa is the least prepared continent to participate meaningfully in former U.S. President George Bush's new world order. As will be demonstrated in later chapters, whatever aspect one considers, wealth, power, security, foreign investment, trade, health, democratic governance, the environment, the information revolution, or the skilled labor force, Africa's prospects give little cause for jubilation. Globalization, past and present, has forced the majority of Africans into strategies of no more than survival, denying millions of people even the right to life. Its logic has entrenched and accentuated grotesque inequalities both nationally and internationally, and fueled social conflict.

The depth of the current crisis in Africa is, to say the least, alarming. In fact, Africa is not just the poorest continent in the world today; it is the only one in a state of decline. It suffers from a multitude of structural vulnerabilities and domestic governance ineptitude: exploitation and underdevelopment, powerlessness, mass poverty, undemocratic global governance, unfair trade, parasitic investment and aid practices, gross mismanagement of economies, corrupt and undemocratic regimes, and suffocation of civil society. It is not surprising that the continent's overall economic performance, as well as its international political and geo-strategic standing, continue to lag behind that of other regions of the world. Its share of global economic activity is not only small but, most disturbingly, declining. After two decades of costly implementation of structural adjustment programs, Africa seems to be sinking further into the dungeon of political, social and economic decay. The continent scores poorly on every major human development indicator: life expectancy, infant mortality and school enrollment. Above all, Africa is defined by diminishing economic growth, growing unemployment, high debt levers, balance of payment problems, a falling share of world trade and adverse terms of trade. Although the continent accounts for about 10 percent of the world's population, its economies account for only 1 percent of the world's GDP.

Even more telling is the fact that the promotion of unrestrained market forces has not only exacerbated existing inequalities between North and South, but it has also generated new ones. Social inequalities in the distribution of economic resources and income are widely seen to be on the increase. The resulting polarization on a world scale is unparalleled in all previous history. In its *1992 Human Development Report*, the United Nations Development Program (UNDP, 1992) determined that, from 1960 to 1989, those countries with the richest 20 percent of the world's population saw their share of the global income rise from 70.2 percent to 82.7 percent, while the share of the poorest 20 percent shrank from 2.3 percent to 1.4 percent. Quite apart from the growth of average incomes at the global level, the deterioration in socio-economic conditions is reflected in the persistent growth in the numbers of those living in poverty, whether measured in absolute numbers or as a percentage of the population. In fact, both the incidence and depth of poverty have been so serious that the World Bank (1991) devoted its *1991 World Development Report* to global poverty. The report predicted that, given the continent's exceptionally high population growth rates (over 3 percent a year) and low economic growth rates, as many as 100 million more Africans could be living in poverty at the turn of the twenty-first century.

At the rate of progress recorded in the 1990s, there are few African countries that are likely to realize any of the United Nations' Millenium Development Goals by the year 2015. Indeed, the future of the continent is marked by uncertainty and despair. The sense of widespread disillusionment has been captured by the concept of 'Afro-pessimism'. For most critical observers, the question that is repeatedly asked is whether or not Africa can survive and overcome the ongoing economic crisis and social decay.

In the ideological and diplomatic realm, one can scarcely fail to notice that Africa's role and influence have noticeably shrunk. As will be argued, the Cold War enabled the countries in the South to exercise some degree of autonomy and to command respect. Even relatively small and insignificant African states were able to exploit superpower ideological conflict in order to advance their various strategic interests, however limited. Moreover, the Cold War offered African countries certain trade-offs and gave them the impression of relative autonomy in the international system. It also allowed them to exert some influence on the international system through various international forums such as the Non-Aligned Movement (NAM), the U.N.

General Assembly, the United Nations Conference on Trade and Development (UNCTAD), and the United Nations Industrial Development Organization (UNIDO). With the end of the Cold War and with the United States as the only superpower, NAM, for example, has lost its ideological and political significance. Its bargaining power and leverage, never great to begin with, has steadily diminished in the post-Cold War era. Equally significant, the independence of the United Nations has been severely circumscribed, as evidenced by the Gulf War and the US-Iraq standoff, in which the premier world organization was used to legitimize U.S. foreign policy interests (Hutchful, 1991; Ravenhill, 1985; Ihonvebere, 2000).

More specifically, Africa has lost key advocates for the South's causes in major international organizations, particularly in the U.N. The former Soviet Union and other East European socialists were often ideological allies of Africa in world affairs. On most issues of concern to Africa, such as decolonization, the struggle for a new international economic order and the democratization of global governance, members of the old Warsaw Pact could be relied on to vote with those forces in Africa that were eager for a change in the nature and structure of the asymmetrical world system. The collapse of communism in Eastern Europe, the disintegration of the Soviet Union and the dismantling of the Warsaw Pact have produced an Eastern Europe far more likely to join the expanding European Union and abide by the wishes of Washington than to heed the yearnings of powerless Africa and the South (Mazrui, 1999:167-168). As will be argued in subsequent chapters, with the conclusion of the Cold War and the end of ideological conflicts, Africa's geopolitical importance seems to be rapidly declining. It will be further argued that, while the East-West confrontation is over, the North-South divide will only deepen and widen. This divide is likely to become the central theme of international politics, as it will become the single greatest threat to world peace and security in the 21st century.

As will also become apparent in subsequent pages, the continent's share of world output has remained low and the domestic market has shrank, due largely to an unfair international trade regime, crippling debt, unproductive foreign investment, as well as pervasive conflicts and unpredictable domestic policy regimes. In the words of Thomas Callaghy, "for the most dynamic actors in a rapidly changing world economy, even a neocolonial Africa is not of much interest anymore, especially after the amazing changes wrought in Eastern Europe and elsewhere beginning in 1989." According to Callaghy, "the African crisis really should be left to the international financial institutions as a salvage operation: if it works, fine, if not, so be it; the world economy will hardly notice" (Callaghy, 1993:221). This unfortunate painting of Africa, extreme as it might look, seems to be the overriding perception among the captains of world finance and industry and in the corridors of power in the major capitals of the world. The purpose of this work, therefore, is to explore and examine what possible futures the continent is likely to face in the context of the current wave of capitalist globalization.

What is New About Globalization?

What is quaintly called 'globalization' came into popular usage in the second half of the 1980s in connection with the huge surge of foreign direct investment (FDI) by transnational corporations (TNCs) and speculative capital investment by transnational banks (TNBs). With all its uncertainties and inadequacies as a concept, it usefully calls attention to a series of developments associated with the on-going dynamics of economic restructuring and political re-configuring at the global level. Contemporary neo-liberal observers tend to claim that the current wave of capitalist accumulation is new and unique. They claim that, whereas the world economy was composed previously of separate local and national economies, from the beginning of the 1980s there was a surge of capitalist accumulation on a global scale (World Bank, 2002).

Although FDI has been around for centuries, the claim is that it is only from the early 1980s that it expanded significantly and much more rapidly than world trade and global economic output. Recent analyses indicate that, for every dollar that goes into trade, well over one hundred dollars go into speculative operations completely disconnected from the real economy! It is also claimed that national economies have been superseded by an expansion of international integration driven by information and transportation technologies. Unlike previous epochs of capitalism, the current wave of globalization is understood as the latest stage of capitalism, in which the authority and capacity of states have been eroded differentially, and various global actors are replacing states in determining well being entitlement on a global scale. Finally, it is claimed that the recent technological revolutions have radically modified work processes and affected the structures of social classes and their perceptions of capital-labor relations (Held et al. 1992; Klak, 1998).

The ideological debate about globalization revolves around whether the present stage of capitalism represents a new epoch or is basically a continuation of the past that can be understood through existing analytical categories of capitalist development. There are essentially two major lines of analysis. On the one hand, there is the functionalist neo-liberal explanation of the current wave of capitalist development. At the descriptive level, this refers to globalization as the widening and deepening of the international flow of trade, capital, technology, information, values and cultural practices within a single integrated global market. As a prescription, globalization is understood as the liberalization of national and global markets in the belief that the free flow of trade, capital and information will produce the best outcome for growth and human welfare. In short, the so-called 'new world order' is portrayed as both inevitable and necessary, the driving force of the development process and harbinger of future prosperity. Whether used descriptively, prescriptively, or both, globalization is presented with an air of inevitability, betraying its historical and ideological roots as well as its underlying class character (Ohmae, 1990; Sassen, 1996; Huntington; 1996).

On the other hand, there are radical writers who tend to dismiss globalization as a useful analytical concept. It is seen as an ideological tool strategically employed to obfuscate the dominant class interest behind it, rather than accurately describe and explain what is going on worldwide. Instead, the current wave of capitalist expansion and integration is understood as but an outcome of a consciously pursued strategy, a political project of a transnational capitalist class, anchored in various institutional structures set up and consolidated since the end of World War II in order to serve and advance its interests. In this regard, the historic, dialectic and logic of capitalism are highlighted and explained. The radical representation of globalization also maintains that, by its very nature, capitalism engenders polarization. The logic of capitalist integration of other technologically weaker economies and societies produces growing inequalities and political consciousness among different members of the system (Petras and Veltmeyer; 2001; Boswell and Chase-Dunn, 2000; Wallerstein, 1974; Pijl, 1998).

In this regard, the opening quotation from the *Communist Manifesto* has two important functions. The first is to remind the reader that, without a strong historical background, the current processes of globalization will be simply explained and understood as a new phenomenon without roots or precedents. Its second and equally important function is to emphasize the point that a more historical approach allows us to appreciate the fact that the current wave of globalization has come into being through complex historical processes which have formed and transformed our economics, ideology, politics and various rationalizations. It is important to note also that, whereas colonialism was repeatedly justified by such silly rationales as 'the white man's burden' and 'civilizing missions,' the current phase of capitalist expansion is rationalized by a whole repertoire of concepts and slogans such as 'the end of history,' 'universal civilization' and 'the inevitability of capitalism' in which markets, democracy and prosperity are said to have put an end to conflict, authoritarian regimes and the reign of necessity. Samuel Huntington even claims that Western civilization is the universal civilization:

> The concept of a universal civilization is a distinctive product of Western civilization. In the 19ᵗʰ century, the idea of "the white man's burden" helped to justify the extension of Western political and economic domination over non-western societies. At the end of the 20ᵗʰ century, the concept of universal civilization helps to justify Western cultural domination of other societies and the need for those societies to ape Western practices and institutions (Huntington, 1996:66).

In order to fully appreciate what is 'new' about the so-called 'new global economy,' 'globalization' and the 'new world order,' one must be entirely clear about what is 'old.' By the same token, in order to understand systemic continuity and change, one must put recent events into a proper historical perspective. Following the world system framework elaborated in the works of Immanuel Wallerstein (1974; 1979), Samir Amin (1975; 1998) and Christopher Chase-Dunn (1998), it is posited that, when capitalism comes onto the scene in history, it does so as a world system. As a result, the study starts by postulating the world economy as the primary unit of analysis, with its own systemic trends and cycles that are discernible only over a long period. By determining the locations of production and distribution of wealth in the world economy, capitalism defines and shapes global patterns of hierarchy, power and inequality. As an analytical framework, the world system seeks also to explain not only the sources of capital accumulation, but also to account for the origins of global poverty, inequality and struggles on a world scale.

Like the classical theory of imperialism, the world systems framework seeks to explain the structure of the world economy in terms of the struggles between the core capitalist political economies in the North and dependent peripheries of the South. As it creates wealth and opportunities for a few, it simultaneously sets the context for conflict, exploitation, domination, disintegration, marginalization, exclusion, fascism, resurgent nationalism and wars against the vital interests of the vast majority of global society. The protests and demonstrations against the World Bank and the World Trade Organization (WTO) in Seattle in November, 1999, the IMF and World Bank Washington D.C. in April, 2000, and similar such protests in Europe and the Unites States in 2001 and 2002 are globally organized protests against global capitalism.

As pointed out earlier, the African continent is not a newcomer to the phenomenon of capitalist globalization and integration. It was perversely integrated into the modern world system from the very start, in the mercantilist phase of early capitalism. From then onwards, the development trajectories of the African continent have come to be determined by the demands and constraints of the imposed capitalist division of labor. The North reserved to itself the roles of industrial production, finance and technology, and imposed the task of primary production and export of raw materials on the South. World system analysts argue that the modern world system emerged in the 16th century following the expansion by conquest of Western Europe's capitalist economic system into Central and South America and the establishment of far-reaching trade links with Eastern Europe and Asia. The core was initially made up of Portugal, Spain, France and England. The major periphery of that time was colonial America, where an outward looking export economy was established, dominated by the European Atlantic merchant capitalists. The mainstays of this economy were sugar, tobacco and cotton based on slave labor in North and South America, and in the European-owned plantations in Mauritius, Reunion and the Seychelles. Furthermore, through the supply of slaves, large parts of sub-Saharan Africa were integrated into the global system in the most destructive way. The slave trade led to the dismantling of earlier, larger state organizations that were replaced by small brutal military systems with permanent wars between them. Africa's underdevelopment is, in large part, attributable to a decrease in population to the extent that it is only now that the sub-continent has recovered the proportion of the global population that it had around 1500 (Wallerstein, 1974; Hopkins, 1982; 1972; Blackburn, 1998).

The second phase of Africa's integration into the modern world system was inaugurated by the industrial revolution in Europe, which had begun in the last third of the 18th century. The new mode of capitalist accumulation attributed special functions to the subjugated peoples. Africa was forced to supply raw materials and agricultural produce, import capital for the creation of infrastructure, and to buy manufactured products made necessary by the destruction of Africa's handcrafts and the subjugation of indigenous agriculture to capitalist demands. Subsequent political independence had only a negligible impact on the mode of economic integration and accumulation. The unequal vertical relationship instituted by colonialism has continued with only minor interruptions. We shall return to this argument in Chapter Two.

Modern World Systems Revisited

The world system framework provides tools of analysis to examine the contemporary global political economy. As was noted above, it defines the world capitalist economy in terms of production and exchange relations, which bind states under their yoke across the globe, brings capitalist and non-capitalist formations alike under its sway, and determines the nature and course of these states' development as dictated by the most powerful state or a coalition of states in any given historical epoch. It further conceives of the world capitalist economy as a single world system, based on economic processes created in 16th century Europe and expanded until those processes encompassed the entire world at the turn of the last century. The political superstructure of this system is a set of sovereign states (and previously colonies and semi-colonies) defined and constrained by their membership in the inter-state network. The modern world system is essentially defined by three structural constants: the capitalist world economy, an inter-state network and the core/periphery hierarchy. No fundamental transformations can occur without replacing these elements. While the scale of the world economic system increases as it expands, its organic structure gets larger without fundamentally changing.

Let us look more closely at each structural constant. The first constant is that the modern world economy is an economic system in which the capitalist mode of production is the central feature of the system as a whole. As a socio-economic system, capitalism has a deep structure and a set of underlying causal tendencies of development. Its first attribute is commodity production. Capitalist commodity production is defined in the Marxist sense as the production of commodities for profitable sale in a price-setting market. The motive force behind capitalist production is accumulation in private hands. The continuous process of private capital accumulation is the *differentia specifica* of the modern world system. The second attribute is the class nature of capital-labor relations. In a capitalist system, the direct producers are no longer in possession of their own means of subsistence and what binds them to the processes of surplus extraction is no longer political command, but rather the requirement to sell their labor power in order to gain this subsistence. The exploitation of labor, which is the basis of capital accumulation, leads to class conflict in the social sphere, class struggles, and ultimately to major social transformations (Wallerstein, 1979; Hobsbawm, 1992).

The initial adoption of a 'Fordist' regime of accumulation and regulation in Europe resulted in a system of mass production of consumer goods and services as well as the scientific management of labor at the point of production within diverse types of nation-states. The creation of a national market was the substance of modern nations and the nation-state system. Securing the nation-state also meant laying down a transport and communications system as a foundation for economic activity. The construction of roads and canals, railways and telegraphic systems became synonymous with nation building. Above all, the national regime of accumulation involved the abolition of 'internal' tariffs, tolls and customs duties and the destruction of pre-capitalist property relations. The mechanisms that facilitated exploitation of foreign nations and peoples were colonial conquest, foreign investment in raw materials, manufacturing and services, which, by way of cheap labor and raw materials, obtained high rates of profits for transnational monopolies based in advanced capitalist countries. It is this economic essence of global capitalist accumulation that sets in motion the social, political and ideological context in which capitalism prospers and sows the seeds of its destruction.

It is important to emphasize that before World War II capital was largely national in character. Corporate interests, as national interests, were jealously guarded at home and abroad by such means as strong armies, tariff barriers, currency controls and citizenship. The two World Wars put an end to all this. The United States restructured the post-war world economy to reflect its own interests. The world representing national corporations only colluded to produce commercial warfare. The creation of the U.N., the International Monetary Fund (IMF), the World Bank and the General Agreement on Tariffs and Trade (GATT) were intended to pre-empt further wars between core countries, and promote liberal democracy and decolonization, private property and to manage global economic liberalism.

It will be argued that one of the most visible characteristics of the current wave of capital accumulation is the disaggregation of production into many sub-units and sub-processes carried out by many firms spread throughout communities, regions and nations worldwide, as described aptly by Kenichi Ohmae (1985) and Gary Gereffi (1994).[5] The accelerating pace of technological development shortens the life cycle of many producers, while corporations have to spend more on research and development to keep abreast of technological development and the period in which corporations may recover such costs keep on shrinking. Therefore, they launch new products in all core markets right from the start to recover their investment before a new product replaces theirs in the market. To reduce the risks involved in research and development, corporations seek and for a while, can obtain, strategic alliances among their would-be competitors. Now, as in the past, while production is dispersed in many communities, regions and nations, the financial and research capacity and control remains concentrated in the world cities located largely in the core regions of the world system.

The second decisive structural constant of the modern world system is that capital accumulation takes place at an inter-state level. Modern states emerged in Western Europe and its colonial territories in the 18th and 19th centuries, although their origins date back to the late 16th century, and the conclusion of the Thirty Years War (1618-1648), which forced imperial dynasties to become sovereign states.[6] These modern states distinguished themselves initially from earlier forms of political rule by claiming a distinctive symmetry and correspondence between sovereignty, territory and legitimacy. For the subsequent period, these states were in interaction with one another in a complex set of shifting alliances and wars. Changes in the relative power of states could upset any temporary alliances, leading to a restructuring of the balance of power. It was during this period that territorial sovereignty, the formal equality of states, non-intervention in the internal affairs of other recognized states and state consent as the foundation stone of international legal agreement became the core principles of the modern international order. The consolidation of this order across the world occurred after World War II with the decolonization process (Hobsbawm, 1992; Kennedy, 1987).

By and large, the rules of the international economy are set by the most powerful states. Hegemonic stability theory holds that imbalanced power tends to produce peace. When there is a strong dominant power, there will be stability, but when that strong power begins to slip and a new challenger rises, war is more likely. Following this logic, one can argue that since the birth of capitalism, there have been repeated attempts by powerful states to achieve hegemony in the inter-state system in order to impose specific norms of inter-state behavior and facilitate acceptance of what is then taken as international collective goods (Koehane, 1980; Gilpin, 1981; Kindleberger, 1981).[7] In the 19th century, Great Britain was the strongest of the major economies. In the monetary area, the Bank of England adhered to the gold standard, which set a stable framework for world money. Britain also enforced freedom of the seas for navigation and commerce, and provided a large open market for world trade until the beginning of the Great Depression.

William Thompson (1988:7) points out that "global wars were fought to decide who will provide systemic leadership, whose rules will govern, whose policies will shape systemic allocation processes, and whose sense or vision of order will prevail." The most successful core nations achieved hegemony by having strong and convergent business class interests which unified state policy behind a drive for successful commodity production and trade with the world market (Chase-Dunn, 1981; Wallerstein, 1983; Modelski, 1978). Hegemonic cycles of the world economy have so far led to the ascendancy to the hegemonic power status at various times of Portugal, the Netherlands, the United Kingdom, and the United States.

In a broader sense, during the period of hegemonic orders, respective powers in the inter-state system tended to act as a constant force to encourage and, if necessary, to coerce other states into pursuing certain policies rather than others. A high degree of international stability was maintained as long as changes in the distribution of economic and military power did not give individual states an incentive to seek the transformation of the system. Such disequilibria have typically been resolved by hegemonic wars waged to change the international structure. Moreover, hegemonic powers tended to be strong advocates of global 'liberalism.' Then as now, largely because of their superior economic and military power, they came forward as defenders of the principle of the free flow of the factors of production throughout the world economy. In general, hegemonic powers have also tended to be hostile to mercantilist restrictions on trade, including the existence of overseas colonies for the stronger countries. They extended this liberalism to a generalized endorsement of liberal parliamentary institutions, political restraints on the arbitrariness of bureaucratic power, and civil liberties. As would be expected, all these values were enforced as long as they did not compromise the overall vital national interests of the hegemonic power (Kindleberger, 1981).

The modern world system tends to operate through a geographical division of labor between the rich core regions and the poor peripheral areas. This constitutes the third, but equally fundamental, constant of a center/periphery hierarchical division of labor in the inter-state system. This is an historically constructed stratification composed of core industrial states in the North, dependent peripheral areas and the intermediate semi-periphery in the South. It was brought into existence by extra-economic compulsion, plunder, conquest and colonization, and it is maintained and sustained by various institutional regimes and politico-military manipulation. Peripheral areas are seen not as pre-capitalist but rather as integrated, exploited and essential parts of the larger system. They can be seen as relations of exploitation and domination. The core economies specialize in the production of goods and services which have high value added, and using highly skilled and free labor. The periphery and semi-periphery states are mainly former colonies and semi-colonies whose production structures are labor intensive, and who utilize unskilled and often coerced labor (Chase-Dunn, 1981; Wallerstein, 1974).

The modern world system framework further posits that semi-peripheral countries, such as the newly industrialized countries (NICs) of South Korea, Singapore and Taiwan, act as a buffer between the core and the periphery. Under certain conditions and in the context of certain politico-economic processes, some peripheral states can be transformed into semi-peripheral ones. Such transformations, or mobility, take place within the context and logic of the system as a whole and as a consequence of the dictates of the dominant state in the world system at a given historical period. They are differentiated from the periphery by their more significant industrial base and productivity, and by strong and capable states. State intervention in the economy and society is very critical and visible. Semi-peripheries produce and import high technology products and services from the core and, in return, export semi-manufactured and fully manufactured products to the core. They also import raw materials from the periphery and export manufactured end products to the core countries. In recent years, they have managed to develop capacities to produce high technology products and directly compete with core economies. The semi-peripheries play an important stabilizing role in the world economy. They tend to depolarize the relations between the core and the periphery. Chase-Dunn (1998) argues that, because their economies increasingly and differentially profit from the world economy, semi-peripheries have a strong vested interest in the endurance of the *status quo*.

But how are these peripheral and semi-peripheral political economies permanently subordinated to and exploited by the core countries? In strictly economic terms, both processes are sustained by the huge transfer of value, i.e. wealth, from the workers and peasants of the periphery to the transnational corporations of the core countries through exploitative production and exchange relations. The low cost of labor in African agriculture, mining, industry and services, for example, helps to create colossal returns on capital invested in these countries. At the same time, at the level of exchange of goods and services, the value of what is exchanged is neither determined by the market mechanism nor by the law of supply and demand and, consequently, prices neither gravitate toward nor deviate from their value. These economic laws and practices tend to operate mainly between economies of more or less equal development, and in which the cost of labor roughly corresponds. In the circulation sphere, international trade between economies at different levels of development and thus, with widely differing costs of labor, is largely influenced by price fixing and corporate collusion among competing transnational firms (Arrighi, 1994; 1999) [8] Workers and peasants in the South have paid a heavy price through high rates of exploitation in the global division of labor. The most prominent of these are sweatshop conditions in the emerging industrialization process. Workers in those sweatshops are paid as little as $3 a day, producing some of the top-label designer clothes and shoes for transnational corporations (Rosen, 2002).

At a political level, post-colonial states remain subordinate actors in a hierarchically organized international system. They have marginal influence in key policy-making organs. As a result, the majority of the states and their people are virtually excluded from the prosperity that globalization purports to offer. In fact, the North-South disparity remains the central facet of the contemporary global order. The 23 percent of the global population living in the North enjoys about 85 percent of the world's income, while the 77 percent of the population in the South enjoys 15 percent. The situation has reached such extremes that the assets of the three wealthiest persons in the world amounted at one point to the GDP of the 48 poorest countries combined (Falk, 1995:57-58).

It is important also to highlight the role of the state in the capitalist accumulation process. Today, as in the past, the state is the principal political instrument of capitalist accumulation. It continues to be the chief administrator of power and holds on to its monopoly by force. It plays a prominent role in organizing national and international expansion through trade treaties, subsidies, technology, labor controls, military intervention and ideological doctrines. Capitalism is, by definition, an ideological project of the ruling class backed by state power and not simply by the natural unfolding of the free market. More specifically, states provide territorially-bound public goods, which, if of competitive quality, help economic enterprises to prosper. This applies not only to small firms, which normally do business largely within the framework of a single state but also to big transnational firms. Although economically spread around the world, TNCs also need a strong political home base in order to compete successfully. It is impossible to conceive of the expansion and deepening involvement of transnational banks and corporations without the prior direct or indirect political, military or economic support of their respective states. In fact, large corporations tend to expand and prosper if they have a strong state backing their interests at home and abroad. However, most states in the periphery preside over the exploitation and plunder of their own countries by transnational corporations. Through bribery and corruption, and through predatory investment regimes and a docile labor force, state managers perpetuate colonial and post-colonial oppression, control and exploitation of their citizens by global capital. It is unremarkable that that these state managers develop a class interest in the very system which they are often reluctant to change.

In conclusion, it can be safely argued that, despite the speed and intensity of transactions in the world economy and despite a proportionate decline in the power and ability of the state and other political institutions to control national economies relative to other periods, the contemporary globalization of capital continues to be defined by the same logic of accumulation for private profit based on the exploitation of labor throughout the world. The reality behind the globalization facade is that it is the latest phase of global capitalist expansion, which is but a continuation of the operation of modern capitalist imperialism on a worldwide basis. The contemporary overzealous attention to globalization as a new phenomenon may seem as too much ado about nothing.

Africa's Possible Futures: An Explanatory Framework
This study seeks to challenge the notion that African societies constitute independent economic and political units, whose development can be understood without taking into account the systemic ways in which they are inextricably linked to one another in the context of larger networks of power structure, material production and exchange. It also seeks to challenge the argument that claims that there have been major transformations in the developmental logic of the world system since the 1970s, which, if prudently

managed, have the capacity to alleviate poverty and underdevelopment for the poor, and to promote democracy for the excluded and disenfranchized. It is the thesis of this work that the forces of globalization and democratization have created, and continue to create, enormous challenges. The challenges of mass poverty, predatory exploitation and subjugation by capital, collapsed states, marginalization and exclusion are indeed Herculean but not impossible tasks to overcome.

As Steven Krasner (1984) argued, periods of crisis require people to make critical choices and such periods tend to give rise to new structures that ultimately canalize future developments. Such critical junctures also open up increased space for deliberate efforts to craft new coalitions and relationships between the state and the economy, and to redefine relationships of power and accountability within respective societies and with the rest of the world. It is therefore argued that the nature and character of the political space created in different situations will have far-reaching implications regarding how development in general is conceptualized, social alliances formed, policies crafted, strategies identified and resources allocated. These dynamics will become apparent as discussions on possible futures are presented in Chapter Four.

Various development policy proposals have been put forward that seek to address the scourge of Africa's marginalization and exclusion. These proposals outline possibilities as well as constraints with respect to possible required political agencies and economic structures. The proposals range from embracing fully the so-called Washington Consensus, which highlights the made-in-the U.S.A. packaging of the neo-liberal scheme of things as the only viable path to economic and social recovery, to the re-colonization proposals for countries considered to be 'basket cases.' Between these two extremes, there are other development policy options that view marginalization and exclusion in positive terms. Instead of screaming and raving, it is argued that Africa should seize the moment for a thorough collective introspection. Globalization, marginalization and exclusion should offer Africa the opportunity to articulate a common vision and a firm, shared conviction to eradicate structural poverty and underdevelopment. The current debates on African Renaissance, African Union, the Abuja Treaty, and the New Partnership for Africa's Development (NEPAD) are a giant step in the right direction. In short, the current crisis in Africa provides a compelling opportunity for the continent's leadership and peoples to redefine its development priorities away from the global integration frenzy, and to focus instead on economic self-reliance, political independence and a new regionalism. The major objective of this work is to examine the fine details of various development strategies and their possible implications.

In order to explore possible appropriate development strategies for Africa, this study seeks to answer the following questions: What are the implications of the new world order for Africa? Does the end of the Cold War imply that there will be a peace dividend for the world at large, let alone for Africa? How can the reality of the continent's appalling circumstances and the growing sense of despair be turned into hope and opportunity? What social and political compacts are likely to guarantee sustainable peace and security on this war-ravaged continent? Can the marginalization and impoverishment accompanying depression be borne indefinitely? How can African political economies, singly and collectively, position themselves strategically to minimize the imminent costs of globalization? If African unity is the continent's sole salvation, what kinds of cooperation and integration arrangements are likely to secure her economic and political emancipation in the emerging global economy? What social and ideological restructurings are required to empower various national, sub-regional and continental actors to take advantage of the current and future changes in the global order? What imaginative and flexible framework of international rules and institutions should be devised in order to preserve the advantages of global markets and competition, while ensuring that globalization works for people and not just for profits? These and similar questions inform and structure the arguments of this book.

Any attempt to engage in the thematic discussion of capitalist globalization and Africa's future is soon caught in wider issues regarding the choice of a theoretical perspective. As earlier pointed out, this study employs an analytic schema of the modern world system. In this schema, it is posited that capitalism develops as a world system rather than simply as separate national political economies. It seeks to provide a long-term view of interactions between the expanding and the deepening of the capitalist system. Africa's participation in the world economy is studied as a sub-system of the larger global system. In this sense, globalization is not some process 'out there,' but is a social construct engineered and channeled by powerful economic, technological and political processes in the service of an increasingly transnational bourgeois class. Though based in the core, this class formation gradually replicates itself and incorporates various leading elements in the periphery. The world system approach has long noted that social relations are not simply internal to discrete nation-states, but are part of the global system of capitalist production established through colonialism, imperialism and the expansion of the European state system beginning in the late 16th century. It is therefore an analytical error to abstract classes and social groups in Africa from these global social relations and argue that they exist within bounded nation-states.

The above argument does not mean that the national economic and political classes in Africa have nothing to do with the fate of its people. Rather, it is to situate them as actors within the framework of the world system within which, in turn, their actions and choices are made. The role of the state and its class interests in Africa is critical to understanding not only the nature of capitalism in the periphery but, equally importantly, in shaping the core-periphery relations. A strong state in the periphery, for example, will seek to structure its relations nationally and internationally either for its own narrow class interests or for broader national development. In the case of the former tendency, it will slavishly respond more to the logic, needs and interests of the world system than to those of its citizens.

The adopted analytical construct also posits that one cannot isolate the processes of change in Africa from those occurring in the world economy as a whole, especially in view of the external economic and social penetration that has characterized African political economies from the pre-colonial, mercantilist period through to the present time. The approach seeks to situate contemporary developments in an historical trajectory in order to account for past and current arrangements. In this sense, globalization is understood with respect to the global, regional and national distribution of wealth, power, conflict and cooperation, and to the way in which political and economic struggles are waged over global resources distribution. As Marx pointed out in his discussion of the method of political economy, one must alternately move from the concrete to the abstract, from the whole to the parts, and then back again. Deduction and induction were both considered necessary operations of analysis (Marx, 1976).

One of the primary objectives of this book is to propose future development scenarios for the African continent for the target year of 2025. The word scenario is derived from a Latin word 'scaenarium,' a place for erecting stages, traditionally used to refer to plot outlines in a theatre used by actors in comedies. Today, the concept is used in the theatre world to refer to scripts for films or plays. Scenario-building studies emerged during World War II as a method of military planning in the United States, when the U.S. Air Force tried to imagine what its opponents might do and to prepare alternative strategies. Slowly, but inexorably, the discipline of scenario building became prominent, initially in business studies and economics and later in political science. Peter Schwartz's classic work, *The Art of the Long View: Planning for the Future in an Uncertain World* defined scenarios as:

> A tool for helping us to take a long view in a world of uncertainty…(they) are stories about the way the world might turn out tomorrow, stories that can help us to recognize and adapt to changing aspects of our present environment. They form a method of articulating the different pathways that might exist for us tomorrow, and finding our appropriate movements down each of those possible paths. Scenario planning is about making choices today with an understanding of how they might turn out (Schwartz, 1991:3-4).

More often than not, states, civil society organizations and businesses find it difficult to plan for the future when they do not know precisely what it will bring. They tend to be so preoccupied with the pressing problems of the moment that it becomes difficult to take a long view. In order to avoid drifting into social, economic and environmental disaster, various futures can and should ideally be planned for. In developing such scenarios, Goran Therborn's study of ideology explains that any constructed worldview should be defined by the answers to the following three questions: What exists? What is good? And what is possible? (Therborn, 1980). Of course, there are those who argue that a science of society is impossible, that we cannot explain and predict social change. Human beings, the object of analysis, are ostensibly intelligent and have free will to do as they please; it is argued that any attempts to predict their behavior are doomed. However, it is proposed that societies change their circumstances depending largely on the conditions handed down to them by history. This work is properly cautious regarding statements about the future. For, in any social relations nothing important is inevitable, but some things are more likely to take place than others. Arguably, historical and contemporary information about Africa is sufficient to allow analysts to predict its possible development futures. Such futures would facilitate the exploitation of better informed decisions, the forging of alliances and the design of socially credible development policies and strategies. The possible futures are multiple. However, they are not a matter of rational choice. They are essentially a product of social struggle.

As Tim Shaw observes, the science of social, economic and political forecasting remains an extremely primitive one. The forecasts that are usually produced represent only possible, not probable, futures (Shaw, 1982:38). This is rather obvious. The quality of the futures we construct and the policy prescriptions we develop depend largely on the quality of the working assumptions we make. One has to identify, on the one hand, elements that are likely to remain the same through the next several decades at the national, regional and world system levels and, on the other hand, elements that are likely to change and move in a different direction. Moreover, one has to specify scenario logics. This involves identifying how driving forces might plausibly behave based on how those forces behaved in the past. Continuations and mutations are the ingredients of one's working assumptions.

Unfortunately, basic assumptions are chiefly dependent on certain key conditions remaining constant, which is unlikely to be the case in today's rapidly changing world. More importantly, difficulties in attempting to predict Africa's future are further compounded by the continent's extreme dependence on the dynamics of the global political economy, which brings into play volatile external factors such as external political alliances, externally induced conflicts, competition and manipulations, commodity prices and the flow of resources. Nonetheless, futuristic studies, despite the inherent flux in their fundamental bases, are likely to improve actors' awareness of possible opportunities and challenges, alliance formation and counter-alliances, and of how best to respond to them. Unlike traditional business forecasting or market research, scenarios present alternative images and explain their full ramifications.

Most scenario-building projects are based on computer simulation models. They deal with a large number of interrelated factors when making forecasts of a particular phenomenon. These models command a significant legitimacy because they are quantitative, dynamic and interactive. Central to quantitative methodologies in futuristic studies are trends and events, and their impact on the system. However, the construction of events or trends is problematic, since both are possible only within peculiar, modern definitions of time and history. In addition to the probabilistic values assigned to the occurrence of an event, and acknowledged by the futures literature, there is a problem with the social construction of events in that an event does not exist independently of an observer and his or her epistemology. The argument that both time and event are constituents of, and not independent states outside of, perceptions and history undermines any notion of objectivity, an assumption that is the hidden thought behind the effort to develop a complex forecasting model. Central to these models also is the view that there is a real world and more of it can be captured or explained by more variables and increasingly complex interactions (Inayatullah, 1990; Armstrong, 1985).

Recognizing the time, data requirements, and the personnel that would be required to develop a complex model, this work has settled for a less ambitious but more practical alternative. The primary objective of this book is not to define the agencies of change and concrete national strategies for development, which would have meaning only in countries facing similar development challenges and at a specific moment in their evolution. More modestly, it suggests a framework for reflection on the debate around different development strategies, actors, interests and options. In this regard, the book seeks to present an analysis of the continent's possible futures by discerning critical development agencies and trends, Africa's past and recent political economy, the dynamics and key players, and the interest of these players in the global, regional and national political economies.

Unlike earlier studies, futuristic studies of Africa undertaken in the 1970s and 1980s - which were either driven by the growing sense of economic crisis in the West (Shaw, 1975; 1982; Mytelka and Langdon, 1979; Legum, 1979), or the imbalances in the North-South relations (Khothari, 1974; Falk, 1975) - this study was begun largely out of a sense of Africa's marginalization, exploitation, exclusion and alienation, trends engendered by the processes of the recent wave of capitalist globalization.

Structural Overview

The remaining parts of the book are divided into four substantive chapters. Chapter Two presents an historical background to Africa's political economy, highlighting different historical phases of Africa's integration into the world system from the very inception of the capitalist system. During the early mercantilist system, Africa participated through the provision of slaves who worked on European plantations and mines in the Americas. The second phase of integration of Africa was that of the colonial period, roughly from 1886 to 1960. The colonial partition and domination of Africa by various European powers brought African peoples into the world economy through cash crop production, mining, and large-scale plantation agriculture. Political independence did not essentially alter the nature of Africa's integration into the world economy. In fact, it further intensified the exploitation of workers and peasants through the export of finance capital, debt payments and unequal trade.

In Chapter Three, we review the on-going debates on capitalist globalization and liberalization and discuss the nature and role of Africa's participation in the emerging global political economy. Various elements of globalization, namely trade, investment, regionalism, security, debt, foreign aid and migration, are used as prisms through which we view the process of globalization and the promise it holds for Africa. In Chapter Four, three possible development scenarios for Africa are presented. They include, first, the nightmare scenario, which discusses the prospects and problems Africa is likely to face by continuing to pursue the current policies and strategies. The second scenario discusses the probability of reforming the institutions of global governance and the global agenda and of promoting enlightened development cooperation arrangements. The third and last scenario discusses the probability of establishing credible regional cooperation and integration arrangements in Africa. We argue that recent developments in the global economy have transformed the importance of an African cooperation and integration strategy from a regional necessity into a continental imperative. The current crisis in Africa vividly demonstrates the illusion, and indeed the impossibility, of independent national development strategies. It is argued that a collective structural transformation is central to Africa's very survival. In Chapter Five we discuss some measures that may enable Africa states and societies to stop and even reverse their growing marginalization within the global system, and to empower them to ward off some of the adverse impacts of Africa's external environment.

CHAPTER 2

AFRICAN HISTORY: AN OVERVIEW

Introduction: Phases of Economic History

We cannot hope to formulate an adequate development theory and policy for the majority of the world's population who suffer from underdevelopment without first learning how their past economies and societal history gave rise to their present underdevelopment (Frank, 1966:17).

In order for a developemnt scenario to be meaningful, one has to take into account the impact of history on the respective societies so as to discern the basic trends that are likely to endure and to put limits on the way in which social and economic changes will evolve. The scope, direction and magnitude of change that a specific society can undertake depends critically on its past, and on the constellation of political and institutional factors that shaped that history. In other words, history provides the broad context and parameters within which scenarios are constructed. Agreeing with the opening quotation from Andre Gunder Frank, Walter Rodney also noted that, "in order to formulate a strategy and tactics for African emancipation and development, we have to understand how the present came into being and what trends are for the near future" (Rodney, 1972:7).

As the opening statement by Gunder Frank notes, the origins of the structural distortion of African political economies, as well as the current socio-economic and political crisis, derive from the nature of historical interactions between Africa and the world system. Samir Amin (1990) and Andre Gunder Frank (1978) distinguish four distinct phases of African economic history: the first period being the pre-mercantilist period (from prehistory to 1500); the second period being the mercantilist period (from 1500 up to 1800) characterized by the slave trade; the third period being (from 1800 to 1950s) defined by European colonization and attempts to establish European-dependent African economies; and the present post-colonial economies (beginning around 1960). Closely following these broad historical phases, this Chapter only provides highlights from the four periods of Africa's integration and changing roles in the world economy, in order to offer an historical anchor for scenario construction and analysis.

Pre-Colonial Africa

Pre-colonial African economic interactions with the rest of the world, especially Europe, date back many centuries before the time when they culminated in fully-fledged colonization in the latter part of the 19th century. Various studies have documented that Africa and the rest of the world were at similar levels of development until the 17th century, with Africa employing basically the same levels of technology as Europe and Asia. In fact, it was Africa that invented writing in ancient Egypt, and Africa that developed mathematics at the University of Timbuktu in West Africa (Diop, 1974; Tordoff, 1998).

Pre-colonial Africa was also characterized by the production of diverse agricultural products, crafts, textiles and mineral-based products. Both internal and external trade on the continent was distinguished by regional complementarities across a broad natural resource base. Thus, a dense and integrated network was put in place, dominated by African producers and traders, which included trade among pastoralists and crop farmers, supply of exports and distribution of imports. In contrast to West Africa, Eastern and Southern Africa had well-established economic interactions with Arabian and Asian countries long before the arrival of the Europeans. Specifically, this part of Africa supplied a range of products, such as gold, copper, millet grains, and coconut to the Middle East and Indian Ocean economies. It is important to note that the quality of many of the processed goods was comparable to products originating from other parts of the world. For example, the type of textiles from pre-colonial West Africa were so sophisticated that they were traded in Central and North Africa as well as in European markets (Amin, 1972; Hopkins, 1973; Rodney, 1972). This short account serves to highlight a long history of integrated and autonomous economic activities in most African regions before 1500. However, the subsequent industrial revolution in Europe transformed global power.

The 16th and 17th centuries and the period leading to the industrial revolution in Europe witnessed the initial reshaping of African economies by European industrial interests. Beginning as early as the mid-1700s, the British economy became the key economy within the core end of the world system. Via institutional reforms (such as enclosures and the Glorious Revolution of 1688), protectionism (Navigation Acts), and the building in India and North America and the Seven Years War (1756-1763), a national market was created, domestic industry and shipping were stimulated, and the foundation was laid from which British capitalism could launch its conquest of the world.

As the first industrial nation, Britain shaped the world economy to her needs, and therefore played a key role in the world system that subsequently emerged (Hobsbawm, 1979). With the onset of the industrial revolution in the rest of Europe, Africa lost its remaining autonomy and was reduced to being the supplier of slave labor for the plantations and mines of the Americas. Between ten and sixteen million Africans were captured and exported to the Americas as commodities between 1451 and 1870. On the import side, cheaper and purer iron bars and implements such as knives and hoes were made available, displacing some of the previous economic activities undertaken by traditional African blacksmiths. The initial integration of the continent did irreparable damage in terms of a reduction in the levels of iron smelting, and even a decline in the mining of iron ore. This organic process ensured simultaneous growth and development for the core of the global capitalist system, but underdevelopment of the periphery (Wallerstein, 1974; 1979).

The African slave trade lost its importance with the maturation of the industrial revolution in Europe. The economic logic of accumulation of capital shifted discernibly from commerce to industry. The impact of the Atlantic slave trade on the underdevelopment of Africa has been adequately treated in the literature. Suffice it to say that the African slave trade and the savagery of slavery, as well as the mineral plunder of the Americas, contributed to what Karl Marx referred to as 'primitive accumulation of capital'. It was considered primitive capital accumulation because it was not a result of the capitalist mode of production, but rather its starting point (Marx, 1976:873).[9] It is little wonder that this particular form of accumulation and subsequent ones radically transformed Europe's political, economic and cultural relationships with the rest of the world. Whereas this stage helped to put in place the basic ingredients for later capitalism, it contributed to Africa's underdevelopment by depleting it of its active population by tens of millions and in some areas, by replacing earlier, larger state organizations with small, brutal military systems that were permanently at war with each other (Rodney, 1972; Blackburn, 1998).

While the African continent sacrificed blood, flesh and other critical resources to aid Europe's economic ascendancy, it remained essentially on the very margins of the resulting economic and social benefits of the modern world system. We do not intend to review Africa's colonial history, but one of the defining features of world capitalist accumulation and integration is its inherent tendency to exploit, pillage, fragment and marginalize relatively weaker actors that participate in the system. In this regard, due to its superior military, economic and technological power, Europe, and later the United States and Japan, exploited and continued to exploit and subjugate Africa, Asia and Latin America for their own economic development, political power and strategic interests. Europeans used the superiority of their ships and cannon to gain control of all the world's waterways, starting with the Western Mediterranean and the Atlantic Coast of Africa and spreading to the Far East. From slave hunting in the 15th century to the contemporary globalization of trade production and investment, the African people and their environment continue to be criminally short-changed.

African Colonization and Marginalization

Arnold Joseph Toynbee, the British colonial historian, once remarked:

> .... The great event of the twentieth century was the impact of Western civilization upon all other living societies of the world of that day. They will say of this impact that it was so powerful and so pervasive that it turned the lives of all victims upside down and inside out ... however ponderous and terrifying (Toynbee, 1948:214).

Indeed, colonialism left such an indelible mark on the future development of the continent and its societies that it has taken them more than four decades since their political independence to make any significant structural changes to their economic and political colonial legacies. As pointed out earlier, the scientific and industrial revolutions that began in England in the 18th century later spread throughout Europe, and marked the beginning of European dominance in global affairs. It was precisely on the basis of these revolutions that Europe acquired technological superiority over the rest of the world, giving it unquestioned dominance in world affairs. The resulting technological prowess allowed Europe to venture to all other continents and conquer territories and peoples of different cultures and civilizations.

This historical conjuncture broadly defined the future basis of capitalism in Europe. It crystallized the formation of modern nation-states and the simultaneous construction of what Samir Amin refers to as 'integrated and auto-centered national economies' through war, revolution and the conquest of weaker societies everywhere (Amin, 1990). On the question of arresting and reversing the auto-centered development of weaker others, Win Wertheim (1992:261) has noted that, during the 18th century, Britain not only imposed tariffs on textile imports from India and China, but also made the wearing of such imports illegal in order to stimulate the British textile industry. In a similar vein, Paul Kennedy (1987:149) further asserts that in the half-century between 1750 and 1900, Britain's share of the world manufacturing output, in which textiles held pride of place, rose from half that of France to par; and by 1830, it had risen further to almost twice the French share.

Gradually, national capital became centralized and concentrated, with small enterprises being engulfed by larger and more powerful ones. The dominant sectors of the economy came under the control of monopoly banks and industries. This process, in turn, gave rise to the formation of cartels, combinations, syndicates, trusts and other forms of monopolies in each of the rising industrial economies of Europe. Similarly, class relations expanded beyond the labor process to become institutionalized in state, colonial and inter-state structures. A mixed system of nation-states at the core and colonial empires at the periphery was the main political structure for three hundred years, until decolonization brought the periphery into the inter-state system as formal sovereign states (Frank, 1978; Amin, 1974).

While Africa's participation in the slave trade has been viewed as the most economically exploitative trade system, European colonialism represents yet another long historical process of perverse integration of the African continent into the global capitalist system through production, investment, trade and politics. The colonial state arose, in part, to advance the interests of its respective metropolitan bourgeoisies against other competing interests and, in part, to suppress and oppress all opposition coming from the colonized peoples in order to ensure cheap labor for capital. The latter objective was accomplished through brute force, including downright genocide, or through dubious treaties of friendship with pre-literate traditional leaders. Jan-Bart Geward (1999) has demonstrated how the Germans annihilated well over 80 percent of the Herero population in the colony of South West Africa (current Namibia) in a single year, 1904. The Herero people were fighting against land alienation and the expropriation of their cattle. Justinian Rweyemamu (1973) reported that, between 1888 and 1906, there were at least eleven major revolts by the people of Tanganyika against German colonial occupation. As would be expected, peasant revolts against an industrial power were bound to be viciously defeated. The brutal crushing of African resistance and the putting down of protests was misleadingly called 'pacification' or 'making peace with the natives.'

Samir Amin (1974; 1990) distinguishes three models of colonization in Africa: the trading economy (incorporating a small peasantry into the world tropical products market by subjecting it to the authority of a market controlled by oligopolies); the mining economy (by which the mineral reserves of Southern Africa were exploited); and the economy of pillage (concessionary companies embarked upon taxing goods and services in transit through the territory under their control, when the local social conditions did not permit the establishment of trade or the exploitation of mineral resources did not justify the organization of reserves intended to furnish abundant human resources e.g. the Congo Basin). With colonialism, the imperative of capitalist accumulation determined almost every aspect of Africa's social formation and organization. At the level of social relationships, the complex criteria of earlier societies, reciprocal obligations, moral order, the oral transmission of knowledge and the reproduction of the physical environment were replaced by the exigencies of capitalism. The maintenance and reproduction of the labor force was left to nature. As a result of this mode of integration into the world economy, Africa's development opportunities were severely circumscribed. As Samir Amin has argued, this mode of integration delayed the commencement of an agricultural revolution.

A surplus value could be extracted from the labor of the peasants and from the wealth offered by nature without any significant investment in machinery or fertilizers, and without guaranteeing the maintenance of the natural conditions for the reproduction of wealth (Amin, 1990). Global capitalism at its industrial stage needed raw materials for its industries, markets for its finished products and new outlets for surplus investment. Africa offered all the above at a high social price. The modernization of the work process was undertaken only where it was beneficial to European interests. Ultimately, European colonialism resulted in the distortion, disarticulation and marginalization of African economies and societies.

Traditional African politics and institutions, like the economy, were severely and deliberately deformed, dominant classes marginalized and cultural forms perverted in order to facilitate the colonial project. The subjugated traditional authorities were later reduced to mere dependent functionaries of the colonial state. It was the judiciary, executive and legislature, all rolled into one. The colonial state was primarily assigned the duties of administration, control and resource extraction. It was corrupt, irresponsible, violent, manipulative, undemocratic and biased in favor of expatriates, foreign investors and minority elements that served its immediate interests of divide-and-rule and exploitation. In short, colonialism undermined and often completely destroyed indigenous political institutions. Even where it took the form of indirect rule, it undermined the traditional sources of legitimacy, since the authority of the traditional rulers was clearly dependent on the power of the colonial state (Davidson, 1989; Ibvembere, 2000).

The end of World War II and the emergence of the United States and the Soviet Union as rival superpowers marked the third phase of capitalist expansion and the integration of the South. It was primarily defined by the emergence of these two superpowers and of anti-systemic forces from the working class and left-wing parties in Europe, as well as from decolonization struggles in the South, and by selective export of capital to old and new ventures in the South. It is important to emphasize that successful capital accumulation in the North was usually accompanied by class struggle from labor unions and left-wing parties demanding social and economic reforms. These struggles led to a series of reforms, including capital-labor accords on the share of labor in productivity gains, the social redistribution of market-generated income, and the legitimacy of the capitalist system based on the provision of basic social programs (welfare, health and education). These labor victories eventually forced sections of capital in the core areas to flow to the South, where relatively cheaper labor and raw materials created a competitive advantage. Such changes in the mode of accumulation made limited import substitution industrialization and economic modernizations possible in several independent states in the South, particularly in Latin America and Asia (Petras and Veltmeyer, 2001).

During this phase of import substitution industrialization, a few countries in Asia experienced upward mobility in the world economy. Thanks to the American containment policy toward communism, countries like Taiwan, Singapore, Hong Kong and South Korea were "not only able to copy Northern technology with impunity and thus build their industries, but they were also able to use the vast expanse of the American market to sell their products," writes Yash Tandon (2000:58). He continues his argument that, "the United States turned a blind eye to this process for it needed these countries to fight communism in the Pacific." However, for most countries, industrialization did not reduce the overall degree of inequality between North and South. This was precisely because the North invariably shifted to specialization into new, more profitable industries such as computers, robotics and biotechnology. Fordist labor strategies that had been declared obsolete by the North quickly came to the rescue of these newly industrialized countries in the South.

The African colonies were not as fortunate. When most economies in the South embarked on import substitution industrialization, much of Africa was under colonial rule, which permitted neither protection of domestic markets nor running deficits. In fact, even the initial processing of primary products was prohibited except in white settler colonies. In the 1920s and 1930s, for example, the British government in colonial Tanganyika blocked a number of individual industrial projects that had been proposed by either Asian or other non-British investors. E.A. Brett (1973:273) quotes part of the debate in the British House of Commons that strongly deplored the idea of establishing competing manufacturing industries in the colonies:

> The suggestion, however, that the colonies should actively promote industrialization is another matter, and requires special consideration, because it has serious limitations. It is obvious that manufacturing countries like ours could not afford to provide free or assured markets for manufactured goods in direct competition with our own. All questions of starting new industries in the colonies must therefore be examined on their own merits and with due regard to the welfare of the colony as a whole and as a primary producer.

Direct colonial control throughout Africa remained skeletal and confined to a few regional and sub-regional administrative centers. Administration was generally through traditional institutions, pejoratively known as 'native authorities.' Only to a limited extent did colonial administrations engage in meaningful nation building. If they did, it was intended to further the growth of the colonial interests and not to promote realistic social solidarity and cohesion. As if the lumping together of heterogeneous communities was not enough, colonialism often resorted to a divide-and-rule policy which sought to play on and strengthen historical differences among communities in order to pre-empt a unified anti-colonial strategy. Slowly but inexorably, popular discontent against colonial rule built up everywhere. It included: a rejection of continued race-based segregation of opportunities for social advancement and access to resources, amenities and services; denial of representation in the structure of governance; and denial of the freedom, liberty and dignity of the African people. These concerns crystallized into a concrete political agenda for decolonization in the 1950s and 1960s (Young; 1994; Tordoff, 1998).

It should be emphasized that Africans were not allowed to participate in national politics, nor could they form political parties. It was not until after the end of World War II that, owing to nationalist pressures for freedom and reform, groups emerged which sought to mobilize the people against colonialism. Some of these nationalism movements were organized around trade unions, peasant movements, or ethnic and religious associations. Political parties emerged out of these diverse groups and movements. Gradually, colonial powers began to open up political spaces for indigenous participation and to conduct some apprenticeship in aspects of democratic rule, such as constitutionalism, multi-partyism, separation of powers and the like. As Crawford Young (1999:16) notes, the partial legalization of formal democratic institutions became part of the decolonization pact "everywhere except in those countries where independence was won by armed struggle rather than negotiation (e.g. Algeria), where the metropole itself was autocratic (Cape Verde, Sao Tome and Principe, and Western Sahara) or both (Guinea-Bissau, Mozambique, Zimbabwe, Angola and South Africa)." We now turn to the discussion of state-society relations in independent Africa.

Political Independence and Domination

For entirely different reasons, the two superpowers that emerged from World War II placed decolonization high on the international political and diplomatic agenda. Whereas the Soviet Union was concerned with winning political and strategic allies among the former colonies, the United States sought to dismantle colonial barriers that militated against joint exploitation of the South. The decolonization process was intensified and hastened by the cultural and political resistance that was staged by colonized people the world over. As Mahmood Mamdani has noted, decolonization in Africa unfolded mainly along two different trajectories, setting apart the process of decolonization in settler colonies from those in colonies without a critical mass of settler minorities. Where settler minorities vied for political power against the native majority and the imperial power - as in South Africa in the Boer War, Kenya at the time of the Mau Mau, and Zimbabwe following the Unilateral Declaration of Independence (UDI) - required protracted armed struggle before nationalists could win state independence. Where settlers did not exist in large numbers, the colonial power had a larger margin of maneuverability to influence the course of transfer of political power (Mamdani, 2001:103).

Beginning in the late 1940s, the anti-colonial struggles in Africa advanced to a stage of popular and protracted resistance in a number of countries. As

Crawford Young (1994) notes, departing with dignity required the colonial state to equip their territories with constitutional structures replicating their own. A pattern of constitutional changes, punctuated by periodic elections, was repeated in the British colonies, with a Westminster model constitution, providing for an interlocking cabinet and legislature, a separate judiciary and an independent public service commission. With the independence of the Gold Coast (later Ghana) in 1957, all other colonies followed suit after 1960 in both the British and French colonies. Moreover, after the defeat of French settler colonial imperialism in Algeria, the people took up arms against Portuguese colonial occupation in Mozambique, Angola and Guinea Bissau. With the collapse of the fascist regime in Lisbon in 1975, Portuguese colonies in Africa won their political independence. In Southern Africa, the people rose up against settler colonialism in Zimbabwe, Namibia and South Africa. In 1980, Zimbabwe became independent, followed by Namibia in 1989. In 1994, a democratic dispensation was finally realized in South Africa when the black African majority of South Africa under the leadership of the African National Congress (ANC) took over the reins of state power (Tordoff, 1998:65-68).

Political independence was an important step in the general struggle for Africa's liberation and one of the major democratic demands and victories of the dominated territories. Symbolically, independent African states acquired national flags, anthems, constitutions, currencies, armed forces and police, and bureaucracy. More substantively, political independence meant the creation of a nation-state separate from the colonizing country. In the post-colonial state, political power came to rest in the hands of a local class or classes that constituted the ruling elite. However, little attention was paid by the new ruling class to deconstructing and recomposing the undemocratic, repressive and inefficient neo-colonial state in order to alter not only the internal relations of power and politics but, most importantly, to reflect the interests of the African majority. The ultimate objectives of independence, namely, democracy, creation of democratic structures, establishment of a credible basis for economic management, and improving the lot of women and other disadvantaged groups, were for the most part quietly abandoned.

Inspired by rapid economic development in the then Soviet Union and China, African nationalist leaders single-mindedly embarked on a project of strengthening the state. Competitive politics, it was argued, was a luxury which poor countries could not afford. The importance of central planning, the capacity of the state to organize and direct development, now called for the concentration of authority, not its dissipation. Moreover, the consolidation of nationhood required elimination of opportunities for fissiparous tendencies to find expression. The doctrine of the single party as the vanguard of African progress gradually took root in most countries. It is not unremarkable that civil society organizations such as the trade unions, and youth, women's and students' organizations that had supported nationalist struggles were either banned or turned into affiliates of the ruling parties. In short, the revolutionary, anti-colonial agenda for the total emancipation of the whole society was betrayed (Fanon, 1974).

Political independence in Africa signified a significant transition in the form and substance of the state. Whereas in a colony, political power exercised by the foreign ruling class went hand-in-hand with imperialist exploitation, political independence ruptured the connection between economic exploitation and political oppression. On the one hand, the state, the apparatus of oppression, came to be managed by an indigenous class situated within the country. On the other hand, imperialist exploitation of the African people continued,[10] which I.V. Lenin (1970) aptly referred to as *Imperialim: The Highest Stage Capitalism*. Symbolically, however, the new African nations assumed membership in the United Nations and entered the Bretton Woods system. They became independent actors on the international stage. However, as will become abundantly clear, the new leadership in Africa faced the daunting challenge of consolidating their newly won political independence and simultaneously promoting economic and social development in their respective national settings. They quickly discovered that the global capitalist grip on Africa had changed, by and large, only in form. Substantively, transnational corporations, the Bretton Woods institutions, international development agencies, the Paris Club and the GATT-WTO assumed indirect control through macro-policy management, investment, technology transfer, trade and debt repayment. It is in this light that Julius Nyerere, the first President of Tanzania, observed that the reality of neo-colonialism becomes obvious when a new African government tries to act independently in order to advance the economic interests of its people. He added:

> For such a government immediately discovers that it inherited the power to make laws, treat with foreign governments and so on, but did not inherit effective power over economic development in its own country. Indeed, there exists various economic activities, which are owned by people outside its jurisdiction, which are directed at external needs, and which are run in the interests of external powers. Further, the government's ability to secure positive action in these fields...depends entirely upon its ability to con-

vince the effective decision makers that their own interests will be served by what the government wishes to do (Nyerere, 1977:5).

The end of colonialism did not automatically bring the end to economic domination and exploitation by finance capital. It meant, however, that the representatives of the colonizing country no longer directly controlled state power. The post-colonial political economies remained firmed trapped in the colonial division of labor and power. It is also important to emphasize that the local ruling classes in various countries gradually consolidated their own class interests that arose from the place they occupied in their respective national social production. Although in the long run the interests of some local ruling classes tended to coincide with those of imperialism as a whole, they were not merely 'servicing agents of imperialist capital' as Yash Tandon (1976) claims. Indeed, various post-colonial states in Africa and elsewhere have exhibited varying degrees of autonomy from particular dominant powers, in line with the conjuncture of class alliances and struggles at different times.

This brings us to a discussion of the nature and character of the post-colonial state in Africa. The colonial legacy of destruction and reconstitution left deep scars on the state of the nation and on its populations. At independence, most states across Africa were defined by the general underdevelopment of their respective national capitalist class. Much of the national wealth remained in foreign hands and the class of indigenous capitalists was only beginning to emerge and consolidate. Secondly, and as a result of the first phenomenon, the working class was also underdeveloped. This pervasive underdevelopment of class formation in Africa chiefly reflected the small proportion of national economic output and employment provided by large-scale agriculture, industry and the service sector. In short, the two major classes of a capitalist society were relatively weakly constituted in the early stages of post-colonial development. The largest proportion of African societies was composed of peasants. By the same token, various social classes that came to control the post-colonial state were equally loosely constituted. The state did not reflect a clear domination of one social class over others. As a result, the control of the state by alternating factions of the petit-bourgeois elements, who sought to use its control for private capital accumulation, became remarkably susceptible to narrow shifts in alignments and realignments. The coups and counter-coups in the 1960s and 1970s were a clear reflection of these shifts and alliances.

Instead of transforming the inherited colonial state, and engaging in a program for dismantling alien and exploitative relations, the new elite used the inherited state power to establish unequal external relations with imperialism and promoted predatory, undemocratic and repressive institutions and policies internally. Most leaders continued to cling to power through a combination of brute force, bribery, manipulation of gullible opposition parties, and surreptious exploitation of ethnic and religious loyalties. Power distribution and resource allocation in virtually all of independent Africa tended to favor only a tiny fraction of the population (Tordoff, 1998; Ake, 1973; 1991).

As would be expected, the Africa people have not been particularly well-served by their respective unstable, poorly constituted and often undemocratic post-colonial states. The track record of most nation and state building for the first forty years of independence was both chaotic and frustrating. It was chaotic in the sense that it became essentially a political history of mixed and often contradictory patterns of development. As several studies have shown, the nature of the post-colonial states in Africa has ranged from the collapsed states of Somalia, Sierra Leone and Liberia to a few robust and consolidating democracies like Botswana, South Africa, Senegal and Mauritius. Between these two extreme cases are nations at various stages: warn-torn nations in the Democratic Republic of Congo, Madagascar, Angola and Sudan; the non-party state of Uganda; and military dictatorships in Rwanda and Burundi. Previous extremes of military dictatorships in Africa included Idi Amin of Uganda, Jean Bedel Bokassa of the Central African Republic, and Francisco Marcias Nguema of Equatorial Guinea. Broadly speaking, most states in the latter category could not boast of a decent economic development record, observance of human rights, or of a discernible pattern of political democratization and consolidation (Chege, 1994; Leftwich, 1993; Soresen, 1991).

Viewed retrospectively, the institutions created and the policies pursued by the departing colonialists had little chance of survival since they were not anchored in solid African social foundations to nurture and sustain them. The nationalists inherited distorted, foreign-dominated and poverty-stricken economies, a weak educational and scientific base, societal instability, vulnerability to foreign penetration, and weak and unstable state institutions. As Peter Anyang' Nyong'o notes "in many cases the political parties ceased to be mass movements and became instruments of political control rather than mobilizers of members of society for popular participation" (Anyang' Nyong'o 2002:90). The authoritarian bent in nationalist politics undermined the political coalitions that had defined nationalist movements in different countries. This was the case with the Kenya African National Union (KANU), the Tanganyika African National Union (TANU), the Uganda People's Congress (UPC), and the Rassemblement Populaire Togolais (RPT) in Togo. In the absence of a vibrant civil society to keep states accountable and transparent, the African ruling classes used the state to advance broader social interests. More often than not, democratically elected governments were intercepted either by long periods of one-party rule (e.g. Malawi, Kenya, Togo and Cameroon), military dictatorships (Nigeria, Rwanda, and the then Zaire), genocide (Rwanda, and Zaire), genocide (Rwanda and Burundi), complex emergencies (Sudan, Angola and Mozambique) or simply by state collapse (Somalia and Sierra Leone).

There were many harsh realities with which independent Africa had to contend. The first was the Herculean task of state-making, nation-building and political integration. In the words of Seton-Watson (1977:1) the major challenge was to evolve "a community of people whose members are bound together by a sense of solidarity, common culture, and national consciousness." Unlike its European counterpart, the nation-state in Africa was a creation of colonialism. Borders were drawn without any consideration for social, cultural, economic, historical, religious, or linguistic criteria. Almost all new nation-states in Africa were comprised of numerous fragmented and often competing nationalities. Colonialism arbitrarily lumped together inveterate ethnic, religious and racial groupings into single territorial entities. Discussing peace and security in Southern Africa, Thomas Ohlson and Stephen Stedman (1994:233) argue that "colonial patchwork borders produced states without nations, often encompassing multiple ethic and language groups into different countries. The fact that borders have not corresponded to nations has contributed to the prevalence of internal conflict in the region." In a similar vein, Jeffrey Herbst (1989) observes that national borders in Africa were largely based either on colonial administrative convenience or intra-imperialist trade-offs. The unfortunate legacy of such boundaries has left an indelible mark on the political evolution of the continent. The post-colonial state has invariably been partial in the competition for and distribution of meager resources among different regions, ethic groups, religious entities, and social classes within these arbitrarily created countries. As a result, such politial evolution soon led to conflicts among different groups as they competed with each other for scarce economic resources and political power.

Indeed, the management of national borders by post-colonial states in Africa has become one of the major sources of insecurity on the continent.

The sacrosanctity of African borders was enshrined in the 1963 Charter that established the Organization of African Unity. It called on all members "to affirm sovereign equality of all member states, non-interference in the internal affairs of member states, and respect for their sovereignty and territorial integrity." Boundary disputes have repeatedly given rise to irredentist and secessionist politics. In recent years, disputes over the precise location of colonial borders have occasioned threats of and actual military confrontations between Nigeria and Cameroon, Somalia and Ethiopia, Eritrea and its neighbors, and Botswana and Namibia.

As noted earlier, political independence conferred on the nascent African states the internationally accepted norms of sovereignty and non-intervention in internal affairs. Although in theory the African states, like their European counterparts, claim supreme, comprehensive and exclusive rule over their territorial jurisdiction, in practice their institutional capacity to impose complete control over their hinterlands and to carry out basic governance functions remained elusive. For many African states, the notion of sovereign control over the territories defined by the borders inherited from colonialism remained a nightmare. Nation-states exist in order to deliver public goods to their citizens: security, education, health services, economic opportunity, environmental surveillance, a legal framework of order and a judicial system to administer it, and fundamental infrastructure requirements such as roads and other means of communication. Almost invariably, effective state control and service delivery in most African countries has largely been confined to the capital cities and a few commercial towns, and the notion of sovereignty has remained largely a legal fiction. After four decades of self-rule, most of them failed dismally to meet the minimal requirements of maintaining order, ensuring the security of their people, collecting taxes and policing the countryside, and could not begin to adequately provide public goods such as health, education and essential economic infrastructure. This lack of effective control and democratic governance markedly increased the risk of conflict and insecurity (Rotburg, 2002:86-87).

Besides the nagging question of sovereign control of its borders and provision of political goods, the post-colonial state was faced with the problem of managing inherited state institutions. Grace Ibingira (1980) argued that, having completely marginalized African traditional institutions and practices, colonialism provided inadequate preparation for Africans to manage the alien state institutions that it had imposed on them, institutions that were not grounded in Africa's political traditions and psyche. The anti-colonial campaigns in many parts of Africa were usually too brief and insufficiently intense to forge a lasting sense of national unity. Not surprisingly, both the institutional and territorial legitimacy of various African nation-states have frequently been hotly contested. In the absence of effective political institutions, power tends to be fragmented. It comes in many forms and in small quantities. As Robert Cox (1987) observes, if it took Europe three to four centuries to build differentiated, autonomous, and centralized political institutions, it would be naive to expect Africans to internalize foreign-imposed institutions in a matter of two generations or so. However, we should hasten to add that this is no excuse for outright misuse of power by some despotic African rulers. In the last three decades, one African state after another has failed, largely due to its leaders' sheer narrow self-interest, to establish an environment in which the legitimate demands of individuals or groups could be satisfactorily addressed, or in which social conflicts would be peacefully resolved.

The rules, norms and institutions that regulate the political behavior and interactions in most African states have remained non-functional at best, and at worst have been arbitrarily changed by the rulers of the day. This mode and style of governance has been described by Robert Jackson and Carl Rosberg (1982) as 'personal rule.' This is a system whereby key politicians take precedence over established institutions and are able and willing to change with impunity the authority of their office to suit their personal needs. It is against this background that Joan Aart Scholte (1999:73) has concluded that, 'African states have been sovereign in name only.' Richard Sandbrook (1985) referred to them as 'fictive states' and Cruise O'Brien (1991) called them 'shadow states.' The institutions that give the state the character to dictate and rule in society are either disrespected or they are simply non-existent. In short, whatever categorization is offered, the common denominator is that most African states have yet to institutionalize the norms, rules and institutions of democratic governance. It is this very weakness that has reduced governance to personal rule in all its infinite variety.

The international political environment in which African states gained their independence was equally inauspicious for state and nation building. It coincided with the height of the bipolar ideological and military confrontational politics of the Cold War. As is well known, during the bipolar era, the Cold War competition and rivalries between two ideological blocs largely shaped the politics and security environment of African states with the mutual suspicion and rivalries of the two superpowers being extended to

Africa. The security of small and weak states was integral to the security calculations of the major powers. Arguably, in the absence of an endogenous power adequate to deter or contain external military threats, most states in Africa relied on tacit coalitions or open alliances with major foreign powers. Despite the rhetoric of non-alignment, most states in Africa picked ideological sides without necessarily creating the broad national political and economic constituencies necessary for sustainable development. By the mid-1970s, more than two dozen African states had entered into bilateral security arrangements with major powers on both sides of the Cold War conflict (Maniruzzaman, 1982:76-79).

In the bipolar world, Cold War competition and rivalries between the two ideological blocs constrained both their behavior and that of their client states, as well as exacerbating some local and regional conflicts. Each superpower, fearing the other might provide decisive support and thereby gain political advantage, was driven to assist one or other party. By the same token, the bipolar structure of the Cold War allowed local disputants to manipulate the superpowers to advance their respective national or regional interests. In this scheme of things, each superpower tended to suppress local African conflicts, out of fear of escalation and concern that open disputes would create opportunities for the rival superpower to intervene in its politically sensitive backyard. By whatever means, big powers did exercise a degree of management to counteract any regional tensions and to keep conflicts within bounds, occasionally even imposing settlements. They restrained their client regimes by stationing troops, extending security commitments, rejecting or limiting the shipment of advanced offensive weaponry, applying political pressure, and using economic rewards and threats of punishment to elicit certain behavior. In the process, foreign powers imposed an artificial and tenuous stability on the continent by propping up the regimes of client states. The blind support by Cold War warriors of many unpopular and oppressive African regimes inevitably led aggrieved groups to carry out *coups d'etat*, and to institute secessionist and irredentist movements and rebellions against the state (Rugumamu, 1997; Thomas, 1999).[11]

It will be argued in subsequent chapters that once the Cold War ended and communism was no longer considered a threat to Western global interests, Africa's intrinsic significance to its former allies seemed to have declined irretrievably. This decline was amply demonstrated by the gradual, yet discernible, patterns of relaxing the vast networks of security alliances, obligations and agreements that bound most African states to competing global security systems. More specifically, the end of the Cold War witnessed a steady abandonment of old dictators and other undemocratic networks constructed to promote Northern interests in Africa. The ensuing break-up of alliances, partnerships and regional support systems exposed weak African states to systemic instability. Predictably, the hollow nature and character of the African state and the unfinished agenda of state and nation building became manifestly obvious. Slowly but inexorably, foreign powers began to withdraw their automatic support from authoritarian African regimes, as well as the concomitant financial, military and political assistance that accompanied that support. In fact, states that had been overly dependent on Cold War patronage, (e.g. Angola, Mozambique, Ethiopia, Zaire, Somalia, and Liberia) began to disintegrate even faster thereafter. Not surprisingly, old conflicts, which for a long time had been buried under the cover of the Cold War, also started to resurface with greater virulence as states grew progressively weaker and small arms and mercenaries became readily available (Wilkin, 1999).

Another significant impact of the end of the Cold War on Africa was the glut in the arms market, especially of small arms and light weapons. Among the contributing factors were the reduction in size of major militaries, the termination or winding down of a number of Cold War conflicts, and the continued dependence for employment and foreign exchange on arms production and arms sales of a high proportion of the population in countries such as Russia, Belarus, Ukraine and South Africa, resulting in the pursuit of new markets, especially in Africa. The availability of arms and mercenaries *per se* does not cause conflicts, but their easy availability tends to change the dynamics of conflict by accelerating the escalation of disputes in conflict-prone environments. Africa became a prime market for both arms and mercenaries (O'Brian, 2000).

Moreover, managing post-colonial economies in Africa turned out to be a headache for most nationalist leaders. As pointed out earlier, they found themselves presiding over economies that had been grossly distorted to suit the interests of colonial powers. Health, education, science, government, law, rail and air transport, agriculture and the financial sector were largely underdeveloped and designed to service the old colonial relationships, rather than to respond to the rising needs and expectations of the African masses. Worse still, little attention had been given to preparing colonies for independence or even self-government. Human capital was poorly developed, especially in terms of technical and professional education. Modern technologies and physical infrastructure were grossly inadequate to enable Africa to put her economies on a stable growth path. Surprisingly, insufficient attention was paid by most African nationalist leaders to seriously interrogating the forms and content of inherited national economies, let alone to analyzing the world economy within which these leaders were marginal players.

Rather than seeking to restructure the colonial foundations of inherited economies, post-independence African economic thinking continued to be trapped in an obsolete international division of labor. It is also important to point out that, for all their rhetoric and pronouncements of idiosyncratic versions of socialism and communism (in Somalia, Mozambique, Angola, Ethiopia and Tanzania), African economies remained largely market economies with varying levels of control (Mkandawire and Soludo, 1999). The nationalist leaders were simply satisfied to indigenize the bureaucracy and to maintain the socio-economic structures and relations established by the colonial state. These were rationalized and justified by the mainstream modernization theory of the time, which counseled integration into the global economy in order to make diffusion of scarce resources, i.e. capital, skills and technology, possible through trade and investment flows.

At the theoretical level, there existed a strong but mistaken belief among African policy makers and their foreign advisors that the world system was governed by objective and fair rules and economic principles. It was further assumed that the system had comprehensive stabilization mechanisms which would automatically offset negative transaction costs on relatively weaker actors. These conclusions were apparent from the initial unquestioned acceptance of the neo-liberal economic models of development that were prepared by World Bank advisory teams for various countries. Economic growth, it was argued, was a function of economic surplus in capital formation and accumulation, through production for national and international markets. The increment of economic surplus, determined by the marginality principle and expressed either in savings, investment and corporate profits, or in increased productivity capacity, would lead to economic expansion. It was also argued that the profit mechanism would be self-regulating and would bring benefits to entrepreneurs, workers and consumers, ultimately enabling them to improve their welfare. Undoubtedly, such thinking was abstracted from the structural neo-colonial context of African development problems. Basil Davidson (1991:13) aptly expressed the dependency syndrome characteristic of many African post-independence development models as follows:

Failure and futilities have occurred with the specific context of the attempt to develop Africa out of the history of Europe or America, and primarily for the benefit of Europe and America, rather than out of the history of Africa for the prime benefit of Africa (Davidson, 1991:13).

Those blemishes notwithstanding, for the first decade and a half of independence, most African countries experienced some modest social and economic development. Despite regular political disruptions by military coups and counter-coups, the continent witnessed significant demographic transformation, including high levels of urbanization, social differentiation, and class formation and consolidation. The dominant development model in the first decade of independence was premised on the existence of a developmental state that had a role to play in setting out plans for development, accumulation and investment. This developmental state sought to bring about social services, industries and infrastructure for the people, while at the same time demanding undivided loyalty from the people. In this regard, considerable investments were made in the social sector, particularly in education and health, in order to redress abject colonial neglect. Enrollment for primary, secondary and tertially education expanded remarkably throughout the continent. A cadre of professionals was produced to administer the post-colonial state as well as to expand the economic and social sectors. Modest industrialization through import substitution was also undertaken throughout Africa. Despite these modest initial achievements, reflected in the indices on health and education, Africa's performance has continued to lag behind all countries in other regions. It will be noted in subsequent chapters that the perverse integration of the continent into the world economy largely explains its inability to effectively manage the forces of globalization (UNCTAD, 2001).

For the initial two decades of independence, Africa's economic fortunes coincided with the general post-World War II economic expansion of the world economy. The buoyant economies of the North provided ever-expanding markets for Africa's primary produce. The industrialization process, which began during the Great Depression in some Latin American countries, was accelerated worldwide during the war and in the 1950s. It took off in some African countries in the early 1960s. On the whole, Africa experienced modest economic growth from the early 1960s until the mid-1970s. While the average growth rate was well below the rate achieved by a handful of East Asian economies, it equaled or exceeded the growth attained by many developing countries in other regions. Moreover, the so-called golden age was an era of considerable global prosperity, favoring rising terms of trade and widespread generosity and competition among the donor community under Cold War ideologies. The development cooperation experiment was launched and, for the next two-and-a-half decades, resources to assist poor countries increased considerably, leading to the creation of a large array of bilateral and multilateral institutions to channel and administer these resources. The Western and Communist powers provided huge sums of foreign assistance to those African states willing to stand against their ideological rival, with no democratic litmus test. Because the newly independent African states were courted for their political support in the evolving international system and encouraged to adopt the political ideologies of one or other camp in an effort to expand spheres of influence, the nature and character of the state was not considered to be an important factor in the relationship between African states and their benefactors (Rugumamu, 1997; 2001).

This does not mean that there were no alternative development strategies to neo-liberalism for Africa. In fact, at the very threshold of independence, Kwame Nkrumah of Ghana made a passionate call for African unity and self-reliance. To Nkrumah, pan-Africanism was an expression of the continental identity and coherence that distinguished regional integration in Africa from that of other regions in the developing world. He sought to unite all those people who bore the yoke of colonialism and continued to be exploited and oppressed under neo-colonialism. This political inspiration was strongly supported by the fact that African states were too weak, too poor and too politically vulnerable to serve the needs of their people. Without continental unity, he argued, the fruits of socio-economic progress would continue to elude Africa. Nkrumah stated:

> In my view, a united Africa – that is, the political and economic unification of the African continent – should seek three objectives. Firstly, we should have overall economic planning on a continental basis, which would increase the industrial and economic power of Africa. So long as we remain disunited, so long as we remain balkanized, regionally or territorially, we shall be at the mercy of colonialism and imperialism ... if we in Africa set up a common economic planning and a joint military command, it will follow that we shall have to adopt a common foreign policy to give political direction to our national continental defense and our national continental economic and industrial development planning (Nkrumah, 1974:116-117).

As a prerequisite to continental economic integration, Kwame Nkrumah's strategic vision sought to create an all-African federation, a coordinated and planned continental economy, a single African government, one defense force and, ultimately, a common strategic doctrine. His grand dream for a United States of Africa received very little support from his gradualist peers who were anxious to preserve their recently gained sovereignty. Although most of his fellow leaders found the idea of continental unity intrinsically desirable, it was not perceived to be practically implementable. During this period, the general consensus within the O.A.U. was to achieve unity by stages. Understandably, the majority of the member-states settled for pursuing less rigorous regional cooperation and integration arrangements based on a gradual and voluntarist approach. They held that economic integration should precede political integration. By the end of the 1980s, the halcyon years of integration in Africa, hundreds of sub-regional economic groupings had been established, but little progress had been made toward the realization of Nkrumah's dream. If anything, as subsequent pages will demonstrate, increasing poverty, marginalization and exclusion were the general trend among most African countries. Surprisingly, the ghost of Kwame Nkrumah did not haunt Africa enough!

Moreover, the onset of Cold War competition on African soil hijacked the concept of development and the development cooperation experiment, holding African nations hostage to East-West rivalries. In the second half of the 1970s, superpower interests in Africa rapidly increased, partly as a result of a Soviet challenge to the Western alliance throughout the South following the American collapse in Vietnam, and partly due to developments in Africa, notably the Ethiopian revolution and Portugal's withdrawal from its African colonies. The Cold War rivalry in Africa was accompanied by a shameful series of self-interested foreign interventions and ruthless exploitation of African conflicts by the Soviet Union, the United States and France. They participated in deliberate instigation or intensification of wars in the former Zaire, Ethiopia, Eritrea, Somalia, Angola, Mozambique and Somalia. By the same token, two alternative ways of achieving development were put forward: one based on market economies and liberal democracy; the other based on central planning and a single party system. In the decades that followed, each side trumpeted its success and sought to enlist poor African countries in its respective camp. Foreign aid, more than any other foreign policy instrument, was extensively employed, either to reward new converts or to punish recalcitrant enemies. Tens of thousands of economically useless projects and programs were lavishly funded throughout Africa as visible symbols of alliance and friendship (Ake, 1996; Nyang'oro, 1999).

Coincidentally also, independent Africa came into existence during the age of regional integration. The period witnessed the establishment of the European Economic Community in 1957, the Latin American Free Trade Association in 1961, the Association of South East Asian Nations in 1976 and the Caribbean Free Trade Area Association in 1968. It is also important to note that the British and French colonial authorities had sought to govern their colonies through federal systems. Thus, the thirteen French territories were grouped into two federations -- French West Africa, whose capital was Dakar, and the French Equatorial African Federation, with Brazzaville as its capital. These were disbanded in 1958. In British East Africa, a customs union was established for Uganda, Kenya and Tanganyika. The union provided for free trade among the colonies and a common external tariff, common communication services, common currency and a common income tax regime. After independence, regional integration experiments became virtually a movement. Within fifteen years of independence, well over twenty intergovernmental multi-sectoral economic cooperation arrangements and over 120 single sectoral multinational and bilateral organizations had been set up. However, by the beginning of the 1970s, most of them had either become moribund or existed in name only (Asante, 1990).

For much of the 1960s and 1970s, African states, multilateral agencies, and donor organizations supported direct state participation in the economy in order to address both entrepreneurial and market deficits. This largely explains why public investment played a major role in the growth of aggregate investment in Africa. State activity spanned every nook and cranny of African economies - manufacturing, services, public utilities and infrastructure. It also explains why generous measures were put in place to protect infant industries and tax incentives were offered to attract foreign investment. As the major shocks of the 1970s set in, such levels of investment were no longer sustainable. In some countries, most public enterprises collapsed, while in others they were sustained through massive borrowing from abroad, which resulted in the huge debts of the 1980s and 1990s (Mkandawire and Soludo, 1999).

The golden age came to an end in the early 1970s and the world entered what Eric Hobsbawm has called the 'crisis decades,' which extended into the 1990s (Hobsbawm, 1994:403). The end of the 1960s marked the onset of a period of disillusionment with the economic and political performance of most African states. When the global system moved into crisis, the conditions in Africa did not allow its countries to keep up even a marginal rate of growth. Simultaneously, Africa's economic fortunes changed noticeably: petroleum prices skyrocketed, the terms of trade with the rest of the world shifted unfavorably, and as misfortune would have it, the weather patterns also changed to Africa's disadvantage. Along with the rest of the developing world, Africa discovered that it had engaged in excessive borrowing from the North and was facing a severe debt crisis. As most economies decayed, debts piled up, investors held back on new capital and not a few donors began to reconsider the role of foreign aid in Africa's development. Viewed retrospectively, the failure of African states to create sustainable and expanding economies led to conflicts among different groups as they competed with each other for scarce economic resources and tenous political power.

With the socio-economic crisis in the late 1970s, a shift in the development model and policy preferences began to take place. In July 1979, African heads of state and government met in Monrovia, Liberia , to examine the economic problems facing the continent and to take a stand on what should be done to address those problems. One year later, they met again in Lagos, Nigeria, and adopted the *1980 Lagos Plan of Action* and the *Final Act of Lagos*. Both documents were mainly preoccupied with the debt crisis, terms of trade, declining aid and FDI flows, drought, and neo-liberal global governance. In short, the African heads of state put the blame for Africa's crisis almost entirely on imperialism, foreign exploitation and domination. They were virtually silent on the gross mismanagement of economies, massive corruption, political intolerance, human rights abuses, and suffocation of civil society. Not surprisingly, the World Bank scornfully rejected outright the general thrust of both documents, which were fiercely criticized for being over-ambitious, and faulted for ignoring the role of the private sector and failing to address the critical role of 'good governance.' In response, the Bank came up with its own report and recommendations, *Accelerated Development in sub-Saharan Africa: An Agenda for Action* (World Bank, 1981).

In its report, the Bank argued that, although structural and exogenous factors had contributed to the worsening of the sub-region's economic crisis, the crisis had, in a large measure, been exacerbated by inappropriate government policies that had adversely affected the efficient functioning of markets. In the World Bank's opinion, by removing government-engineered distortions, increasing internal efficiency and creating a stable macroeconomic environment, governments could strengthen prospects for long-term productivity improvements, thereby helping to check the effects of adverse

international conditions (World Bank, 1981). These policy reforms came to
be known and codified as structural adjustment programs (SAPs). The Bank
recommended a 'rolling back of the state' and 'unleashing the markets' as
the right policy strategy to promote economic growth, structural change,
and poverty elimination in Africa. In retrospect, it is clear that it was through
the implementation of structural adjustment programs that African economies
became further integrated into the new wave of the globalization process.
As David Reed concludes, structural adjustment policies virtually became
economic policy instruments for the globalization process in the South. They
championed the notion of 'globalism' or 'one world,' in which a single market
for goods, capital, services, skills and technology prevail:

> The impact of structural adjustment has transcended the national context for which it
> was designed and has played a fundamental role in restructuring the world economy.
> Policy lending, coupled with a new trade regime, has been the driving force in realigning
> major sectors of the developing world and Central and Eastern Europe in their relations
> with the highly industrialized nations, opening new capital and commodity markets,
> altering the functions of the state, and changing the terms on which working people offer
> labor (Reed, 1996:19).

As weak and dependent actors in the world economy, most African
governments reluctantly agreed to implement the IMF/World Bank structural
adjustment policies beginning in the early 1980s; they accepted direct outside
interference in their economic policy management in exchange for desperately
needed financial assistance. By the early 1980s, the Soviet Union was
reconsidering the magnitude of its overall commitments to the South, and
was beginning to scale back its financial obligations.[12] Many African countries
found themselves adopting not just short-term stabilization measures but
also long-term programs of structural adjustment designed to transform their
economies along free market lines. This development caused a sea change in
the role of the state, relative to both local and regional governance on the
one side, and multilateral institutions and NGOs on the other. From then
onwards, the international financial institutions took effective control of a
significant portion of the continent's policy management process. The
institutions imposed and closely supervised a comprehensive regime of
currency devaluation, privatization, market pricing, and macroeconomic
stabilization. African countries were rendered particularly vulnerable by the
massive debts they had acquired during the 1970s and early 1980s. This
increased the power not only of creditor countries, notably the United States,
Germany, France and the United Kingdom but, most importantly, the role
of the Bretton Woods institutions that came in to perform the role of debt
collectors.

The external intervention by multilateral financial institutions, governments of dominant powers, TNCs and a host of other non-governmental actors has undermined the sovereignty and the moral authority of the African state. The SAPs are usually so heavily packaged that they foreclose any options for policy modification by states. Simply put, states were under siege, with little leeway to devise policies that could consolidate their political power base or simply protect the interests of the poor. Deep cuts in the state's provision of employment and social services have eroded their previous social base still further. They are no longer in a position to pursue socially desirable objectives such as nation building, economic growth or equity. Moreover, SAP policies and programs have undermined the state's sovereignty by limiting the resources available for basic social services and public security, and even political patronage.

Failing to shelter its citizens from the crisis of the 1980s, the state increasingly lost its legitimacy and came to be perceived as a predatory institution acting as a middleman between society and the international system, instead of as an apparatus that safeguards and promotes the interests of society. This, in turn, meant that the post-colonial state could hardly pursue its national project of consolidating its ideological legitimacy, building political alliances, relating to its opposition, or securing the cooperation or support of autonomous centers of power. In short, most African states are now regarded as 'irrelevant,' as 'houses of banditry,' or as 'purveyors of indifference and cruelty' (Cheru, 1989; Davidson, 1992; and Olukushi and Laakso, 1996).

Furthermore, SAP policies and programs were based on the assumption that the privatization of inefficient and nepotistically managed public enterprises was one of the ways of combating corruption and reducing the state's financial obligations. In due course, the international donor community added political accountability to the economic conditionalities already imposed by SAPs. The disbursement of donor aid came to be conditional on greater institutional transparency, and broader political representation, government accountability and good governance, broadly defined. In this sense, the North arrogated to itself the moral superiority that endows its institutions with the presumed ability to provide solutions to the problems of the South. The older notions of 'manifest destiny' or 'imperial missions' easily come to mind. In its typical hypocritical style, the World Bank in 1989 advised African countries of the need to attack corruption and mismanagement to promote the autonomy of the judiciary and create an enabling environment for resource mobilization, democracy and participatory politics. This is what Dani Rodrik (1999:148) describes aptly as "forced harmonization."

It is important to note that international development and financial agencies failed to develop any set of objective criteria against which to measure the performance of good governance. Nor did they bother to consult broadly with aid-recipient countries on how best to operationalize the political conditions they set. Not surprisingly, in the absence of a coherent international policy different donors interpreted them differently in different situations. Critics were disconcerted by the selective and arbitrary application of the political conditionality doctrine. During the 1990s, major development cooperation programs between the European Union and developing countries was suspended in eight countries: Burundi, Liberia, Nigeria, Rwanda, Somalia, the Sudan, and Haiti. This involved the withdrawal of all financial and technical assistance, except humanitarian aid. In two of these cases, Liberia and Somalia, total suspension occurred *de facto*, rather than as a result of a formal decision, due to civil war and the collapse of each national government. In other cases, aid for new projects was suspended, while current projects remained unaffected. Such partial measures were taken in Gambia, Mali, Niger, Togo and the then Zaire. Even more disconcerting, while the United States cancelled debts for Poland and Egypt, it resisted doing so for African countries that were showing discernible democratization results (Oxfam, 1998).

Notwithstanding the rhetoric about local ownership and attempts to forge less asymmetrical relationships between donor agencies and their African recipient countries, the Bretton Woods institutions installed foreign technical advisors in various central ministries in order to closely monitor the implementation of SAP policies and programs. In the absence of countervailing institutions, international technocrats (who were not accountable to the local electorates) took the driver's seat in macro-managing SAPs. This unfortunate practice of according greater importance to accountability to donors than to national legislators and citizenry is grossly incompatible with internationally accepted democratic norms. Moreover, such excessive intervention eroded the moral authority of African states in their attempt to manage national affairs of critical importance. The erosion of sovereignty, in turn, inhibited internal policy and political debates about possible policy mixes and their timing and sequencing. As a result, the domestic consensus and coalition building required for sustainable economic reforms were severely undermined. This is what has been referred to as the rollback not only of the state, but most importantly, of the independent aspirations of the peoples of the South. As Susan George notes in the preface to *Dark Victory*:

> Rollback meant an end to Third World pretensions. There was to be no more talk of a New International Economic Order, binding codes of conduct for foreign investors, mandatory transfers of technology or managed commodity prices. The South was to return to that quiescent state from which it should never have been allowed to emerge. The unruly would be disciplined and the rebellious cowed (in Bello, 1994:x).

The initial expectations that SAPs could bring rapid economic recovery and poverty reduction were unrealistic. A minor economic turnaround occurred in a few African countries, but most of them slipped backwards into growing poverty and marginalization, ecological degradation, de-industrialization and political instability. The most obvious and debilitating effects of economic adjustment were often urban social unrest and violence. Many adjusting countries found themselves with 'IMF riots,' usually as a result of rising food and transport prices or user fees for basic social services. Not surprisingly, by 1993, twenty countries in Africa were below their per capita income of about twenty years earlier.

The rolling back of the state from key areas of the economy and from providing basic social services left behind huge gaps that could hardly be filled by either the private sector or by the kind of multiple coping strategies that would not have fitted the requirements of the economic adjustment model. SAPs assumed the existence of institutions sufficiently robust to administer the program and cushion their impact. As one study by the United Nations Research Institute for Social Development noted, "the flexibility and capacity of private sector institutions were often overestimated, and the process of adjustment so debilitated many state institutions that they were incapable of making the necessary contribution to ensuring the functioning of adjustment measures" (UNRISD, 1995:10).

By the end of the 1980s, confronted with the failure of many adjustment programs, the Bretton Wood institutions went a step further away from technical matters of economic policy to political mobilization of civil society in favor of SAPs. This took the form of high profile social safety nets designed to protect social groups seriously affected by adjustment. Ghana's SAP was the first in Africa to formally integrate the Program of Action to Mitigate the Social Costs of Adjustment (PAMSCAD) with the joint initiative of the government, the World Bank and the U.N. Children's Fund (UNICEF). One World Bank study noted that PAMSCAD, with resources of more than $80 million, only reached about fifty thousand beneficiaries or 0.3 percent of the population. The program was terminated in 1993 (World Bank, 1996b). Given the huge size of the affected population in African countries and the amount of resources set aside for the purpose, one wonders if any progress will ever be made in alleviating mass poverty.

Civic groups and opposition politicians seized the opportunity created by the weakening of the old autocratic regimes and the more supportive international atmosphere to push for political reforms. These agitations were to result in the end of single party systems and military rule in most of Africa. They also led to the outright overthrow of some long serving autocratic regimes in several countries. The state was perceived not only as parasitic but also, and most importantly, as redundant and useless developmentally. In Benin, and later across West Africa, national conferences were held to renegotiate the fundamental social contract that legitimized political power. A return to civilian rule, elections, and multi-party democracy followed these conferences. Elsewhere in Africa, pressure for political reform, particularly elections, made democratic procedures a crucial new element in African politics. It is, therefore, of little surprise that non-state actors have taken an ever-larger part in the affairs of the continent and have further eroded the sovereignty of these discredited nation states. Moreover, the World Bank, which, after 1988 openly focused on the political dimensions of development, gave the process of democratization in Africa a major moral boost. By advocating good governance, gender equality, decentralized power, human rights, and the need to check corruption and waste, the Bank massively energized the pro-democracy advocates on the continent.

In addition to international financial institutions and organizations such as the U.N., other international civil society organizations such as Amnesty International, Oxfam, Transparency International, Jubilee 2000 and Human Rights Watch exerted an enormous influence on what was once considered the prerogative of the state. Links have been established among transnational NGOs, local activists and individuals that are collectively committed to global justice on a range of issues. One of Transparency International's most important and enduring contributions, for example, has been to help place corruption firmly on the agenda in national politics, in academic research and in the policies of international financial institutions. Its publication, *Corruption Perception Index* (CPI) has become a must-read document worldwide. Committed to high principles and unwilling to make allowances for context, human rights NGOs have been critical of almost all African governments.

They have managed to put pressure on states accused of violating individual and group rights, as well as on those states that might sanction them (Khotari, 1984; Scholte, 1999). In short, civil society organizations have added a fresh voice to those traditionally consulted in the national and international decision-making processes.

Most telling, particularly from the mid-1980s, is the fact that NGOs have demanded recognition by international institutions. In the process of claiming a transnational or a sub-national constituency, they have carved out a role for themselves in several sectors, and have taken the lead in responding to complex international emergencies. Moreover, since 1999 some international civil society organizations have turned their attention to the excesses of the market, as evidenced by the work of Jubilee 2000 on the debt issue and calls for civil disobedience at the Seattle WTO meeting, and at the World Bank/ IMF annual meetings in Washington, to highlight unfair trade practices by the rich nations.

In Africa, NGOs became the main agencies for delivering and managing humanitarian assistance to the extent that collectively they were transferring more resources, in net term, to the South than was the World Bank. It has been estimated that NGOs disbursed over 10 percent of all public aid in 1994 (approximately $8 billion), surpassing the volume of the combined U.N. system ($6 billion), excluding the international financial institutions. This trend has been encouraged mainly by the increasing willingness of northern donor governments and multilateral institutions to direct official aid away from presumably predatory African states and through NGOs. Typical relief programs, for example, involve a contractual relationship between an international bilateral or multilateral donor and an NGO, whereby the latter acts as an implementing agent of the former in an agreed program of assistance (Duffield, 1994:58-60).

Above all, the dynamics of SAPs and globalization have further undermined most African states' ability to provide essential public goods. As will become increasingly apparent in the next few lines and paragraphs, state collapse in several countries is clear testimony to institutional decay. While there is an imperative for developing countries to integrate into the global economy and reform their economies, the policies that they have been encouraged to adopt have often undermined political stability and public security. The downsizing of police forces in African countries, as a result of either a cessation of conflicts or the adoption of economic policies that necessitate reduced security expenditures, has given rise to a security dilemma in various African countries. Such a dilemma becomes apparent when some groups in society start to sense that they have to take care of their own security. When they perceive that the state is either incapable or unwilling or both, they understandably and predictably take their own measures for protection. This perception has led to the proliferation of domestic security companies and self-defense militia in many African countries. In addition, inappropriate demobilization and reintegration of armed services personnel after the ending of conflicts has sometimes led to the creation of a number of mercenary forces seeking employment in foreign conflicts.

Kalevi Holsti (1996) has observed that the end of the Cold War left weak states not only bereft of internal legitimacy, but also unable to manage military challenges from warlord neighbors, unruly strongmen, rebel movements, mercenary forces, or frustrated subjects. Once such irreversible, destabilizing spirals of violence reach a crucial threshold, they often degenerate into traumatic state collapse and lawlessness. In order to defend themselves from such threats, some collapsing states in Africa have resorted to hiring private military companies, security companies, or even mercenaries. By the same token, in the absence of adequate and reliable public security, private businesses and prominent individuals in society have become increasingly reliant on the services of private security firms for their protection. The Angolan government, for example, made it part of its constitution that foreign investors provide their own security arrangements (O'Brian, 2000:54). This clearly demonstrates how far some weak African states have been forced to go in privatizing national security!

Citizens depend on states and central governments to secure their persons and free them from fear. Because failing states are unable to establish an atmosphere of security nation-wide, non-state actors have moved in to fill the void. The rise in demand for the services of private military companies and security firms has meant that national security in most of Africa has increasingly and exclusively been reserved for specific individuals and influential societal groups, while being virtually denied to the rest of society. At the same time, the monopolization of public security by influential private individuals has engendered a proliferation of armed non-state actors, including rebel movements, insurgents, warlords, guerilla groups and mercenary forces. For these groups, security is undertaken for and on behalf of some groups of the population, as opposed to and to the exclusion of others. A convergence of interlinking influences and actors, including the availability of small arms and the prevalence of war entrepreneurs, is now causing chronic militarization of society and undermining peace efforts in Angola, Côte d'Ivoire, Liberia, Sierra Leone and the Democratic Republic of Congo, to mention but a few.

As will be discussed in subsequent Chapters, with the increasing reluctance of Northern governments to intervene militarily in situations where they do not have any major strategic interests, new types of security entrepreneurs have emerged to fill the gap. Since the end of the Cold War, there has been a worldwide proliferation of what are alternately referred to as 'private military companies' (PMCs) or as 'private security companies' (PSCs). More often than not, these forces are employed without appropriate legislation in terms of accountability, transparency or codes of ethics. According to a study by David Isenberg (2000), by 2000, there were as many as 90 private security military forces of varying types operating in Africa alone, mostly in war-torn countries where oil companies and other major transnational companies are required to organize their own security. Some of the most popular private military companies include: Military Professional Resources Inc. and DynCorp. from the United States; Defense Systems Ltd and Sandline International from the United Kingdom; and Silver Shadow and Levdan from Israel.

The South Africa-based security firm Executive Outcomes (EO) had the greatest success in Angola and Sierra Leone, where insurgent activities had jeopardized diamond production. In these two cases, sovereign states invited private military companies to maintain security in their own countries (Chabal and Daloz, 1999; Reno, 2000). As Jean-Francois Bayart and colleagues insightfully conclude in their essay on kleptocracy in Africa, "one of the consequences of this particular conjuncture of factors is an erosion of the very foundations of political regimes...of states themselves" (Bayart et al, 1999:1). The monopoly of legitimate use of physical force has slipped away from some African states. In the words of political economist Samir Amin, the immediate development prospects of Africa are in doubt:

> If the 1960s were characterized by the great hope of seeing an irreversible process of development launched throughout what came to be called the Third World and in Africa particularly, the present age is one of disillusionment. Development has broken down, its theory is in crisis, and its ideology a subject of doubt (Amin, 1990:1).

As noted earlier, Africa's post-independence politics were tumultuous. In fact, there are few African countries of which it can be said that they have not experienced one form or another of political instability in the last forty years. The unresolved national question, the illegitimacy of borders, lack of participation and corruption fuelled political grievances in every country.

No sooner had independence been won than the continent, particularly sub-Saharan Africa, became a theatre of endless bloody ethnic conflicts, *coups d'etat,* wars, famines and refugee flows. The political survival of African leaders became the only precondition for pursuing any other goal. Their insecurity meant, in Robert Jackson and Carl Rosberg's apt phrase, "the seamanship often mattered more than navigation: staying afloat was more important than going somewhere" (Jackson and Rosberg, 1982:18). Exclusive focus on the disaster-ridden countries of the continent in the last few decades is bound to lead to despair and despondency. It is little wonder that recent African political economies provide abundant material for predicting doom and gloom. Africa's badly shattered economies can partly be explained by three decades of political instability. Viewed retrospectively, therefore, the political history of instability and corruption in the DRC, Somalia, Angola, Liberia, Sierra Leone, Rwanda, Burundi and the Sudan was nothing more than a prescription for disaster. The pervasive insecurity in Africa was further exacerbated by frequent droughts and famines, and later, and perhaps more ominously, by the spread of the HIV/AIDS pandemic. Africa seems to have been cursed!

It needs to be emphasized that recent economic and social performance indicators by the World Bank in Africa give no cause for jubilation. Unlike any other region in the world, macroeconomic performance in Africa has been remarkably poor since the beginning of the global recession in the early 1970s. The overall rate of growth has often been slow, or at times negative. Output per capita has declined, average incomes fallen, and inequalities have increased in most countries as the proportion of the population living in poverty has grown at a faster pace. Experiments with structural adjustment programs have not been successful in establishing the conditions for sustained growth. They have dismantled state-mediated mechanisms of capital accumulation, but have not succeeded in putting viable alternative mechanisms in their place. Above all, barely any African economies have experienced sufficient structural transformation to make any dent in the relevant economies' levels of poverty. One of the major manifestations of this problem is limited export diversification. Almost all African economies remain highly dependent on primary production and export. In the World Bank's classification of economies by major export categories, not a single Africa country belongs in the 'export of manufactures' league (World Bank, 1996:53-54). Export earnings have been dominated by one commodity in several countries. With such a narrow production and export base, Africa's participation in international markets has remained limited. Indeed, as will be pointed out in Chapter Three, reliance on one or two low value agricultural export commodities leaves African economies extremely vulnerable to volatility in commodity prices.

Conclusion

The euphoria of the immediate post-independence era was palpable. It was not for nothing that the 1960s were called the 'African decade.' 'Seek ye first the political kingdom,' admonished Kwame Nkrumah, one of the giants of that age, 'and all else will follow.' Alas, this was not to be. Of the 48 countries of sub-Saharan Africa, for example, 39 are in the low-income category and none falls in the high-income league. Of the ten in the middle income group, eight (Mauritius, the Seychelles, Botswana, Namibia, Swaziland, Lesotho, Gabon, and Cape Verde) have a combined population of less than six million, or merely one percent of the region's total. The other two are South Africa and Angola. Botswana, Gabon and Cape Verde owe their limited success to the discovery and exploitation of oil and diamond reserves. As is well-known, South Africa is a special case and the national per capita figure says very little about the situation of the vast majority of the people in that country. Race disaggregated per capita income figures would doubtless have a different story to tell. As for Angola, it has been consumed by a civil war since its independence. The endemic political instability in the country did not then, nor does it now, augur well for economic growth and poverty reduction. Swaziland and Lesotho's growth records appear solid but their role as a labor reserve for the Republic of South Africa makes the basis of their economic performance ambiguous. All in all, the impact of Africa's economic participation in the world economy during the three decades of political independence leaves a lot to be desired.

It is argued in the concluding Chapter that the solution to Africa's current woes lies equally in local as well as in transnational politics and transnational action. World market integration and transnational activities are driving virtually all new social movements and organizations to face up to the challenges of capitalist globalization. Already, there are thousands of anti-systemic movements and forces in the world organizing against polarization and refusing to submit to the consequences of exploitation and marginalization. Given the obvious failure of the neo-liberal development model in peripheral economies, the case for its continued application is indefensible. Since the Earth Summit of 1992, U.N. conferences have accepted significant policy inputs from grassroots movements. Such groups have networked to produce a common agenda, with the Internet providing the technical framework for these struggles.

The focus on world politics means more than just emphasis, for politics in the world system is more important than was the case previously. Social and trade union movements not only need to be transnational in order to be effective globally, they also will be required to nurture unity of political purpose and a shared vision. Arguably, fundamental changes in the world system happen only at a global level. Labor, peace, environmental and women's movements, for example, are increasingly transnational in organization and response. At a global level, these progressive movements share key interests and goals that entwine them inherently with democratization at the center of the entire transformation edifice. Surely, as will be submitted later, alliances and the coordination of struggles will not happen automatically. One tack would be to focus on issues of world concern and with the greatest global resonance, such as poverty, women's issues and environmental destruction, forming strategic alliances with transnational women's organizations, labor unions and environmental organizations in order to wage a war against the forces of globalization.

Strategically, however, it will be argued that transformational struggles in Africa will require structurally reconfigured national political economies. This will include instituting democratic governance, respecting human rights, protecting the rule of law, and promoting social equity. It will also include promoting effective states that ensure high and stable economic growth, provide public goods and social protection, raise the capability of people through universal access to education and other services, and promote gender equality. Before presenting various development scenarios, the next Chapter discusses the the salient features of contemporary globalization, outlines the institutional frameworks governing them, and assesses the impact of the current wave of globalization on African economies and politics.

CHAPTER 3

GLOBALIZATION AND AFRICA's MARGINALIZATION

Introduction

The continent's long-time role in the world system – to export raw materials and to import manufactured goods – has served to define its position and orientation. Its position at the periphery is largely a function of its relationship to the center. And its orientation – outward looking, toward external exchange and criteria – is an aspect of this incorporation. African states have engaged in foreign trade rather than domestic development, in satisfying 'international demand' rather than internal domestic needs. This inheritance of extroversion has a profound implication for the present performance and future potential for the continent (Shaw, 1975:369).

As noted in Chapter One, globalization is a highly charged issue. Debates surface everywhere in public discourse. Malcolm Walters (1995:1) asserted, for example, "that globalization may be the concept of the 1990s, a key idea by which we understand the transition of human society into the third millennium." However, interpretations abound. At one extreme, globalization is seen as an irresistible and benign force for delivering economic prosperity, security and liberty to people throughout the world. At the other, it is blamed as a source of all contemporary ills from economic inequalities associated with unfettered markets to social decay. Surprisingly, for a concept that is ubiquitous, there does not appear to be any precise or consensus definition. Its popularity stems in large part from its ambiguity and, like all popular concepts meant to cover a variety of phenomena, globalization has many meanings. There is little agreement on its definition, basic concepts, evidence, explanation, or implications and policy prescriptions. But, for all its imprecision, "globalization has become the most satisfactory descriptive label for the current historical era" (Falk, 1999:1).

The concept holds a widespread appeal in social science discourse, as attested by thousands of publications on the subject. Discourses on globalization have become a prime site of struggle between, broadly speaking, neo-liberals who celebrate its presumed fruits, and radical critics who claim that there have been no major transformations in the developmental logic of capitalism as a world system. The radical critics claim that globalization is nothing less that the continuation of the operation modern capitalist imperialism on a world-wide basis. To be sure, this crude dualism tends to present two conflicting interpretations from among diverse arguments and opinions. However, these two analytical categories, refer to ideal-type constructions. They help us order a field of inquiry and identify the primary areas of consensus as well as contention.

This Chapter examines only some of the critical socio-economic issues and trends of globalization and their impact on Africa's current and possible development prospects. It is not possible to cover all the significant dimensions of capitalist globalization in this study. However, let us now consider the role and impact of some of the major driving forces of globalization such as global regionalism, geo-strategic and diplomatic configurations, international trade, foreign direct investment, official development assistance, debt crisis, technology development and diffusion, and international migration on Africa's development. The aim of this chapter is to sharpen our understanding of those key issues, actors and trends that directly impact Africa's search for sustainable development.

Globalization Contextualized

There has been only gradual development and consolidation of a new and deepening phase of capitalist development between 1945 and the present, but this accelerated after the end of the 1980s. Unlike the previous waves of development, the contemporary phase has spread everywhere and is the only dominant economic system at the moment. Arguably, with the collapse of the Soviet Union and the end of communism in Eastern Europe, the conversion of European social democrats to neo-liberalism and free market conservatism and the imposition of SAPs on the economies of the South have left capitalism as the "only game in town." Radical critics of the globalization thesis, who study the longer-term aspects of capitalist development, are not surprised by the current expansion, the growing magnitude, or the deepening of inter-regional flows and patterns of social interaction. As the opening quotation from Tim Shaw notes, capitalism as a social order has a pathological expansionist tendency; in order to survive and maintain profits, capital has to expand to new markets. Its constant drive for global reach is, by definition, the internal logic of capitalism as a socio-economic system. Much as Marxist writer Giovanni Arrighi recognizes the spectacular expansion of the 1980s, he remarks that "it does not appear to be a revolutionary tendency at all" (Arrighi, 1994:300).

There is, of course, a general rise of regionalism, liberalization of international trade, masive cross-border financial flows, greater concentration and centralization of capital and production, and a move from Fordist to post-Fordist regimes of production and labor management. But, as Paul Hirst argues, many of the indices of 'globalization' (such as trade and investment patterns) reveal a stark concentration only within the OECD states. He concludes that, "it is the advanced industrial economies that constitute the membership of the global economy" (Hirst, 1995:7). On this basis, Winfried Ruigrok and Rob van Tulder (1995:151) support Hirst's thesis by noting that, in fact, we should speak of 'triadization' rather than globalization of the world economy. There is an increasing organization of world economic activity within the three core blocs, each with its own centre and periphery; namely: the Europeean bloc, the Asian Pacific and the Americas. The current changes, while significant and distinctive, are not unprecedented and do not necessarily involve a move toward a new type of economic system. The mere increase in the magnitude of transfers does not implicitly mean any significant change in the behavior or in the relationships of the major actors, namely capital and labor. In fact, current processes have done little thus far to challenge the hallmarks of capitalism, that is, an economy centered on the exploitation of labor and on surplus accumulation.

The basic criticism of globalization arises from a common sense but often forgotten observation: the international economy is not global yet. Markets, even for strategic industries and major firms, are still far from being fully integrated. Capital flows are still restricted by currency and banking regulations, the mobility of labor is undermined by immigration controls and xenophobia, and multinational enterprises still keep most of their assets and their strategic command centers in their historically defined home nations. As for the countries of the South, their economies remain predominantly dependent on the markets of the North, making them dangerously susceptible to changing conditions in global markets; more than 50 percent of Asian exports, 75 percent of Latin America's exports and well over 75 percent of Africa's exports are destined for Northern markets (UNCTAD, 1999).

The notion of globalization has come under spirited attack from many quarters. Specifically, the trailblazing works by Paul Hirst and Graham

Thompson (1999), David Held and others (1999), and Ankie Hoogvelt (1997) have argued that globalization is not a supra-human process created by abstract and unchallengeable market forces, or by intangible and uncontrollable technological forces. These critics argue that the emerging global system is not only a societal construct, driven and shaped as required by the dominant national, international and transnational players, but that it is also, and more importantly, a convenient ideological myth which serves to justify and legitimize the neo-liberal project. In this sense, globalization is interpreted primarily, but not exclusively, as the latest stage of capitalism, compounding the inequalities of power and resources already in place and also creating new imbalances. The process is supported by a liberal ideology that places a premium on individual choice in the market place. These writers have come to the conclusion that, in fact, the level of integration, interdependence and openness of national economies in the present era is not unprecedented. The current wave of globalization is but one of a number of distinct conjunctures in the history of the international economy that have taken place since an economy based on modern industrial technology began to be generalized from the 1860s.

There are also substantive disagreements about the role and importance of transnational corporations in the globalization process. Since the days of the East India Company in the 18th and 19th centuries, international firms have been the main global link between producers and consumers. What has changed noticeably over the years is not the character but the extent of the global reach of these international firms. While most liberal writers recognize the unparalleled scale of these corporate activities, critics dispute the extent to which they remain nationally identified, or genuinely transnational. Their economic power relative to states, in setting the ground rules for their activities is also disputed. Critics have concluded that none of these corporations are truly 'global,' 'footloose,' or 'borderless' (Ruigrok and van Tulder, 1995; and Hirst and Thompson, 1996). As far as the OECD countries are concerned, transnational enterprises remain largely confined to their home territory in terms of overall business activity, that is, in terms of location of sales, affiliates, declared profits, research and finance. A brief glance at the Fortune 500 list of the world's largest companies would confirm that only a few of them have headquarters outside the United States, the United Kingdom, Germany, Japan, or France.

By the same token, critics argue that capital markets were more integrated at the beginning than at the end of the 20th century. An important study by

Martin Feldstein and Charles Horioka (1980) found that the hyped freedom of capital movement has not integrated international finance as much as many believe. They observed that if the world economy were really integrated in financial matters, then national savings rates and investment rates would no longer be correlated and interest rates around the world would be more nearly equal. Moreover, critics argue that in a perfectly integrated international financial system, the cost of capital (discounting the risk factor) would be approximately equal everywhere. Instead, significant national differences in capital costs remain characteristic of the world economy. In short, there is overwhelming evidence to suggest that the current international economy is less open and integrated than the regime that prevailed from 1870 to 1914 - - the so-called *'belle epoque.'* [13] Gradually, however, the international economic regime of the *belle epoque* collapsed due largely to incompetent policies, unemployment and nationalism that drove governments into war and beggar-thy-neighbor protectionism.

Moreover, critics of the globalization thesis also argue that capital mobility is not producing massive shifts of investment and employment from advanced to developing countries as neo-liberals would wish us to believe. Rather, foreign direct investment, technological capacity, industrial production and markets are all highly concentrated among the advanced industrial economies of the European Union, Japan and North America. These major economic powers, in the triad, have the capacity, especially if they coordinate policy, to exert powerful governance pressures over financial markets and in other economic arenas. Global markets are thus by no means beyond regulation and control, even though the divergent interests of the great powers limit the current scope and objectives of economic governance. Most countries in the South remain essentially marginal to both investment and trade, apart from a small minority of newly industrialized countries. Some studies have projected that losses from globalization would be outweighed by gains, but invariably, those losses will be concentrated in a group of countries that can least afford them.

The impact of the globalization process is both uneven and contradictory. On the one hand, some countries and, to an even greater extent, corporations have been considerably more able than others to reap the potential trade, investment, technological and transformational benefits of global restructuring. As the 1996 UNDP *Human Development Report* perceptively observes, globalization is not a positive-sum game but rather 'a two-edged sword - with winners and losers' (UNDP, 1996:82). The distribution of costs and benefits is asymmetrical across countries, sectors, firms, factors, classes and individuals. For some, it brings the promise of integration into a thriving world economy and society. Globalization forces have led to creative processes producing new technologies, devising more and better tradable goods and services, and expanding the range of opportunities. To others, it means increasing inequality and prospects of chaos, disorder and poverty.

The costs and benefits to various national economies and firms differ widely, depending on a matrix of factors that include the structural power of these economies in the global system, resources, geo-strategic advantages and economic strength. Strong states not only influence the nature and pace of globalization but, they also have relatively greater control over their integration into the world economy. Not surprisingly, the world has become more polarized, and the gulf between the poor and the rich countries has widened even further. Of the $23 trillion global GDP in 1993, about $18 trillion was accounted for by countries in the North, and only $5 trillion by the South, even though they have nearly 80 percent of the world's people. Worse still, the gap in per capita income between the North and South tripled, from $5,700 in 1960 to $15,400 in 1993, adjusted for inflation (UNDP, 1996:2).

It is important to stress the point that in the contemporary world, the old geographical boundaries of social and economic prosperity between North and South have been breached. There are more direct consequences of capitalist marginalization and a greater concentration of poverty in most of Africa than in any other region of the world. However, similar patterns of inclusion and exclusion are observable in the countries in the industrial North. Due to the onslaught of technology and capital, the South has visible islands of consolidated capitalist development in countries like South Korea, Taiwan and Singapore. Similarly, the patterns of unequal development have spread to the developed industrial North. The economies of the North are gradually becoming highly differentiated and complex. Cities like New York, London, Paris, Rome and Chicago exhibit a new social architecture containing large areas in which economic and social conditions are similar to those of many countries and cities in the South (like Rio, Delhi, Lagos or Nairobi) with many people unemployed, hungry, illiterate, homeless and completely marginalized. This new social architecture is re-arranging the world into winners and losers of globalization.

The emergence of widespread resistance to globalization, particularly on debt and poverty issues, as well as anti-globalization protests at every major

WTO/World Bank governors' meeting, comes as no surprise. Neo-liberal reforms have spurred the development of a wide spectrum of non-governmental organizations that are at the forefront of efforts to block those reforms. Some labor unions and opposition political parties have also mobilized against neo-liberalism. In some countries, revolutionary groups have emerged with the explicit objective of scaling back market reforms. Governments thus have to grapple with protests and demonstrations, strikes and work stoppages, land seizures, riots, and civil disobedience and even armed rebellion. Unless globalization is tamed, so the argument goes, a 'new barbarism' will emerge as conflicts spill over into the global 'zones of peace' fuelled by intensifying poverty, exclusion, disempowerment and wealth inequality (Petras and Veltmeyer, 2001; Onimode, 1989).

Worse still, the process of globalization is transforming fundamentally, though differentially, the authority and capacity of states to set the social, political and economic agenda within their respective territorial boundaries. The decision-making authority is slowly but inexorably being ceded to such actors as the IMF, the World Bank, transnational corporations and the World Trade Organization. These institutions, of course, are not autonomous actors. Rather, they represent the interests of leading states. For the majority of states in the world, this reallocation of authority to external actors is merely an intensification of the loss of control of vital matters falling within the domestic domain. The IMF/World Bank-sponsored policy programs, for instance, have forced almost all African economies to the very fringes of the global economy and have left the majority of poor citizens living miserable lives. International competition for market shares, FDI and jobs has forced national governments, particularly those in Africa, to reduce taxation on TNCs and, with it, the social services that protected the very poor. They have also cut those public services and regulations that protected the environment. Above all, the globalization drive has forced governments and firms to 'downsize' or 'restructure' to ensure that the cost of labor is kept low.

Admittedly, there have been some interesting theoretical insights like Samir Amin's (1974) 'accumulation on a world scale' (1974); Andre Frank's (1966) 'development of underdevelopment,' the 'production of the capitalist system thesis' of Immanuel Wallerstein (1974); Arrighi Emmanuel's (1972) 'unequal exchange' and Walter Rodney's (1972) 'dependency theory.' All these theoretical insights sought to provide frameworks to explain and interpret the inner structure and dynamic of capitalism, as well as the nature of relations between the 'center economies' and the 'periphery economies' of the same system. The exaggerated claims of the globalists do not stand up to any rigorous test. As Paul Hirst and Grahame Thompson argue, "if the theorists of globalization mean that we have an economy in which each part of the world is linked by market sharing close to the real-time information, then it began not in the 1970s but in the 1870s" (Hirst and Thompson, 1999:9-10). In the same vein, Giovanni Arrighi (1999:55) concludes that the examples of economic expansion and integration of the last two decades should not be construed as novel "except for their scale, scope and complexity."

In support of globalization and liberalization, the neo-liberal orthodoxy has become almost the only development model and mobilizing ideology in Africa. It is claimed, and even widely believed that globalization is an inevitable part of the inexorable rise of the global village. There is no alternative to the rationality and efficiency requirements of the market. In the words of Francis Fukuyama, "...the triumph of the West, of the Western idea, is evident first of all in the total exhaustion of viable systematic alternatives to western liberalism" (Fukuyama, 1989:3). According to this thesis, the only hope for the rest of the world is to imitate the most successful countries as quickly as possible and abandon all ideas of alternative approaches, solutions and visions. In this regard, the deregulation of markets and prices, privatization of enterprises, the downsizing of governments and the liberalization of trade have become indispensable policy initiatives that are expected to enhance both efficiency and welfare in all countries. In short, more rather than less globalization is the principal remedy for eradicating global marginalization, poverty and underdevelopment.

Under these circumstances, the capacity of African countries to create and sustain their own economic niches would appear to be very limited. As the following sections demonstrate, the continent lacks not only the requisite policy instruments and institutional and technical capacity to reap the much-heralded benefits of globalization but, most importantly, individual national economic units are inadequate to respond decisively to the structural asymmetries and inequalities of the global capitalist system.

Global Regionalism and Africa's Exclusion

The recent embrace of regionalization is a political and economic response to globalization, as states try to control at a regional level what they may have failed to manage at a national level. National policy agendas are circumscribed, both by resources and level of development, and by the global rules and policies. Regionalism refers also to a process of policy coordination, harmonization and adjustment designed to facilitate closer economic and political interdependence, and to manage the externalities that arise from it (Haggard, 1995). In fact, the past two decades have witnessed a resurgence, revitalization or expansion of regional economic cooperation and integration groupings at the global level. Of over 250 economic integration agreements that have been reported to WTO, the majority of the countries that are a party to these agreements are often seeking to create free trade areas (WTO, 2003). Calculated policy and institutional responses to the challenges of globalization have had a particularly effective regional character in the core nations of the North. Regionalism is also seen as a force that helps channel the resources of economies and people into activities where they are likely to excel. It is a force that softens the effects of globalization by pooling state policies in order to compensate for the loss of national policy sovereignty. As James Mittelman claims, "regionalism today is emerging as a potent force in the global restructuring of power and production" (Mittelman, 1999:25). In other words, regionalism is a negative reaction to the forces of globalization.

Ideally, regional economic integration represents an exercise in international economic relations, driven by economic mechanisms, but frequently with political objectives as the underlying force. There is even one view that the new regionalism can be distinguished by its emphasis on the non-economic and political dimensions. The political ambition of creating territorial identity, political convergence, collective security and regional coherence now seems to be the primary, neo-mercantilist goal of the new regionalism (Mistry, 1995:13). One can also note the curious way in which former enemies or previously excluded members, such as the Republic of South Africa in Southern Africa and Vietnam in South East Asia, have entered the main regional organizations, if only for their long-term self-interest. This wave is often referred to in the literature as 'the new regionalism' and is characterized by increasing scope, diversity, fluidity and non-conformity (Hettne and Inotai, 1994).

One of the classic economic arguments behind the creation of regional cooperation and integration arrangements is that they provide mechanisms through which intra-regional trade expansion and accelerated development can be achieved. Indeed, the orthodox theory of regional economic integration was firmly based on the static and dynamic gains to be derived from such arrangements. It is often stated that by widening markets and enhancing trade expansion, regional trade arrangements result in a clearer division of labor, and improve efficiency and encourage competition, product specialization and entrepreneurial skills development. The customs union concept constitutes the foundation of the theory. It involves the creation, in linear succession, of increasingly advanced stages of economic integration: a preferential trade area, then free trade area, customs union, common market, economic union and finally, a political union. The market forces that are set in motion at one stage are expected to have spillover effects to the next stage so that the entire implementation process becomes an economic necessity (Viner, 1937).

Three distinctive global trends in the development of regional cooperation and integration arrangements are discernible: North-North, North-South and South-South. North-North cooperation is represented by the European Economic Community, which was established by the Treaty of Rome in 1957 and ultimately transformed into the single market of the European Community in 1992. The European Single Market Act (1986) has played a key role in the resurgence of regionalism on a global scale. The prospects of 'Fortress Europe' created shock waves in the rest of the industrialized world, particularly in the United States and Japan. In the words of T.N. Srinivasan, "open regionalism is nothing but an oxymoron" (Srinivasan, 1998:340). These two global economic giants were concerned that, once the European Union had established a free trade region among its members, there would be increasing temptation and opportunity for retaining barriers to non-members in order to induce tariff-jumping foreign investments. Despite the protestations of the European Community that it would continue to meet the requirements of the General Agreement on Tariffs and Trade, the United States reacted by establishing an institutional framework - the North American Free Trade Area (NAFTA) to facilitate the regionalization of the North American political economy. NAFTA, an economic arrangement among the United States, Canada and Mexico, belongs to the North-South type of economic cooperation and integration.[14]

Once launched, the regional movements in Western Europe and North America undoubtedly contributed to the spread of regionalism elsewhere in the world. By the late 1990s, there were approximately 180 regional agreements and almost all members of the WTO were included in one or more formal regional agreement (Gilpin, 2001:341-43). Rather than operating solely to facilitate the free exchange of goods and services, the process of bloc formation has been perceived as the functional equivalent of the colonial imperialism of past centuries, with rival core powers attempting to fortify their respective geopolitical positions by aggressively supporting strategic alliances and coordination in order to pre-empt and out-compete non-bloc enterprises. In fact, all other countries are afraid that the emerging 'tripolization' of the world economy dominated by Fortress Europe, NAFTA, and Pacific Asia will increase regional protectionism, trade and investment diversion and that the protectionist interest groups (of agriculture, steel and textiles) will slow down the process of multilateral trade liberalization. This has been referred to as 'the 21st century mercantilist regionalism' (MacNeill, *et. al.*, 1991). These three regional trading blocs have come to be known as the 'Triad'. The triad accounts for about 70 percent of world GDP. NAFTA and the EU each account for about 25 percent. The Asian region, led by Japan and the newly industrialized countries (NICs) including China, the fastest growing economy, accounts for about 18 to 20 percent of world GDP. In this regard, the global economy revolves around these three economic powerhouses. They are deeply integrated in terms of their geopolitical proximity, investment, technology, trade and security coordination.[15]

The South-South integration groupings are by far the most numerous and the least effective. In Latin America the list includes, among others: the Latin American Free Trade Area (LAFTA), which was replaced by the Latin American Integration Association (LAIA) in 1981; the Central American Common Market (CACM); the Andean Community (AC); the Caribbean Economic Community (CARICOM); and the Southern Cone Common Market (MERCOSUR). In Asia, the groupings include: the Asia-Pacific Free Trade Area (APFTA); the South Asia Association for Regional Cooperation (SAARC); and the South Pacific Forum (SPF).

Since its inception in 1958 and most recently through the Multinational Programming and Operational Centers (MULPOCs) the Economic Commission for Africa (ECA) has promoted wider economic integration in Africa. Surprisingly, no region in the world can claim to have more of these regional cooperation groupings than this continent. The major regional initiatives include: the Arab-Maghreb Union (AMU); the Economic Community of West African States (ECOWAS); the Economic and Monetary Union of West Africa (UEMOA); the Economic Community of Central African States (ECCAS); the Central African Economic and Monetary Community (CEMAC); the Common Market for Eastern and Southern Africa (COMESA); the Southern African Development Community (SADC), the East African Community (EAC); and the Intergovernmental Authority on Development (IGAD). African governments have historically neglected to conduct in-depth evaluations of the potential impact of joining a regional bloc. In fact, the tendency has been to join any and all blocs to which they have had access, without carefully assessing the costs and benefits involved. With the exception of the Southern African Customs Union (SACU), all other sub-regional cooperation and integration arrangements in Africa have performed dismally. The common market goal was ambitious and has remained elusive, with most regional arrangements failing to achieve targets within the adopted timetable. As Peter Anyang' Nyong'o argues, the failure of nearly every initiative toward regional cooperation has been a result of flawed conception, defective policy formulations and haphazard execution of such policies (Anyang' Nyong'o, 1990:6).

The fears of marginalization arising from regionalism in the South are supported by hard evidence. The emerging triadization of the world economy will increasingly favor regionally-based factor movements as well as investments in a wider economic space, as well as promoting economic growth mainly for relevant member states. This argument is partly demonstrated by the geographical patterns of intra-firm alliances. Of the 4,200 intra-firm strategic cooperation agreements signed by enterprises worldwide in the period 1980-89, for example, 92 percent were between enterprises from Japan, Western Europe and North America. Marginalization is also partly demonstrated by intra-regional capital flows. During the 1980s and 1990s, the triad accounted for around four-fifths of all international capital flow (Group of Lisbon, 1995:71).

Moreover, as the E.U. record indicates, regionalism has witnessed unprecedented growth and has provided the impetus for industrialization and economic recovery among member countries. Between 1958 and 1970, for example, intra-E.U. trade increased by 600 percent. To be sure, the E.U. is the model in this regard. As a result of integration, non-E.U. firms that face quantitative restrictions on their exports have increasingly turned to investing in production facilities within the E.U. The integration process already has a significant effect on existing production patterns. The upsurge in U.S. investment in the E.U. reflects on the profitability of past investments. Moreover, the growth of Japanese investment in the E.U. equally reflects on the consideration by Japanese industrialists as to their anticipation of the threat of what would otherwise be imposed on imports from non-E.U. countries. Above all, it reflects the medium and long-term prospects for growth in the E.U. In a similar vein, Robert Hine (1992:120) has noted that the United States' arrangements in NAFTA contain "exclusionary provisions against third parties, particularly through the local content requirements and strict application of the rules of origin." Trade and investment within each of these three regions tend to be larger than with any other single region. At the same time, inter-bloc transactions are expanding geometrically. And, as will be argued in subsequent pages, unless Africa accelerates the pace and intensity of its sub-regional and regional integration projects, the capacity of individual countries to participate meaningfully in the emerging global economic trend is severely limited (Rugumamu, 1999b).

As Harald Sander (1996) has observed, regionalism is almost by definition discriminatory against non-members. Given the proclivity of the triad toward regionalism, Africa faces monumental obstacles relative to its access to collective security, investment, technology and markets. Already, the E.U.'s enlargement eastward provides new and more dynamic investment and trade opportunities than the combined African, Caribbean and Pacific (ACP) group. In this regard, at least four cautionary observations are in order. First, and as earlier noted, as world productive resources become increasingly concentrated in the three mega-blocs, Africa's access to them will become further circumscribed. Weak competitiveness and low productivity will inevitably push her out of the market. Second, rapid advances in the frontier areas of science and technology will generate new waves of industrial revolution in the triad. These, in turn, will further compound Africa's underdevelopment and will exacerbate its marginalization and exclusion. As will be pointed out later, rapid technological advances will hasten the obsolescence of the mainstays of Africa's economies. The demand for natural resources and cheap labor will decline progressively as the acquisition, application, and manipulation of new frontiers of knowledge intensifies. Third, as the globalization process deepens, the developmental gap between Africa and other more dynamic regions and countries in the South will further widen. The latter's enhanced capacity to acquire, absorb, adapt and diffuse technologies will permit them not only to enjoy the economic spillover from the triad, but also, and more importantly, to participate effectively in the emerging global economy and collective security. As John Ravenhill (1993:59) predicts, with few prospects for a significant reversal of Africa's economic decline in the coming decade, and with new investment and trade opportunities for the E.U. opening up further into Eastern Europe, most African states, individually and collectively, are likely to continue to decline significantly as economic and security partners for a gradually integrating Europe.

The progress achieved in Africa's integration efforts in the first three decades of independence has been uneven at best and unimpressive at worst. The share of intra-group trade, for example, has remained low: growing from 2.9 percent in 1970 to 7.84 percent in 1992 within ECOWAS; declining from 8.0 percent in 1970 to 6.8 percent in 1996 but registering a modest increase in 1998 within COMESA; and showing a modest growth from 2.6 percent in 1970 to 6.0 percent in 1997, within SADC (ECA, 1999:2-4).[16] Several economic studies have narrowly explained Africa's poor integration performance as largely a function of structural factors. The competitive nature of the primary commodity-producing, small, low-income economies with little manufacturing capacity, the weak financial sectors, and a poor intra-state and inter-state transport and communications infrastructure, all contribute to economies that have little to trade with each other, yet are locked into the North-South trading relationship (Rwegasira, 1996; Aly, 1994).

Besides economic explanations, Africa's post-independence political history offers equally plausible insights into the problems of cooperation and integration on the continent. As the rest of the world continued to make significant strides toward cooperation and integration in the 1970s and 1980s, most of Africa was embroiled in bloody inter-state conflicts and destructive civil wars and haunted by the specter of collapsed states. These unfortunate developments occurred despite the fact that, since the establishment of the Organization of African Unity (O.A.U) in 1963, successive leaders had sought to build a united and secure Africa. For a variety of reasons, the political will to integrate was rarely supported by the requisite commitment to translate declarations into concrete actions. This lack of political commitment manifested itself in member countries developing their own strategies, plans and priorities, which scarcely reflected regional cooperation imperatives. Lack of commitment was also demonstrated by the constant failure to abide by integration rules and regulations.

Although African countries continue to speak of collective action for regional integration, very few of them have consciously designed their national plans to be consistent with the promotion of effective integration for development. Most of them do not even have a developed national institutional apparatus for coordinating, harmonizing and monitoring their involvement in the different inter-governmental organizations to which they belong. Lack of political commitment has also been reflected in tardy payment of budgetary contributions. Not surprisingly, some regional groupings have been unable to discharge their functions smoothly due to constant lack of funding. With all indicators pointing to further marginalization and exclusion, regional cooperation and integration received a new impetus in Africa after the signing of the Abuja Treaty in 1991 to establish the African Economic Community by 2025. As will be pointed out in later sections of the book, by 2000 the Treaty had already accumulated dust in most African capitals as the rest of the world became more integrated through trade, investment and digitization. Indeed, let us take a closer look at Africa's performance in the technology sector.

Technology Development and Africa's Marginalization

The first industrial revolution in the 18th century was driven by steam power and the textile industry. It was later strengthened by the development of railways and given a powerful new impetus by the arrival of electricity and the rise of science-based industries. Globalization today has been made possible by another wave of technological change: information and communication technology (ICT). Even more than energy technologies and biotechnology, ICT is considered the principal source of the 'third industrial revolution' that began with the microelectronics revolution in the 1960s. The successful marriage of computer technology and telecommunications or 'digitalization' is one of the defining features of contemporary globalization. For better or worse, it has had a revolutionary impact on the way societies live, conduct business and learn. This convergence has brought about the information age, the so-called 'knowledge era,' the 'new economy,' the 'information society' and, above all, the 'digital divide' between the global haves and have-nots.

Technology was arguably created, developed and diffused in response to specific market pressures. Research and development, personnel and finance all tend to be concentrated in the North, led by transnational corporations and following the global market demand dominated by high-income consumers. Since the mid-1970s, the world has witnessed radical technological innovations in microelectronics, biotechnology and new materials. In the absence of a standard terminology, these technologies are variously called 'frontier,' 'high,' 'advanced,' or 'emerging technologies.' As a result, the relevant research effort has also tended to neglect opportunities to develop technologies for those people with low purchasing power. The OECD countries, with 14 percent of the world's people, accounted for 86 percent of the 836,000 patent applications filed in 1998, and 85 percent of scientific and technical journal articles published worldwide (UNDP, 2001:39). As in the case of trade and investment, there are serious imbalances in the access to information, knowledge and technology.

The main characteristic of the emerging technologies is that they have a major impact on several other technological systems and on many economic and social activities. The new and emerging technologies are changing the context and the mode of industrial production. As a result, new international patterns of industrialization are emerging. The knowledge-based economies are generating powerful spillover effects, often spreading like wild-fire, setting off a chain reaction of new innovations. The sources for higher productivity are increasingly dependent on knowledge and information as applied to production, and this knowledge is increasingly science-based. The knowldge-intensive and high technology industries (electronics, semi-conductors, etc.) and the service sector (software development, financial services and call centres) have become the fastest growing sectors in the global economy. Successful economic development will eventually require that countries become able to enter and compete in these sectors. For the poor countries of the South that have not put in place innovative public policies in order to cope with these technologies, the same technologies could easily become a source of exclusion, not a tool for progress. By the same token, the needs of the poor could remain neglected and new global risks may be left unmanaged (Castells, 1998).

Over the past two decades or so, production has become more and more knowledge-intensive, as investment in intangibles such as research and development, software, design, marketing and management have come to play a greater role in the production of goods and services. Not only has the nature of production changed, but competition has also become more innovation-based and globalized as markets have been liberalized everywhere. This has accelerated the pace of technological change and increased the burden on firms to engage in a continuous process of innovation in order to survive (Mytelka, 1999). Production in OECD countries is dramatically shifting from material goods to information-processing activities, thus fundamentally changing the structure of those societies to favor economic activities that focus on the manipulation of symbols in the organization of production and in the enhancement of productivity. In 1990, for example, about 47.4 percent of the employed population in the United States, 45.8 percent of those employed in the United Kingdom, 45.1 percent of those employed in France, and 40.0 percent of those employed in West Germany were engaged in information-processing activities, whether in the production of goods or in the provision of services.

The organization of production in particular, and of economic activity in general, has changed from standardized mass-production to flexible customized production, and from vertically integrated large-scale organization to vertical disintegration and horizontal networks between units. Investment, production, management, markets, labor, information and technology are organized across national boundaries. Some 65,000 TNCs (with 850,000 affiliates) are the key actors behind these global production systems. With the spread of the Internet, e-mail, low cost international phone services, mobile phones and electronic conferencing the world has become more interconnected (Castells, 1993).

The revolution in information technology has combined with organizational changes at the global level to produce a new world information economy. ICT has spread in varying degrees to many service industries, including office and related service activities, banking, insurance, telecommunications, computer and construction services. The characteristics of ICT are particularly attractive. It cuts the costs of information processing, speeds up data transmission, decreases the size and increases reliability of equipment, while enhancing the importance of software. The programmability, interactivity, and networking capabilities of ICT have radically changed the ways in which goods and services are produced and delivered. More specifically, economies of scope, flexible production lines and greater customization of products are made possible through the application of this important technology. The information society index (ISI) for the year 2001, assembled by the International Data Corporation (IDC) and the World Times, identified 55 countries (accounting for 97 percent of global national product and 99 percent of ICT expenditures) as among those with the basic infrastructure needed to take advantage of the information age. The failure of most African economies to respond resolutely to the challenges posed by these new technologies will obviously mean increased marginalization in the future (Soubra, 1993:26-28; Franda, 2002:8-12)

In the emerging global economy, the structure and logic of the information economy defines a new international division of labor. It is based less and less on the location of natural resources, cheap and abundant labor, or even capital stock, and more on the capacity to create new knowledge and to apply it rapidly via information processing and telecommunications to a wide range of human activities. Thus, information technology and the ability to use and adapt it are critical factors in generating and accessing wealth, power and knowledge in our time. The structure of production has been reorganized into networks that span the world. It is organized among separate players – subcontractors, suppliers, laboratories, management consultants, education and research institutes, marketing research firms and distributors. These dense and complex interactions create value chains that drive the technology-based global economy. In the labor-intensive industries, for example, TNCs design the product, specify the product quality and then out-source its production to local firms in developing countries. They also exercise control over the quality and timing of production, which is often subjected to changes in design and volume. This is a global 'just-in-time' production system. In these circumstances, countries and firms lacking access to modern telecommunications systems cannot effectively participate in the new global economy. As will be demonstrated, Africa is, by and large, almost excluded from participating effectively and meaningfully in the global political economy that is largely influenced by the emerging technological revolution (Stonier, 1983; Boyer, 1987; Castells and Tyson, 1989).

Not only is Africa by far the least computerized region in the world, but it also lacks the minimum infrastructure required to make use of computers. Before moving into electronics, Africa will need to put in place a reliable electricity supply. Between 1971 and 1993, the commercial use of energy in Africa rose from 251 kilowatts per capita to 288 kilowatts per capita, while in developing countries as a whole, consumption more than doubled, from 255 kilowatts to 536 kilowatts per capita. This compares unfavorably with a consumption of 4,589 kilowatts per capita for industrial countries (UNDP, 1996:183). Furthermore, the critical aspect of computer use is its networking capability, which relies on telecommunications infrastructure and network connectivity. Africa has the world's least developed information and communications infrastructure, with just 2 percent of the world's telephones and fewer than 2 telephones per 1,000 inhabitants. On average, there is one telephone line for every 200 people in Mali and Niger, while in the DRC there is one line for every 1,000 people (Jensen, 1999). Moreover, in mid-2000, there were 5 million mobile cellular telephones in South Africa and about 400,000 in the rest of Africa. However, very few of these were connected to the Internet and no international roaming agreements or facilities for data communication were provided by any mobile telephone companies (Franda, 2002:14).

One can safely add that, if the physical infrastructure is lagging behind, the human skills to operate information technology remain totally inadequate in most of Africa. As Fernando Cardoso observes, the problem is that the South's great competitive advantage, which ensured its initial integration into the international market, albeit in a condition of dependence, has lost its importance. That advantage was abundance of arable land, mineral resources and cheap labor. These traditional advantages have become inconsequential. In his own words:

> So the South is in double jeopardy - seemingly able neither to integrate itself, pursuing its own best interests, nor to avoid 'being integrated' as servants of rich economies. Those countries (or parts thereof), which are unable to repeat the revolution of the contemporary world, and at the same time cannot find a niche in the international market, will end up in the 'worst of all possible worlds.' They will not even be worth the trouble of exploitation; they will become inconsequential, of no interest to the globalizing economy (Cardoso, 1993:156).

If one excludes South Africa, in January, 2000, about 25,000 computers were permanently connected to the Internet in Africa. This meant the entire continent of Africa, excluding South Africa, had far fewer computers connected to the Internet than did New York City. In South Africa there was one Internet user for every 46 people in 2000. For the rest of Africa, there was one user in every 1,468 people, compared with an average of approximately one in every two people in North America and one in every four people in Europe. In other words, approximately 2 percent of the population of South Africa had some form of access to the Internet in 2000, whereas less than 0.1 percent of those in the rest of Africa had access. These figures place the entire continent at the very bottom of the list of world regions with connectivity to the Internet. As pointed out earlier, the major reasons the vast populations of Africa have been unable to gain access to the Internet include the lack of basic telecommunications and other Internet-related infrastructures, the extremely high cost of using those facilities that do exist, and the lack of skills, resources and awareness necessary to enable people to use the Internet for any purpose (Franda, 2002:12-13).

Even more devastating is the potential of the biotechnology industry. Global consumers will soon have a choice between Kenya AA coffee, which is the current favourite purchase for those with taste for the organic, and bio-coffee beans made in laboratories in the United States. Moreover, the development of the high fructose corn sweetener using immobilized enzyme technology is probably the best known example of a trend which may well become widespread in the 21st century. In this case, the threat is to relatively high-cost sugar producers, but similar substitution is possible for vanilla, cocoa, palm oil products, peanuts, pyrethrum, and many other traditional crops. Although not all such substitutes are economically feasible yet, the possible dangers for many African countries are clear. Low-cost subsistence producers, comprising a significant proportion of a country's working population and contributing a significant amount of foreign exchange earnings, could be wiped out, leading to huge problems of structural adjustment in precisely those countries least able to cope (Clark, 1990:915).

In the emerging setting of accelerating technical change and economic liberalization, sustained growth necessitates continuous skills and technology upgrading in all countries. In African countries in particular, this calls for an enormous effort to improve institutions, factor markets and infrastructure. It also calls for the capacity to support continuous policy interventions to strengthen institutional capacities to deepen and broaden technological competencies, and where necessary, to promote local enterprise. To be sure, a conducive environment for transnational corporations has not always entailed a level playing field with domestic enterprises in all activities. The two sets of firms often operate in segmented markets for information and capital, and face different learning processes. The situation in the diplomatic sphere is also not favorable to genuine African development interests.

Geo-strategic and Diplomatic Isolation

There are essentially two competing positions that seek to explain the emerging and possible future role of the African continent in global security and diplomacy. On the one hand, there is a school of thought that claims that, with the conclusion of the Cold War, Africa's importance and relevance in global politico-strategic concerns has diminished markedly. The race to win ideological and strategic allies in the South in general, and in Africa in particular, seems to be over. In the emerging global geo-strategic configurations, Africa's intrinsic political value as an ideological spoil or diplomatic asset to the United States, Japan, or the E.U. seems to be almost negligible. Not least, the Security Council has gradually developed not only lackluster responses to Africa's complex emergencies but, most importantly, the individual major powers have become reluctant to get embroiled in large scale overseas interventions perceived to be of low strategic import.

Barry Buzan (1991:435) argues that Africa's geo-strategic importance has become virtually marginal to the vital interests of the North. Gone are the days when the Non-Aligned Movement (NAM) occupied the moral high ground in international diplomacy. The movement's demands were debated seriously in major international fora and, indeed, neither side in the Cold War divide could ignore NAM's aspirations. With the termination of the Cold War, NAM's strategic and diplomatic significance has not only waned but, most importantly, its collective bargaining capacity with the North has been irreparably eroded (Hutchful, 1991). In the coming years and decades, the South is likely to suffer from acute strategic inattention.

Relatedly, the end of the Cold War and the disintegration of the socialist bloc has resulted in the loss of a major constituency for Africa's causes in the United Nations. On most critical issues of concern for Africa, the former members of the Warsaw Pact could be relied on to vote with those forces in Africa that were eager to promote structural changes in international politics. In this sense, therefore, the disintegration of the former Soviet Union and the dismantling of the Warsaw Pact have left Africa without a reliable and powerful bloc of supporting countries in the United Nations system (Mazrui, 1999:168).

While the Cold War created sufficient diplomatic and ideological space for African states to articulate and defend their respective national interests, the Soviet Union was a reliable and strong ally in the global struggle against imperialist exploitation, injustice and foreign domination. In recent years, there has developed a visible tendency toward the diplomatic isolation of the African continent. The new Russia seems to be preoccupied with a different set of priorities. This emerging lack of concern and attention was evident at the U.N. Conference on Environment and Development (UNCED), where Africa's pressing development needs were rarely given serious attention or passionately supported by Russia. Important questions - such as democratic global governance, the dumping of toxic waste, debt, market access, commodity prices, foreign aid, the economic impact of globalization and desertification - were given only fleeting consideration. Fantu Cheru notes that Africa's marginalization at these important meetings was further compounded by the inability of its delegates to organize themselves effectively at the caucus level in order to articulate their shared interests (Cheru, 1996:150).

The growing understanding between the two superpowers after the late 1980s and the dissolution of the Soviet Union in 1991 marked the beginning not only of the withdrawal of the Eastern European states from Africa but, most importantly, the decline in the North's geo-strategic interest in the continent. Gradually, these countries reduced their level of commitment to Africa. By the early 1980s, the Soviet Union was reconsidering the magnitude of its Third World commitments, and beginning to scale down its financial obligations. A discernible pattern of Soviet disengagement was becoming clearer; it had became full-scale withdrawal by the end of the decade. Withdrawal was graphically manifested in a systematic downgrading and/or closure of embassies, as well as deep slashing of development cooperation resources. Not surprisingly, foreign military bases in sub-Saharan Africa were closed down one after another, and Africans were constantly counseled by the North to fend for themselves (Gulvin, 1996; Rugumamu, 1999a). More tragically, the growing disinterest in, disregard for, and lack of commitment to Africa was further demonstrated by the Northern foot-dragging responses to the crises in Rwanda, Burundi, Angola, Sudan, Sierra Leone and Côte d'Ivoire, as compared to swift responses to the crises in Kuwait, the former Yugoslavia, and in the republics of the former Soviet Union. Without doubt, with the conclusion of the Cold War, Africa's geo-strategic significance had dramatically waned.

In the post-Cold War period, the United States, Europe and Japan seem to be slowly but steadily diverting their attention and resources away from Africa in favor of those regions of the world with which they have closer cultural, economic and strategic connections. The fast liberalizing economies of Eastern Europe, Russia, China and East Asia are more favorable than those in Africa that are ravaged by warlords, inflation, poverty, corruption, and informality. Furthermore, the ethnic fissures in the former Yugoslavia and throughout Eastern Europe have generated significant dangers and problems for Western countries, particularly Western Europe and the United States. The flow of war-battered migrants from these ethnic wars threatened to destabilize Western European societies, as demonstrated by the violence perpetrated against immigrants in Germany in the 1990s. Understandably, the E.U's preoccupation with the security problems in the Balkans takes precedence over the crises in far away Africa. Due to geographical proximity, the Mediterranean and Middle Eastern states are similarly likely to receive more E.U. attention and resources in the years to come. The E.U. countries have recognized that they may put their own security at risk if they fail to preserve their neighbors and Europe's periphery from sliding into misery and anarchy. To be sure, these states are closer neighbors than sub-Saharan African countries. The current European security concerns with both regions stem from the flow of illegal immigrants from North Africa as well as the specter of radical Islamist movemements and alleged terrorism (International Institute for Security Studies, 2002:129).

More specifically and in a similar hands-off pattern, France more than Britain, has been slowly but inexorably disengaging herself from Africa. The close and warm Franco-Africa relations can no longer be automatically expected. Historically, France exerted its influence through cultural, economic and military channels. Institutionally, the Franc zone pegged the currency of France former colonies in Africa to the French franc at a fixed exchange rate, and the Ministry of Cooperation exclusively handled Franco-African technical, strategic and cultural affairs. In this scheme of things, one of Paris' strategic roles in Africa was the provision of military support to the French-speaking African countries. In fulfilling her 'gendarme role' on the continent, France maintained security and defense agreements and stationed troops in several African countries, including the Central African Republic, Côte d'Ivoire, Djibouti, Gabon and Senegal. France also used her interventionist forces in Chad, Western Sahara and former Zaire (now the DRC). This elaborate network of agreements and logistical support structures enabled the French army to intervene at least 30 times in Africa in the last four decades. All this is now history. The year 1994 started with a 50 percent devaluation of the CFA franc, which had been tied to the French franc since 1948. Worse still, it was decided that future French aid to Africa was to be conditional on formal compliance with IMF/World Bank conditions. Above all, in 1998, the Ministry of Cooperation was demoted and placed under the Ministry of Foreign Affairs. Taken together, these three policy measures sent a clear message to African leaders that there would be no more special and exceptional favors from Paris (Gulvin, 1996).

As the Cold War has thawed and the EU has expanded eastward, France has tended to pay growing attention to Eastern and Central Europe. Obviously, this shift in interest is consistent with the central role that France wishes to play in the larger Europe. Simultaneously, Paris has increasingly adopted a more guarded stance on the use of her soldiers in solving Africa's domestic problems. Only in situations it considers to be characterized by special circumstances (e.g. Rwanda in 1994 and Côte d'Ivoire in 2004) has France used its soldiers in African conflicts. This policy has been referred to pejoratively as 'compassion fatigue'. France, like its allies in the North, is arguing that the security problems of Africa have to be resolved by Africans on their own terms and by taking full responsibility for the outcome of their actions. In fact, she is one of the leading EU member-states that proposed the creation of a special African intervention force to be equipped, trained and financed by Europe and the United States, but using African solders (Guy, 1995; Chafer, 2002). In short, Africa is generally being left to its own devices.

On the other hand, there is another school of thought that claims that there are both positive and negative compelling factors that are likely to force states in the North and other critical constituencies to continue engaging intimately with Africa, if only for their own security and long-term economic self-interest. Fewer ethnic and religious wars, refugees and illegal immigrants who overstretch social and other services, and fewer complex emergencies in Africa would undeniably be good news for everyone in the North. In the long run, a policy toward Africa of containment and quarantine of the effects of global poverty, disease, global warming, despair and violence would be self-defeating for the North. Imaginary walls against 'external evil' are naïve and short-sighted policy options. Indeed, the former U.S. National Security Advisor, Anthony Lake, warned that "...we care about Africa because of the enormous potential of the people, traditions and its resources...we care because the great global challenges of tomorrow can be seen in the challenges facing Africa today" (Lake, 1995:13). In short, the inescapable argument is that Africa is too important for the North to delink with it diplomatically or simply ignore it. John Saul and Colin Leys (1999) come to a similar conclusion to that profered by Lake. They note that "African countries will present increasing dangers for the rest of the world...and, as this becomes clear, Africa will gradually move back toward the head of the aid queue." The flow of narcotics and refugees, and the rise of terrorist activities are likely to drive industrialized countries to constantly watch over or directly meddle in the activities of African countries.

In the wake of the 11 September 2001 terrorist attack on the United States, everyone seems to have been reminded that development, security and peace are inseparable. Underdevelopment and extreme poverty tend to be breeding grounds for despair and violence, thus undermining peace and security for the North and South alike. The American-led international coalitions against the Taliban regime in Afghanistan and in the Gulf War against President Saddam Hussein of Iraq give solid credence to the argument for the North's continued diplomatic and economic engagement with the South. Although globalization may discourage conflict among those who directly benefit from it, it dialectically enables transnational networks of terrorists with apocalyptic objectives to operate on a global scale.

Above all, the outbreak and spread of deadly diseases, such as HIV/AIDS, Ebola, SARS, and cholera in Africa have direct repercussions for the societies of the North. Poverty and miserable living conditions in Africa, as elsewhere, serve as incubators for these and other diseases that can and do spread to the North. Moreover, the destruction of the global environment is likely to compel the core countries of the North to pay close attention to what happens in the South. The world's forests, most of which are located in the South, combined with its biodiversity, will make it imperative for the North to try to find ways to exploit and/or preserve these resources and, as a consequence, respond to at least some of the demands of Africa. In this regard, major actors in core countries in the North will have no choice but to engage with Africa meaningfully, if only for their own survival. But this enlightened thinking has yet to emerge and take root. In the short-term, the current single-minded obsession to build and maintain a global anti-terrorism coalition will mobilize the world community, not to seek to eradicate the root causes of insecurity in the South that often lead to political alienation and ultimately terrorism, but will simply be used as an excuse to pursue narrow self-interest and punish any regime that the North defines as 'a rogue state.'

The euphoria of the new world order was not only ephemeral but also deceptively unrealistic. The great surge of hope that the 'peace-dividend' would be channeled into improving human security for the many millions who exist without any control over their social, political, conomic, or physical environment has already evaporated. The 1990s saw troops, resources and the political capital available for U.N. peace operations in the South in genera , and in Africa in particular, decline markedly The idea of reviving the collective security apparatus of the United Nations as envisaged in the U.N. Charter has long been forgotten. In fact, the former U.N. Secretary-General, Boutros Boutros Ghali in a 1992 report entitled, *An Agenda for Peace*, had provided far-reaching recommendations regarding the U.N.'s intervention in internal conflicts and its programs of humanitarian assistance. Reflecting the new spirit in the Security Council, the report called for the establishment of peace enforcement units. Consequently, the number of U.N. peacekeeping operations increased from five in 1988 to seventeen in 1994, and the number of countries contributing military and police personnel increased nearly threefold from 26 to 76 over the same period. This period also witnessed an increase in the peacekeeping budget from $230 million to$3.6 billion (Omach, 2000:79). Above all, the post-Cold War optimism would seem to have been initially vindicated by the successful, U.S-led U.N. operations in the Gulf War.

However, the initial optimism about the role of the U.N. in conflict management lasted only briefly. The debacle of the U.N.'s peacekeeping efforts in Somalia in October of 1993 radically changed Western intervention policies in Africa. From that point on, the United States and other large contributors have required the U.N. Security Council to be more selective in its approach to intervening to resolve conflicts, especially of the internal variety that has been wreaking so much havoc in Africa. Following the unfortunate Somali experience, the West has gradually withdrawn from direct participation in Africa's conflict-management endeavors. There has developed, in fact, a distasteful mood of 'Afro-pessimism' and 'conflict fatigue.' Since then, the Security Council's slow and sometimes feeble initial approaches to the internal conflicts in Sudan, Burundi, Rwanda, Sierra Leone, Angola and the Democratic Republic of Congo have reflected the more cautious approach of the United States. Unexpectedly also, the North further demonstrated an outright willingness to appease Jonas Savimbi following his rejection of the election results in Angola in 1991. It also demonstrated inaction in the face of genocide in Rwanda, vacillation during the refugee crisis in the Democratic Republic of Congo, and reluctance to act even when the elected governments of the Congo (Brazzaville) and the Côte d'Ivoire were overthrown. Furthermore, it showed a willingness to accept governments with dubious electoral mandates and poor human rights records when such governments suited the North's interests in stability, as was the case in Ethiopia, Uganda and Gabon (Ottaway, 1999).

In the Supplement to the *Agenda for Peace*, the former U.N. Secretary-General, Boutros Boutros-Ghali noted that the U.N. does not have the capacity to embark on peace enforcement everywhere conflict breaks out. As a result, the concept of 'farming out' peacekeeping, both to regional organizations and to willing coalitions of member-states began to gain favor. Regional arrangements, as outlined in Chapter VIII of the U.N. Charter and in other U.N. policy statements, have come to play a significant role in the maintenance of international peace and security. Subsequently, an implicit policy emerged which encourages so-called 'layered responses' to conflicts: local and national organizations are expected to respond initially, followed by responses at the sub-regional and regional level and, ultimately, the level of the broader international community is engaged. According to the architects of this policy, the aim is to encourage African initiatives that seek African solutions to African conflicts (Deng and Lyons, 1993:4). It is little wonder then that, instead of familiar U.N. blue berets, peacekeepers in Sierra Leone fought under the banner of the Economic Community of West African States (ECOWAS). By the same token, when the warring parties in the Democratic Republic of Congo gathered in Lusaka, Zambia, in July of 1999 to sign a cease-fire pact, they endorsed an agreement initiated and mediated by the

Southern African Development Community (SADC), with the U.N. playing an ancillary role. In fact, Africa is the only continent being called upon by its former Cold War allies to set up its own international force for peacekeeping and humanitarian assistance. In short, the burden sharing strategy sought to make the obvious point that the responsibility for mitigating conflicts in Africa should lie first and foremost with Africans themselves and their collective organizations (Clever and May, 1995).

Stung by the Somali eexperience and prompted by the desire to reduce costly interventions in distant, non-strategic locations of the world, the United States launched the African Crisis Response Initiative (ACRI) as a response to what it perceived to be 'persistent political turmoil in Africa.' The substance of the initiative was to train and equip between 5,000 and 10,000 African troops for rapid deployment in an African crisis. The ACRI was not intended to be a standing force, but rather a rapid-response, contingency force that could be quickly assembled and deployed under U.N. and/or then O.A.U, now A.U. auspices. Its broad mission was to carry out humanitarian relief and peacekeeping operations. Its more specific aims were to establish and provide personnel to manage 'safe areas' in conflict zones and to ensure the delivery of humanitarian assistance, operating under the U.N. Chapter VI mandate. In addition to providing equipment and training, the United States committed itself to contributing airlift assistance to increase mobility and communications as well as to enhance intelligence, command and control abilities (Frazer, 1997:109-110).

The U.S. proposal was immediately and enthusiastically embraced by European powers, particularly Britain and France, as well as by some African countries. The U.S. European Command (EUSCOM) was designated to serve as the agency that would manage military training programs in sub-Saharan Africa. It sought to enhance the capability of selected African military forces by enabling them to respond to crises by participating in peacekeeping operations in Africa. In this regard, the U.S. Congress passed the African Conflict Resolution Act in 1994, calling for the provision of material and technical assistance to help institutionalize African conflict resolution capabilities. The resources were to be provided to the then O.A.U, sub-regional organizations and national governments. Countries that were initially earmarked to participate in the ACRI program included Senegal, Malawi, Uganda, Ethiopia, Mali and Ghana. It was hoped that ACRI would eventually create the feeling among Africans that regional states and organizations were playing a more active and responsible role in conflict management and resolution and that the West would no longer be embroiled in complex and never-ending African conflicts. Some African countries, including South Africa, Nigeria and Tanzania, were initially wary of the initiative, suspecting that it was simply a means to persuade Africans to implement policies and decisions not of their own making.

Ealier responding to similar global concerns and anxieties, African heads of state had agreed in June, 1992, that the O.A.U should establish its own Mechanism for Conflict Prevention, Management and Resolution. Remarkably, for an organization that had avoided involvement in internal conflicts, the new O.A.U Mechanism had a clear mandate to concern itself with such conflicts as well. As then O.A.U Secretary General, Salim Ahmed Salim remarked, "given that every African is his brother's keeper, and that our borders are at best artificial, we in Africa need to use our own cultural and social relationships to interpret the principle of non-intervention in such a way that we are able to apply it to our advantage in conflict prevention and resolution" (Salim, 1992:11-12). At the O.A.U. 1993 Summit, African heads of state formally approved the Mechanism. It was charged with anticipating and preventing conflicts, and engaging in peace-making and peace-building activities. In order to monitor incipient conflicts and to act proactively, an Early Warning System on Conflict Situations in Africa was established in 1995. The dilemma has been how to translate the security information gathered into concrete initiatives. In fact, the effectiveness of the Mechanism was limited not only by the scarce resources at its disposal to develop systems and finance peace-making operations but, most importantly, by the lack of a solid organizational mechanism and structural capacity to single-handedly manage a myriad of continental conflicts. In the short and medium term, the geo-strategic and diplomatic isolation of the continent seems more imminent now than any meaningful and engaged collaboration with the North. A similar situation of marginalization manifests itself where matters of foreign aid are concerned.

Foreign Aid and Africa's Continued Dependence
Official development assistance (ODA) plays an essential role as a complement to other sources of financing for development, especially in African countries with little capacity to attract private direct investment. ODA is the largest source of external financing in sub-Saharan Africa. It has the potential to help a poor country to reach adequate levels of domestic resource mobilization over an appropriate time horizon, while human capital, productive and export capacities are enhanced. Moreover, ODA can be

critical for improving the environment for private sector activity and can thus pave the way for robust growth. Above all, it has the potential for supporting education, health, public infrastructure, agriculture and rural development and for enhancing food security.

As observed earlier, it was widely hoped by many developing countries that the conclusion of the Cold War would engender peaceful resolutions to many long-standing political conflicts, especially in Africa, and that the post-Cold War period would allow for a significant portion of the 'peace-dividend' to finance enlightened development cooperation. These hopes and expectations have largely been shattered. According to Nicolas van de Walle (1999:339), the current mood in donor societies is "one of great frustration and growing cynicism." He further claims that, "the legitimacy of the aid enterprise will continue to erode, without clear evidence that aid is helping Africa to move forward." Roger Riddell (1999:311) also claims that there is "serious and perhaps growing doubt about aid to Africa." By 2002, most national ODA levels were far below the long-standing target of 0.7 percent of GDP, with an average of only 0.3 percent.

The World Bank (2000:23-237) supports the same view by asserting that the rise in donors' disenchantment with the African continent "...partly is explained by the belief that aid to Africa has done little to raise growth or reduce poverty." Indeed, the inability to show practically any economic achievements for decades of development assistance, however limited and ideologically charged, may have frustrated some naïve sectors of the donor community. What these explanations fail to uncover are the ideological imperatives on which the aid regime was ultimately anchored. The end of the Cold War has undermined the very foundations and rationale for the international order that prevailed after the late 1940s. In fact, the ideological origins and objectives of foreign aid and development cooperation cannot be understood outside the Cold War context. Of course other motives apart from ideological confrontation also played a role, not so much in initiating foreign aid programs as in sustaining them once the original principle had been accepted (Rugumamu, 1997). Obviously these trends are contrary to to the more recent Monterry Consensus which states that "mobilizing and increasing the effective use of financial resources and achieving the national and international economic conditions needed to filfil internationally agreed development goals...will be our first step in ensuring that the twenty-first century becomes the century for development for all."

During the five decades of the post-World War II period, foreign aid was promised, given, withdrawn or denied to support 'trusted ideological allies' even when some of them blatantly pursued unacceptable domestic policies. After 1949, preventing countries from going down the 'communist road' became the central tenet of U.S. foreign policy (Baldwin, 1985:327). It sought to cultivate or, where necessary, to implant an indigenous elite that could carry on the communist containment from within. The end of the East-West ideological confrontation spelled the end of rent drawn from the threat of shifting allegiance. While the late President Mobutu Sese Seko of former Zaire was reportedly amassing one of the world's largest personal fortunes (which was invested outside his own country), decades of large-scale foreign assistance left not a trace of progress. Zaire (now the Democratic Republic of Congo) is just one of several examples where a steady flow of aid either ignored or even abetted incompetence, corruption and misguided policies.[17] It is not surprising that the Cold War left a legacy of ineffective aid, partly in the form of loans that had accumulated into large debt stocks and partly in the form of compromised state institutions. Writing immediately at the end of the Cold War, Keith Griffin concluded that, "the debt burden, not economic development, has become the legacy of forty years of foreign aid" (Griffin, 1991:678). We shall return later to the politics of aid and debt.

With the end of the Cold War, the old rationale for development cooperation in general, and for aid in particular, virtually disappeared and new threats to states in the North and new development problems, opportunities and agenda have emerged. The evidence so far would tend to suggest that the imperatives of human solidarity, poverty alleviation, humanitarian assistance and the promotion of democracy and human rights do not possess the same mobilizing power that the Cold War once had to rationalize foreign aid. There is no doubt that international aid flows have gone into a steady decline in real terms since the conclusion of the Cold War. Rather than increase the quality and quantity of aid to poor developing countries, particularly those in Africa, donors have increasingly focused on their immediate domestic and regional issues, such as facilitating the transition of the former socialist states to market economies, helping immigrants and refugees, cutting the international flow of narcotics, reducing national fiscal deficits, stimulating trade, and improving education, health care and the like. Paradoxically, Africans are now being advised not only to learn how to do more with less aid, but also to look for alternative sources of development financing (Rugumamu, 2001a; 2001b).

Even as the ability to use aid effectively increased in most of Africa by the early 1990s, the international aid levels began to decline. More ominously, there is little evidence to suggest that donors were preparing for a sustained increase in their aid budgets to support Africa's development efforts.[18] Cuts in aid budgets have been accompanied by the slogan 'trade not aid,' together with exhortations for countries in the South to participate fully in the global market place. Even though foreign aid is a tiny fraction of donors' budgets, it has been one of the first items for the axe. Between 1990 and 1998, for example, the overall ODA fell by one-third in real terms. Apparently, the pressure to prune development budgets has evolved into a dogma that aid should necessarily be cut. The share of net ODA in the GNP for the OECD countries declined to 0.22 percent in 1998, compared with 0.35 percent in the mid-1980s. The total net disbursement from Europe to sub-Saharan Africa fell from 52.1 percent of the members' total aid budgets in 1988/89 to 44.4 percent in 1998/99 (OECD, 2000: Table 33). The cuts were particularly remarkable for big donors like the United States, France and the United Kingdom, who reduced their aid budgets, measured both as a share of their GNP and also as a share of their total budgets that went to Africa. The aggregate result of these changes was that net disbursements to Africa declined markedly. Measured in 1998 prices and exchange rates, the total bilateral aid from the 15 E.U. members went down from $8.8 billion in 1988/89 to $5.4 billion in 1998/99 (OECD, 2001: Table 29).

More specifically, there has been a fall in the real value of E.U. aid to sub-Saharan Africa from $2.1 billion in 1988/89 to $1.6 billion in 1999, measured in 1998 prices and exchange rates. The reduction in the E.U. aid is better appreciated when it is recalled that on 1 January, 1995, three affluent countries, Sweden, Austria and Finland, joined the European Union. The decline is even more telling when one compares these figures with what went to other regions. Sub-Saharan Africa's share of total E.U. development aid dropped dramatically from 61 percent in 1988/89 to 31.3 percent in 1998/99, while aid to other geographical regions grew from 39 percent to 68.7 percent during the same time period (OECD, 2001:Table 29). As pointed out earlier, enduring strategic geopolitical objectives have continued to influence the direction of aid flows.

France, the biggest European donor, reduced its total ODA/GNP aid commitment from 0.63 in 1992 to 0.39 in 1999. Within this shrinking budget, the share of French ODA going to Africa was reduced from 51.8 percent in 1988/89 to 34.2 percent in 1999 (OECD, 1999). Germany, the second biggest European donor, reduced its ODA/GNP from 0.38 percent in 1992 to 0.26

in 1999, while at the same time the share of German aid going to Africa was reduced from 31.3 in 1988/89 to 27.7 in 1999. This resulted in a reduction of net disbursement from Germany to Africa from $1.3 billion in 1988/89 to $939 million in 1998/99, measured in 1998 prices and exchange rates (OECD, 2001: Table 29). Like France and Germany, the British ratio of ODA to GNP fell from 0.31 in 1992 to 0.23 percent in 1999. Measured in 1998 prices and exchange rates, British aid to sub-Saharan Africa decreased slightly during the 1990s, reaching $784 in 1999 (OECD, 2001: Table 29). The decline was especially sharp with regard to the United Sates whose aid was a mere 0.08 percent of its GNP in 1997. Four countries, namely Denmark, Norway, the Netherlands and Sweden, have had a commitment clearly superior to the rest. They are the only countries which carry out the famous United Nations resolution that calls on developed countries to give 0.7 percent of their national income as international aid.

Despite the falling level of aid to African countries, the region is still, on average, the most aid-dependent of the major world regions. In 1997, net disbursement of concessional resources to sub-Saharan Africa amounted to US$16.4 billion. Foreign aid as a percentage of the gross GNP of sub-Saharan countries averaged five percent in 1996-1997, down from 10 percent in the 1980s but still the highest of any major developing region (OECD, 1999). However, it is important to note that these figures understate the real decline since they include debt forgiveness, which is officially counted as aid. This is not really aid since most of the forgiven debt would not have been repaid anyway.

Critics of foreign aid have welcomed the decline of aid flows, arguing that aid is less effective than private investment and commercial loans in stimulating long-term economic growth. They charged that foreign aid reflected naïve assumptions about world politics and insisted that aid programs should be either related to narrowly defined donor self-interest or eliminated outright. Other critics point to the dubious Cold War record of subsidizing autocratic regimes, fostering neo-colonialism and inflaming regional conflicts. Still others focus on the self-serving and wasteful use of official development assistance. They expose the pervasive practice in which nearly all of the bilateral aid to Africa was tied to the purchase of over-priced donor goods and services. Such critics have further exposed the bloated and overly heavy bureaucracies of many aid agencies that often spent much of the aid on themselves and misappropriated funds for luxurious capital-intensive projects that do little to improve overall living standards. To all these critics, the apparent global rise of private capital as the principal mechanism for transferring wealth from rich to poor states has been perceived as an encouraging trend (Hook, 1996; Thorp, 1971).

With radical changes in global politics and other interests, the direction and composition of aid resources are also changing. The composition of aid flows is shifting from project assistance and structural adjustment loans towards humanitarian assistance and peace-building. Emergency aid has risen sharply since 1990, peaking in 1994 at some $3 billion bilaterally and $2.5 billion multilaterally, with a further commitment of $3 billion to peacekeeping. However, the increasing share of aid going to emergency assistance means that the amount of ODA devoted to promoting development actually declined in the 1990s (World Bank, 2000:72). The pie is not only diminishing, it is also being distributed among a greater number of recipients! At the same time, relatively less aid is earmarked for the South, in order to make room for other priority regions. Africa has emerged as the net loser in these developments. In the late 1980s, it was envisaged that aid to Africa would grow in real terms. But net transfers per capita have fallen from $32 in 1990 to $19 in 1998 (World Bank, 2000:71).

Moreover, the immediate post-Cold War period has witnessed a steep rise in the number and frequency of civil conflicts, of new challenges to development, and of new demands on dwindling aid budgets. This is not the whole story. Following the collapse of the Soviet bloc, it became increasingly apparent that the former communist countries would need substantial assistance to help manage their transitions to market economies. In all likelihood, the Federal Republic of Germany will continue to concentrate its aid and private investment resources on its own backyard, the former East Germany and other Eastern European countries. These new demands on the E.U. aid budget are likely to drastically reduce the funds available in the long run to regions of less priority, such as Africa.

Paradoxically, as aid budgets became increasingly parsimonious, expenditures devoted to the aid administration of bilateral and multilateral programs increased from $2 billion in 1990 to $3 billion in 1996. The increase in administration costs in part reflects a greater emphasis on social programs, which often are labor-intensive. Higher administrative costs are also a clear manifestation of donor supervision at a ridiculously detailed level. As some Lomé Convention studies have shown, with the end of the Cold War, the E.U. introduced political conditionalities as well as cumbersome administrative procedures down to fine operational details. The principle of co-management administration proved more theoretical than real. Development prioritization and project planning as well as management came to be largely influenced by the donor's side, with joint management remaining only on paper (McQueen, 1998; Raffer, 1999).

The damaging consequences of the overall decline in aid have been compounded by three related problems. First, the decline has been the steepest in the poorest countries, with the share of aid going to low-income countries falling from 45 percent in 1991 to 28 percent in 1996. Obviously, this is inconsistent with the internationally declared goal of reducing poverty. Second, basic education and health, two of the greatest priorities in terms of developing more equitable patterns of globalization, account for less than 5 percent of the overall aid effort. Third, a large share of development assistance, 40 percent of the total, is spent on technical assistance, much of it in the donor countries (Oxfam, 2000). Ultimately, one is left wondering who is helping whom in the international aid regime.

Finally, with the conclusion of the Cold War, new thinking is gradually emerging in the 'aid industry', a thinking that seeks to make aid more effective in reducing poverty. Since the publication of the 1990 *World Development Report* by the World Bank, structural poverty reduction has once again taken center stage in development cooperation. In the post-Cold War era, the Bank ushered in a new poverty agenda by articulating the importance of policy reform. It also provided the new basis for a better aid strategy. Poverty reduction, particularly among rural populations, has become one of the primary organizing principles in the aid process since the 1990s. Almost all major bilateral and multilateral aid donors and recipients have recently embraced this relatively novel development philosophy.

In order to reduce poverty, the report recommends that external assistance should be more tightly linked to the assessment of overall nation-wide efforts being made on the poverty reduction front (World Bank, 1990:iv). It further proposes a three-pronged policy thrust. The first is the rekindling of economic growth. However, since the benefits of economic growth might not trickle down as had previously been assumed, the report suggests that growth must be labor-intensive in character. This emphasis in the new poverty agenda cautions governments against over-subsidizing capital, which leads to capital-for-labor substitution. However, it should be quickly pointed out that the key issue in this strategy is not to increase labor intensity but to raise the returns of labor. The second prong in this proposal suggests a change in the composition of public expenditure. Governments should help the poor by increasing the share of expenditure that goes to education, nutrition and health by specifically increasing the share of education and health spending that reaches the poor. In other words, the aim would be to assess how much each dollar of public money would contribute towards poverty reduction. The third prong would provide social safety nets, special government schemes targeted toward the poor who are unable to enter the labor market.

Although there are general agreements in the literature on the means to achieve significant poverty reduction, three disturbing differences of opinion remain unresolved. First, there are issues concerning the questionable legitimacy of external agencies in determining sensitive policy agendas such as the anti-poverty crusade. Arguably, any effective implementation of a major domestic policy requires a well-planned mobilization campaign of key national actors and various political constituencies. In this regard, only national governments with relatively high degrees of legitimacy would have the capacity to mobilize various domestic constituencies for such an undertaking. Rajni Kothari gives similar compelling arguments concerning the limitations of foreign actors in determining national development policies. He argues that foreign agencies can influence, but not determine, national political agendas. He further warns:

> History has shown very clearly that one cannot constructively transform a society from outside. All genuine social transformations have been initiated from within the society, even though in many cases the genesis for such transformation lay in the cross-fertilization of ideas and experiences from different societies (Kothari, 1993:152).

Second, and more poignantly, it is argued that sensitive policy interventions, such as the anti-poverty agenda, which is driven largely by international agencies such as the World Bank, UNICEF or UNDP, is lacking on other important grounds. According to John Toye and Carl Jackson (1996), such a policy should ideally be home-grown and command broad national support. As the deprivation of particular groups becomes politicized, they acquire a level of support far beyond what obtained earlier. In other words, enlightened politics and informed broad public discussions are more likely to play a unifying role in the anti-poverty agenda in any country than are foreign international agencies. More specifically, they recommend:

> .... Any international efforts, like that of the World Bank to promote poverty reduction in particular countries must face up to the implications of one very central difficulty. It is perhaps not fully appreciated that the poverty reduction agenda has received high political priority in the now developed countries only at particular historical moments and under well-defined conditions. Research shows that the attitude of the elite was critical. They took action on poverty alleviation issues because they shared a consensus around three

beliefs. They were that (i) the welfare of the elite and the welfare of the poor were interdependent, and the elite was not able to insulate itself from the living conditions of the poor; (ii) the poor did, in fact, have the means to affect the welfare of the elite, principally by three methods namely crime, insurrection and epidemic disease; and (iii) some actions by the state would be efficacious in reducing the threat to the welfare of the elite posed by the behavior of the poor (Jackson and Toye, 1996:57).

Thirdly and finally, the World Bank's prescription for progressive economic integration of developing countries into world markets, and the benefits thereof for the poor, is far from being generally accepted. The instability of commodity prices, the increasing decline in the demand for them in the West, the weak bargaining power of poor countries *vis-à-vis* multilateral agencies, and the constraints on economic recovery imposed by onerous debt burdens make it extremely difficult for African economies to grow on the basis of an outward orientation. As noted earlier, since the early 1970s, economic growth in the North has been increasingly associated with new technologies rather than the use of natural resources such as energy, agricultural raw materials and minerals. Understandably, continued dependence on primary commodities and foreign assistance as engines of development has few prospects, if any. This demands that we examine the prospects for an increase in foreign direct investment in Africa.

Foreign Direct Investment and Africa's Exploitation

One of the driving forces of globalization is foreign direct investment (FDI).[19] Since the early 1980s, the policy environment worldwide has been far more condicive to the growth of FDI. The number of countries adopting significant liberalization measures toward FDI increased steadily. According to the UNCTAD's *World Investment Report 2000,* foreign direct investment by TNCs was due to surpass one trillion dollars in 1999 (UNCTAD, 2000). These movements, however large, operate through many of the older networks of banks and corporations that pre-date the current boom in globalist expansion. Understandably, the growth of FDI has been unevenly distributed. Growing theoretical and empirical evidence suggests that, due to the segmentation in global markets, certain regions may not benefit from capital movements. One can distinguish two sets of factors that might induce capital to move to any particular country or region: the 'push factors' in a capital exporting country and the 'pull factors' in the capital receiving country. The push factors include the rates of return in the capital-exporting country; low interest rates push investors into the world market in search of lucrative investment opportunities. The pull factors include high interest rates of return and financial stability in the capital importing country (Fernandez, 1993).

The European Union, the North America and Pacific Asia, referred to as the Triad, constitute the core of FDI flows. These three power blocs are not only the major global investors, they are also the major recipients of investment. Well over 80 percent of worldwide FDI flows remain within this economic power triad, which is clearly where the thrust and dynamism of globalization takes place. This growth reflects the development of new technologies, falling transport costs and the emergence of global production systems under the auspices of transnational corporations. The growth in the number of cross-border mergers and acquisitions is made possible by large organizational networks, new electronic technologies and competitive forces. Private international capital flows, particularly foreign direct investment along with international financial stability, are vital complements to national and international development efforts. Foreign direct investment has the potential to contribute toward financing sustained economic growth over the long term. It is especially important for its potential to transfer knowledge and technology, create jobs, boost overall productivity, enhance competitiveness and entrepreneurship, and ultimately eradicate poverty through economic growth and development.

While FDI has the potential to generate enormous gains for development, its benefits are often lost in the pursuit for narrowly defined corporate interests. Unlike trade, international investment does not come under any internationally binding regime. Experience has amply demonstrated the predatory macro-economic impact of unregulated private capital flows, particularly short-term flows. The East Asian crisis of the 1990s drove home the point that this vulnerability does not disappear with the rise of overall sound economic management. As will become increasingly apparent, corporate behavior is too important to be left to voluntary codes and standards of ethical behaviour defined by the corporate sector itself (Rugumamu, 1989).

As investment becomes more and more concentrated and centralized among the core powers, considerably few countries in the South are likely to benefit from such skewed flow patterns. These include most of the NICs and second-tier NICs, where there exist strong developmental states, an educated workforce and a developed economic infrastructure. Most of Africa remains largely excluded at a time when flows are growing substantially all over the world. As Paul Collier and Catherine Pattillo put it, "until recently, Africa has been an unambiguously capital-hostile environment...and was rated as the most risky environment in the world by commercial risk-rating agencies" (Collier and Pattillo, 2000:3). The behavior of governments is said to constitute a major source of these risks, both because governments can capriciously alter public policies and because they can threaten the security of property rights.[20]

Ordinarily, FDI is potentially the most valuable source of private capital transfer to Africa. However, at its worst, FDI can exploit unfair labor practices, evade taxes, pollute the environment and produce high profits with few benefits for the local economy. Generally, growth and poverty reduction through foreign investment has been relatively poor, due in part to the institutional weaknesses and in part to global trends toward reduced regulatory controls in foreign investment. The latter is aggressively pursued at a multilateral level, through the investment regime of the WTO and, at a bilateral level, through the conditionalities attached to IMF and World Bank loans. More disturbing is the fact that the history of foreign investment in Africa raises serious questions about its contribution to human security. Many operations have been subject to critical scrutiny. The activities of Shell Oil in Nigeria came under the media spotlight in November, 1995, when Ken Saro-Wiwa, the leader of the Ogoni people, was executed by the government. Saro-Wiwa, a human rights activist, was campaigning for the recognition of the rights of the Ogoni as well as the restoration of environmental sanity in his homeland. Ogoniland provided about 80 percent of Nigeria's oil income but its people did not see any tangible benefits accruing to the Ogoni people as a whole (Smith, 1997).

Although the rates of return on FDI have generally been much higher in Africa than in any other developing region, the continent's image as a location for foreign direct investment has not been favorable over the years. UNCTAD (1999:17) confirms that the profitability of foreign affiliates of major corporations in Africa has been high and that, in recent years, it has been consistently higher than in most other host regions. However, Africa has often been associated only with pictures of civil unrest, starvation, deadly diseases and economic disorder. Indeed, this image has given many foreign investors a negative perspective on Africa as a whole. Africa's weak economic performance in the 1970s and 1980s is also reflected in its poor record of foreign direct investment flows. Despite some stabilization in flows since 1994, the continent has continued to struggle in order to make up for the ground it lost during much of the 1970s and 1980s. The World Bank survey of 150 foreign executives in East Africa concluded that investing in Africa was a highly risky venture even for the most daring capitalist. Some of the major factors cited in the study include an unreliable investment environment, the lack of production and commercial infrastructure, economic policies that penalize exports and investment for the sake of local business interests, and lack of human capital (World Bank, 1994).

While this picture is not entirely fictitious, and for some countries these unfortunate conditions do prevail, it is not an accurate portrayal of all African countries. By 1999, elections that were rated more or less free and fair were held in more than 40 states on the continent. Some countries, such as Mauritius, Uganda, Tunisia, Botswana and Senegal, have enjoyed decades of sustained economic prosperity and steady flows of FDI. However, for much of the past two decades, FDI flows into Africa have increased only modestly from an annual average of almost $1.9 billion in 1983-1987 to $3.1 billion in 1988-1992, $6.0 billion in 1993-1997 and $9 billion in 1998-1999. Investments by TNCs in Africa are still only 1.2 percent of global FDI flows and 5 percent of total FDI into all countries in the South. About 70 percent of FDI in Africa in 1999 was concentrated in only five countries, namely, Angola, Egypt, Morocco, Nigeria and South Africa (UNCTAD, 1995; 1999).

Whereas flows to developing countries as a group quadrupled, from less than $20 billion in 1981-1985 to an average of $75 billion in the years 1991-1995, flows to Africa only doubled during the same period. As a result, Africa's share within total flows to developing countries dropped significantly from more than 11 percent in 1976-1980 to 9 percent in 1981-1985, 5 percent in 1991-1995 and 4 percent in 1996-1997. The deterioration of Africa's position is also reflected in the ratio of FDI to GDP. In 1970, Africa had attracted more FDI per $1,000 of GDP than developing countries in Asia, Latin America and the Caribbean. Although both the value of its FDI flows and the FDI/GDP ratio grew for most of the time between 1975 and 1997, by 1990 Africa had fallen behind other developing regions and the continent has remained behind since then. The gap became even more pronounced during the 1990s when the worldwide surge in FDI flows into developing countries largely bypassed the region (UNCTAD, 1999:2-3).

Indeed, Africa's FDI share is the smallest of the developing regions and compares unfavorably with that of Southeast Asia, which received $81 billion in financial flows in 1996, about two-thirds of the developing countries' total FDI in that year. China received over $16 billion, while Singapore received $9 billion. In fact, the overwhelming majority of new investment activity in Africa in recent years has consisted of the acquisition of existing assets, often resulting from the privatization of state enterprises. Such short-term rise in foreign investment has a limited scope (UNCTAD, 1997:21-23).

Paradoxically, this low rate of foreign investment flows to Africa has coincided with various aggressive attempts at liberalizing investment policies, privatizing public assets, and signing bilateral investment promotion and protection treaties. A number of African countries have initiated economic reforms aimed at creating favorable foundations for foreign investment, such as ensuring political and economic stability. Most countries have taken steps to increase the role of the private sector, for example, by privatizing state-owed enterprises. In addition, they have taken steps to restore and maintain macroeconomic stability through the devaluation of overvalued currencies and the reduction of inflation rates and budget deficits. All these measures aim to protect and promote FDI and to clarify the terms under which foreign investments can take place between partner countries. African countries also accelerated the conclusion of double taxation treaties in the 1990s. These treaties make it more attractive for foreigners to invest in a country by helping them to avoid paying taxes twice on the same transaction. Finally, the majority of African countries have signed multilateral agreements dealing with the protection of FDI, such as the convention that established the Multilateral Investment Guarantee Agency (MIGA) and the Convention on the Settlement of Investment Disputes, which standardizes procedures of negotiations between states and nationals of other states (Elbadawi and Mwega, 1998; Collier, 1998).

As with economic growth generally, what matters with foreign investment is its quality. Successful developing countries, particularly the NICs, integrated foreign investment into active industrial and technology development policies. Such policies included: local sourcing requirements, which help build forward and backward linkages with local industries; export performance requirements, so that corporations cover the foreign exchange costs of imports; and restrictions on majority ownership together with technology transfer requirements. However, the ability of most African economies to emulate the NICs and generate linkages is currently compromised by the SAP conditions, and it is likely to be further eroded by the current multilateral investment regulatory regime.[21] The WTO regime has been accompanied by a distinctive bias in favor of deregulation. Above all, the recently stalled Multilateral Agreements on Investment (MAI) seeks to significantly extend binding legal rights and, thereby, to open markets for investors. As Yash

Tandon notes, should the Agreement come to pass, Africa will lose over TNCs:

> MAI means essentially that Africa will have no control whatsoever on how FDI comes into the country and how and in what sectors it operates. There will be no obligation on it to transfer technology, none to hire local workers at managerial or lower levels, none to purchase from local sources, none to fix a certain percentage of its production to local or external markets. Foreign capital will have better than "national treatment" when it comes to externalizing their profits, better protection against any possible threat to appropriation by the state and guaranteed access to courts to demand compensation in cases of such appropriations. MAI would outlaw policies of indigenization...for such would constitute treating foreign capital differently from national capital (Tandon, 2000:70).

In spite of the extensive efforts made to create the right policy and institutional environment for private capital inflow from abroad, foreign investors and lenders have generally shied away from the African continent. In the short and medium term, this trend is not likely to change, given Africa's multiple vulnerabilities to shocks, lack of business support services, weak physical, social and administrative infrastructure, and the small-scale nature of the would-be investment projects. This gloomy assessment is made worse by the debt overhang.

Africa's Debt Crisis and External Control

International aid and debt relief have a central role to play in distributing development opportunities within the global economy. For almost three decades, however, unsustainable debt servicing has been allowed to undermine development efforts in most poor African countries. Huge indebtedness has crushed all possibilities for economic growth by diverting scarce resources needed for health, education and infrastructure as well as contributing to the continent's further marginalization in the global system. The North's lack of genuine concern for Africa's plight is abundantly manifested in the casual attention it pays to Africa's debt crisis. Its rhetoric has not always been backed up with sufficient resources and political will. Until this is achieved, it may be argued, no aid and investment effort is likely to succeed. As the South Commission rightly observes, "debt has become a form of bondage, and the indebted economies have become indentured economies - a clear manifestation of neo-colonialism" (South Commission, 1990:227). True, the roots of the debt crisis in Africa can be traced to a mixture of internal and external policies, but the reproduction of the crisis and the inability to implement prescriptions for effective debt management are inextricably linked to the internal structures of power and politics.

The African people were drawn into debt in entirely dubious ways. These include the use to which borrowed money was put, the variable interest rate at which most foreign debt was contracted during the 1970s, and the loaning of resources to undemocratic and unaccountable regimes. In the 1970s, the process of recycling billions of petro-dollars at low interest rates encouraged unprecedented expansion of borrowing in most African countries. Big bankers awoke to the delight of international lending, and developing countries were eager to accept these seemingly 'cheap loans,' channeling them into ambitious but often non-viable projects. This atmosphere of relatively easy resource availability discouraged financial prudence on the part of both creditors and debtors. On the one hand, the creditors were more anxious to find borrowers than they were to ask how the loans were to be used by the debtors, since most of the loans were state guaranteed and, therefore, involved no apparent risks. On the other hand, debtor countries paid little attention to the returns from the borrowed funds as long as those funds financed some of the capital flight by their own governing groups, maintained the high consumption levels of state functionaries, or simply propped up the value of the national currency to make foreign goods cheaper and to encourage imports (Rugumamu, 2001d; Onimode, 2000).

Foreign loans provided a large and relatively inexpensive source of finance for ambitious yet unsustainable industrial programs, for increases in the size of state bureaucracies and for the expansion of the social sector. Politically visible white elephant projects, such as elegant airports, wide roads that led nowhere, importation of expensive luxury goods and the accumulation of sophisticated weaponry, made more political sense to politicians than did either economic growth or poverty alleviation (Onimode, 1989). Worse still, part of the loan money was looted by the Mobutus, Abachas and Mois of this world and laundered in European banks. It has been estimated, for example, that well over $98 billion, illegally acquired by Nigerian leaders, family members and cronies of these leaders were stashed away in foreign banks. Neither the World Bank, the International Monetary Fund, nor the international development agencies raised an eyebrow at such unethical practices (Aluko, 2000:2).

In fact, since the early 1980s, Africa's debt burden has become increasingly onerous and unmanageable. The amount of debt and the increasing inability to service it has led creditors and suppliers to impose severe payment conditions on debtor economies via the Bretton Woods institutions. The austerity policies of the major governments, such as those of Reagan in the

United States and Thatcher of Britain, caused inflation to fall, real interest rates to rise, raw material prices to fall, and the value of the dollar (in which most loans were denominated) to rise. The real interest rates in global markets remained at relatively low levels during the 1970s. According to the World Bank (1990:15), average real interest rates for the 1963-1989 period were as follows: 2.63 percent, 0.91 percent and 5.85 percent, for the periods 1963-1973, 1973-1979, and 1980-1989 respectively. At the same time, the average annual growth of exports for sub-Saharan Africa was 6.62 percent during the 1965-1980 period, but this rate fell sharply to -0.8 percent during the 1980-1987 period. The maturity period for loans was shortened from 6.7 years to 4 years and the grace period was reduced by 36 percent. The overall grant element in the period in question was also down by 82 percent (World Bank, 1989:172). With rising interest rates, and shortened maturity and grace periods on old and new credits and loans, the size of Africa's debt rose to unmanageable proportions.

The total external debt of the continent rose from $111 billion in 1980 to $310 billion in 1997. Its rapid growth has been excessive in relation to both gross domestic product and exports. The ratio of Africa's external debt to gross domestic product, for example, increased from 14.5 percent to 67.5 percent between 1971 and 1997. Measured against the export of goods and services, the debt service ratio increased from 0.63 percent to 21.3 percent between 1971 and 1997. All other relevant debt indicators demonstrate that over the 1971-1997 period, debt service obligations, particularly for sub-Saharan African countries, reached unsustainable levels. For most of these countries, the low capacity to service their debts is vividly reflected not only in the massive build-up of arrears and high service ratios but, most importantly, in the number and frequency of rescheduling arrangements. The cumulative burden of these payments has been nothing short of staggering, particularly for the heavily indebted poor countries (HIPCs), most of which are in sub-Saharan Africa. Debt repayment typically absorbs over one-quarter of an HIPC's national budget. That some African governments should spend more repaying their rich creditors than in providing basic services is both morally wrong and economically senseless (African Development Bank, 2000).

Compared with other debtor developing regions, particularly Latin America and Asia, the size of Africa's external debt has, on the whole, been relatively small. However, given the size, structure and vulnerability of African economies, Africa's debt is more unsustainable. Goran Hyden (1987:24) has noted that the double tragedy of poor African countries is that not only is their foreign debt overwhelming relative to their domestic economic capacity, but it is also too small to give them any real bargaining strength in the international arena. As if that were not enough, creditor nations, as well as banks, insist on treating the debt question on a country-by-country basis, in a divide-and-rule fashion, which ensures that debtors are kept in the weakest possible bargaining position. One is strongly convinced that little is likely to be accomplished until African countries bring their collective strength to bear at the international bargaining table. The implementation of the New Partnership for Africa's Development initiative would seem to be aimed at seeking to do just this.

Africa's more recent debt has been accumulated from loans contracted with multilateral financial institutions, especially the IMF and the World Bank, for private banks are not attracted to poverty. In fact, part of this debt resulted from the borrowing associated with externally sponsored economic structural reform programs. In 1980, for example, IMF/World Bank debt equaled 19 percent of Africa's total debt. By 1992, this debt accounted for 28 percent and by 1998 it had reached 32 percent. Worse still, until 1996, multilateral debt could not be formally rescheduled or diminished and significant arrears were accumulated. Much of the rest of Africa's debt was bilateral or government-guaranteed, private, medium- and long-term debt, which could be rescheduled through the Paris Club of Creditors.

As pointed out earlier, this difficult external debt burden and the resultant desperate need for foreign exchange made African countries dependent on a variety of external actors, all of whom used their leverage to demand economic, and later, political liberalization. Beginning in the early 1980s, the IMF was used as the vehicle to ensure that African countries repaid Northern commercial bank loans. In exchange for structural adjustment loans, borrowing countries were expected to implement IMF-mandated policy reforms, including the liberalization of domestic trade regimes, relaxation of foreign exchange controls, privatization of basic services and an end to social subsidies. In the final analysis, African states became increasingly more accountable to foreign creditor nations and multilateral financial and development aid agencies than to their own people. Equally importantly, they became less able to respond to the basic needs of their people, including health, education and security, as they religiously implemented externally mandated policy reform measures.

Unsustainable debt has created serious foreign exchange constraints for most poor sub-Saharan African countries. Of the 32 countries classified by the World Bank as severely indebted, low-income countries, 25 are in sub-Saharan Africa. The sub-region's total external debt rose from $60 billion in 1980 to $219 billion in 1997. Its annual debt servicing absorbs between one-quarter and one-third of foreign exchange earnings. Although debt service ratios have started to fall in a few countries, this is largely because of a widening gap between scheduled payments, which amount to over 50 percent of the export earnings of some African countries, and the actual payments. As a result, arrears have been accumulating at a frightening rate. In addition, the accumulation of arrears has also contributed to another dimension of the debt problem, namely an unsustainable debt stock, which deters investment and undermines economic stability. Apart from diverting domestic financial resources, debt servicing has resulted in the diversion of development assistance, with bilateral aid from E.U. member countries being used to finance the debt owed to the IMF and the World Bank. It has been estimated that around one-quarter of bilateral aid, some $9 billion annually, is currently being used directly to finance debt repayments (World Bank, 1998).

As one UNCTAD Report (2001:36) has noted, if the net resource flows and net resource transfers are combined with leakages, it turns out that in the past two decades Africa has not received any net transfers of real resources from the rest of the world. It estimates that for each dollar of net capital inflow to sub-Saharan Africa from the rest of the world, some 25 cents went back as net interest payments and profit remittances abroad; more than 35 cents leaked into capital outflows and reserve build-ups, while 51 cents constituted losses. These figures imply that there is a net transfer of real resources from Africa to the rest of the world. Surely, a system which, on aggregate, is responsible for growing net resource transfers from the poorer to the richer parts of the world is hardly likely, politically or economically, to add to international stability, not to mention justice. This conclusion brings to the fore the internal logic of capitalist development and the inability of liberal global governance to deliver on economic growth and poverty reduction in African countries.

The resultant debt bondage irretrievably tends to compromise the debtors' national sovereignty, however broadly defined. Debtor countries were prevented from defaulting by a series of renegotiations of their debts with creditors. Through these renegotiations, the Paris and London Clubs of creditors have held debtor governments at ransom. As pointed out earlier, the most pernicious aspect of structural adjustment conditionality has been the curtailment of the autonomy of the African state. The IMF and the

World Bank have *de facto* usurped the national sovereignty of the African states as they have increasingly assumed the role of national policy management. It is worth remembering that even the highly indebted poor countries initiative was designed by creditors and was largely controlled and managed by them as well. They have the power to decide who gets what, when and why. Although Uganda reached the so-called 'completion point' in its debt management process as early as 2000, the Paris Club could not cancel its debt. The decision to delay the cancellation process was prompted by the U.S. State Department's request to the Paris Club following the fighting between Ugandan and Rwandan troops in the Democratic Republic of Congo. Incidentally, Uganda had previously been deferred due to 'donors' anger' over the government's decision to purchase a presidential jet at an estimated cost of US$30 million (Jubilee 2000, 2000:10-11).

It is the firm conviction of this author that, irrespective of whether or not Africa's external debt should be paid, such payments cannot and will not be met given the structural, political and economic constraints imposed by the current phase of global capitalist accumulation. Karamo M. Sanko (1990:26) goes further, to insist that "even if all the debt is cancelled today, many problems which led to the current crisis will continue to exist. Therefore, major policy changes in both the creditor and debtor nations are required in order to generate long-term economic prosperity in Africa." If economic growth, poverty reduction and sustainable development are indeed at the heart of the emerging development cooperation crusade, then the very conditions that give rise to stagnation and marginalization should be tackled head on. These include, on the one hand, the unequal international division of labor, lack of access to Northern markets, falling commodity prices, declining investment and net transfer of resources to the North through debt servicing obligation. On the other hand, Africans have to grapple with widespread corruption, economic mismanagement, misplaced priorities, unnecessary defense and security expenditure, and above all, undemocratic political systems and institutions. Nobody would expect the same leaders who piled up the billions of dollars in foreign debt by looting their treasuries to pursue policies that would resolve the debt crisis. The need for a new and broad-based democratic dispensation in Africa has become, indeed urgent.

In the present circumstances, however, Africa should negotiate to pay its accumulated debts only as a result of economic growth, not through reduced consumption and austerity as is the current practice. Moreover, realistic debt relief must not be conditional upon controversial structural adjustment measures that, in many cases, have made the poor poorer. For countries with such limited revenue bases and such intense levels of deprivation, resource transfers from Africa to rich countries usually carry high opportunity costs. Such costs are reflected in the notorious imbalances between the ever growing spending on debt repayment and the declining public spending on health and education in many of these poor countries. As discussed above, such unpropitious socio-economic realities, as well as the exigencies of social justice and morality, provide compelling arguments against debt repayment.

Moreover, for Africa's low-income, disease-stricken, debt-stressed, primary commodity economies, the arguments for debt cancellation are disarmingly straightforward. Debt repayment is economically exhausting, as it continues to block future development; it is politically destabilizing as it threatens social harmony. And it is ethically unacceptable, as it hurts the poorest of the poor. Worse still, much of Africa's accumulated debt is a result of ill-conceived, creditor-supported development projects and programs, flawed policies and strategies that originated from development cooperation agencies in exchange for Cold War support, as well as short-sighted policy decisions by African leaders. In all fairness, therefore, Africa's unsustainable debt should be accepted as a shared responsibility of creditors and debtors alike. Given the size of Africa's debt, its total cancellation would have only a negligible impact on international financial institutions and markets (Rugumamu, 2001:48).

Finally, it should be emphasized that most of the poor Africans, who now bear the brunt of debt payment, did not directly benefit from the loans that gave rise to the debt crisis. Its cancellation, if carried out in ways that directly benefit the poor and the excluded, would lift them out of their current abject poverty. It is against this background that major debt cancellation campaigners are calling for a new, more disciplined approach to international borrowing and lending that will break the damaging cycle of reckless lending and unsustainable borrowing. It has also been repeatedly argued that an international insolvency body be established that would be entrusted with resolving the debt crisis. The principle that individual and corporate debtors should not be left to the mercy of creditors is widely accepted. The same principle should be extended to sovereign debts. It would go a long way toward attacking the complicity of Northern banks and some corrupt African leaders likely to engage in money laundering. Unfortunately, previous and current loan transactions were, and continue to be, shrouded in secrecy. This cloud of secrecy explains, to a large extent, why it has become almost impossible to recover most of the resources that were illicitly diverted to European and American banks.

In this regard, the debt problem can be effectively brought to the top of the global agenda if it is politically linked to the fundamental political problems facing the continent, such as broad-based democratization and internal socio-economic restructuring, in order to create a viable environment for meaningful recovery. *The African Charter for Popular Participation in Development and Transformation* (ECA, 1990) argued that the crisis was, in many ways, more political than economic. It had to do with the lack of empowerment of popular organizations, absence of accountability of leaders to the people, the suffocation of civil society, the non-involvement of women, youth and the rural majority in decision-making processes, and the general opposition of most African governments to democratizing their societies. The internal linkage can be successfully exploited only when the African continent acts as one and speaks with one voice. Once again, the imperative of cooperation and integration to fight against all forms of marginalization comes to the fore. This observation is even more pertinent in the arena of international trade.

International Trade and Africa's Marginalization

Increasing international trade is another important organizing characteristic of the new wave of globalization and one of the major causes of Africa's marginalization. In contrast to financial market liberalization, there are compelling efficiency grounds for trade liberalization. Trade is considered an important engine for economic growth and can play an important role in the development of poor countries. It enhances a country's access to goods, services, technologies and knowledge. And, by stimulating the entrepreneurial activities of the private sector, trade can create jobs, speed up learning processes, attract private capital flows, increase foreign exchange earnings and generate resources for sustainable development and poverty reduction. Unfortunately, the current rules and practices governing international trade operate in a manner which gear the whole international trade process toward serving the corporate and political interests of the North, resulting in a highly unequal distribution of the benefits of world trade. Michael Todaro draws a similar conclusion:

> The principal benefits of world trade have accrued disproportionately to rich nations and within poor nations disproportionately to both foreign residents and wealthy nationals… (world trade) reflects the highly inegalitarian institutional, social, and economic ordering of the global system, in which a few powerful nations and their multinational corporations control vast amounts of resources…trade, like education, tends to reinforce existing inequalities (Todaro, 1981:358).

The extraordinary expansion in world output since 1945 has resulted in large part from the massive liberalization of world trade, first under the auspices of the General Agreement on Tariffs and Trade (GATT) established in 1947, and now under the auspices of the World Trade Organization (WTO) which replaced the GATT in 1993. Tariff levels in high-income economies of the North have come down dramatically, and now average approximately 4 percent. Tariff levels in low-icome economies of the South have also been reduced, everaging 20 percent. Non-tariff barriers to trade such as quotas, licenses and technical specifications, are also being gradually dismantled, but rather more slowly than tarrifs.While world output has expanded fivefold, the volume of world trade has grown 16 times at an everage compound rate of just over 7 percent per annum (Africa Development Report 2004:118-119).

World trade expansion did not occur uniformly accross countries, with the North and only a small group of 12 countries drawn from the South accounting for the lion's share. In contrast, the majority of countries in the South did not experience significant trade expansion. World exports increased from $61 billion in 1950 to $3,447 billion in 1990, and to $6,700 billion in 1998. As noted above, throughout this period, growth in world trade was significantly higher than the growth in world output. The share of world exports to world GDP rose from 6 percent in 1950 to 12 percent in 1973 and 16 percent in 1992 (Nayyar, 2002). It should come as no surprise that international trade, like international investment and finance, is concentrated in the triad. As an illustration of the intertwining of trade flows, in 1992 the E.U. exported goods and services worth $95 billion to the United States and imported $111 billion. The E.U. exported $96 billion to the Asia Pacific region and imported $153 billion. As for the United States, it exported goods and services worth $128 billion to the Pacific Rim and imported a staggering $215 billion. If one adds financial interdependence, technology transfer and alliances, and joint ventures between firms, it is obvious that the core of the global economy is a tightly interdependent network among the United States, Japan and the E.U. (World Bank, 2002). Around this triad of power, wealth and technology, the rest of the world is organized in a hierarchical and asymmetrically interdependent web, as different countries and regions compete to attract their capital, human skills, technology and markets for goods and services (Castells, 1998; Collier, 1998). It will be argued that world trade policies and practices not only deprive the poor people of economic opportunities through various trade barriers, but also destroys livelihoods by dumping highly subsidized surplus products on the markets of poor countries.

Most African economies face serious problems as a result of their dependence on a narrow range of products, principally primary commodities and minerals. Approximately in about one-third of sub-Saharan African countries, agricultural exports in 2000, for example, accounted for about 75 percent of export earnings and the share of commodities in the export totals of some individual countries frequently exceeds 90 percent. In the early 1990s, less than a third of all African countries were dependent on a single primary commodity for at least 50 percent of their total exports. Oil producers, such as Nigeria, the Congo, and Angola had become less diversified in their trade over time, to a point where oil accounted for more than 90 percent of their exports. Worse still, most of the poorest African countries have been reliant on a single low-value agricultural commodity; cashews accounted for 91 percent of Guinea Bissau's exports, coffee for 66 percent of Burundi's exports, cocoa for 92 percent of Sao Tome's exports, and cotton for 57 percent of Mali's exports. Reliance on a single commodity has left African economies extremely vulnerable to volatility in commodity prices (van de Walle, 2000:265-268; UNCTAD, 2001a-4-7).

Sub-Saharan Africa's importance in global trade declined over the past 30 to 40 years. Exports from the sub-region accounted for 3.1 percent of world exports in 1955, but by the late 1990s, its global share had fallen to about 1 percent, implying annual trade losses of $65 billion at current prices. Part of this outcome reflects a declining global demand for key agricultural export products but a part is also due to a substantial erosion of her global market share. Indeed, if sub-Saharan Africa had merely maintained its 1962-64-export share for major products, the sub-region's exports would now have more than doubled their current value (Yeats et al., 1996:38-41).

While Africa's export performance in terms of volume of growth was inferior to that of other developing regions for the last two decades, it has been hit, more than any other region, by deteriorating terms of trade. This is at the core of the continent's marginalization. While world commodity prices often shift up and down erratically, there is one long-term tendency; the prices of manufactures have tended to rise, while those of raw materials have tended to fall. As a result, African countries, which export mainly raw materials and import manufactures, have suffered particularly large falls in their national terms of trade. Ultimately, this reduces their real income and share in world trade. For non-oil exporting sub-Saharan countries, cumulative terms of trade losses in 1970-1997 represented almost 119 percent of regional

GDP, a massive and persistent drain of purchasing power (World Bank, 2000:20; UNCTAD, 2001a: 6-8). This secular decline in Africa's terms of trade is one of the major reasons for the marginalization of the continent. Martin Khor (2001:28) has gone even further to conclude that the deteriorating terms of trade "probably constitute the single largest mechanism by which real economic resources are transferred from South to North."

In order to reduce dependence on traditional commodity exports, an increased number of African countries have been moving into exports of processed goods and manufactures. However, their recent industrial performance has been extremely weak. They could hardly compete against imports by transnational corporations. Growth of manufacture value-added averaged only 3 percent per year in real terms from 1980 to 1997 and exports contribution to GDP has slowed steadily over that period, from 3.7 percent annually in the first half of the 1980s to 2 percent annually in 1989-93. As a consequence, African economies remain the least industrialized in the world. In 1990, industry accounted for about 30 percent of output in Africa, compared with 37 percent for all low- and middle-income countries worldwide. Manufacturing, the most dynamic element in industry, accounted for a particularly small share of total industrial output. This poor performance is especially marked in exports, where Africa's performance is almost non-existent (African Development Report, 2004).

Africa's poor record of manufactured goods is is not only a clear reflection of the underdevelopment of Africa's industry but, most importantly, the consequence of escalating tariffs on manufactures considered 'sensitive' by the North. In fact, tariffs on manufactures are far higher than the average rates on products of particular export interest to the South, in particular on processed food products, tobacco, some beverages, fruit and vegetables, food-industry products including fruit juices and canned meat, and textiles, clothing and footwear. Such measures act as disincentives to investment aimed at value addition locally, while at the same time discouraging diversification (UNCTAD, 2001b; Stein; 1992).

Over the last three decades, the trend in raw material prices (in constant dollars) has been one on the decline, with the decline especially sharp during the 1980s and 1990s. This trend has been caused, in considerable measure, by a decrease in the rate of growth in world demand for these materials. In turn, the lower rate of growth in world consumption reflects a major change in the structure of world demand brought about by technological change and also marks a shift in the composition of world output. Although these developments have had an adverse impact on raw material producers in all countries, their effects have been especially severe for those sub-Saharan African countries that are heavily dependent on raw materials for their foreign exchange earnings. As noted previously, the composition of output in industrial countries has been shifting from agriculture and manufactures to services. Since raw materials constitute a much smaller proportion of the value of services than they do of agricultural and industrial production, the shift in production composition has significantly contributed to the decline in the growth of world demand for raw materials (Mikesell, 1988; Clark and Juma, 1991; Castells, 1993).

The conservation in the use of materials and the substitution of new materials for traditional ones has also contributed heavily to the reduction in consumption of raw materials exported by African countries. Most substitutions do not involve an increase in the demand for one raw material that offsets a decrease in demand for another raw material of equal value. Instead, such substitutions entail replacing a traditional raw material either with a synthetic one or, if with another raw material, then with one in which a significant portion of its value derives from processing and energy. Synthetic fibers have been substitutes for cotton, wool, jute and sisal. Synthetic rubber has replaced natural rubber. With the exception of natural rubber, all agricultural raw materials were less competitive in relation to synthetics in the 1980s and 1990s (Castells, 1993; 1998. Specifically, Raymond Mikesell's study, referred to above, shows that, over the last 30 years, conservation and substitution of traditional metals has occurred very rapidly due to developments in material technology and requirements for new and improved products. High-strength, low-alloy steel has replaced carbon steel and cast iron for consequent savings in car weight. Aluminum has replaced copper and plastics, and composite materials have been substituted for metals in auto production. Metals technology has produced thinner-walled and smaller-gauged copper tubing, and the revolution in the design of electrical and electronic circuits has resulted in a reduction in the use of copper wire. Above all, the conversion of telephone lines using copper wire to ones using fiber-optic cable is likely to have a devastating impact on copper-dependent economies such as the Democratic Republic of Congo and Zambia (Clark, 1990:914-919; Mikesell, 1988:154-155). The economic future for primary commodity exports is dim. According to Castells' projection:

> The more economic growth depends on high-value-added inputs and expansion in the core markets, then the less relevant become the economies which offer limited, difficult markets and primary commodities that are either being replaced by new materials

or devalued with respect to their overall contribution to the production process. With the absolute costs of labor becoming less and less important as a competitive factor, many   countries and regions face a process of rapid deterioration that could lead to destructive reactions. Within the framework of the new international economy, a significant part of the world population is shifting from the structural position of exploitation to a structural position of irrelevance (Castells, 1993:37).

To further illustrate the case of unequal trade, let us briefly examine Africa's more recent trade relations with Europe. By 2000, around 51 percent of Africa's exports were to the E.U. and 17 percent to North American markets while intra-African trade accounted for only 8 percent of the total exports of the region. In order to have guaranteed supplies of raw materials at stable prices, beginning in 1975, the European Union entered into a special development cooperation relationship with its former colonies in Africa, the Caribbean and the Pacific (ACP). This arrangement was formalized as the Lomé Convention. As of 2000, about 92 percent of the products originating from ACP countries entered the E.U. market duty-free. If agricultural products, which were subject to a tariff quota with zero duty, are included (protocol products such as sugar, beef, bananas and rum), this percentage rises to about 99 percent. The only exceptions are products that come under the E.U. Common Agricultural Policy (CAP), such as tomatoes, carrots, onions and the like. Whereas the majority of the E.U. exports to ACP countries consists of manufactured and capital goods, ACP countries export largely agricultural raw materials, minerals, and crude oil - clear evidence of a relationship in the colonial mold (Asante, 1981; 1990; Parfitt, 1996).

Many developing countries, including those in Africa, enjoy preferential access to most industrial country markets, under the Generalized System of Preferences (GSP) and selected provisions in regional and multilateral agreements. Yet, despite the preferential access to the E.U. market that was offered under various Lomé Conventions, ACP exports to Europe have deteriorated during the past two-and-a-half decades of trade and aid cooperation. These preferences are neither unlimited nor permanent. The ACP's share of total E.U. imports fell from 6.7 percent in 1976 to 3 percent in 1998. This reflected the declining share of the ACP in world trade, which was cut in half from 3 to 1.5 percent during the same period. In volume terms, ACP exports grew by less than 4 percent, while those of non-ACP developing countries grew by 75 percent (ACP Report, 1998; McQueen, 1996). Moreover, the UNDP (1996:84) reports that since the early 1970s, the least developed countries have suffered a cumulative decline of 50 percent in terms of trade with the rest of the world. For developing countries as a group, the cumulative terms of trade losses amounted to $290 billion between 1980 and 1991. Much of this catastrophic fall was due to the decline in real commodity prices. In 1990, for example, they were 45 percent lower than in 1980 and 10 percent lower than even the lowest prices during the Great Depression of 1932.

The Lomé Convention put in place the commodity export stabilization program, STABEX, that was deliberately offered as an alternative to the UNCTAD IV demand for commodity price stabilization. The scheme covered 44 commodities, all of which were either unprocessed or semi-processed. Like an insurance scheme, it was designed to compensate for export earnings shortfalls of selected commodities. Only when export earnings fell below 7.5 percent of the average for the previous four years could the country in question request a financial transfer. Even then, such transfers could be denied when it was the opinion of the E.U. that the decline in export earnings was caused by a trade policy that discriminated against the E.U. A policy, for example, that directs primary commodities towards domestic processing and that discourages the export of such commodities in their raw state can be considered discriminatory. Lynn Mytelka and Steve Langdon (1979:197) long ago concluded that the STABEX system was both an incentive to maintain present levels of production in these specific commodities and a disincentive to diversifying commercial agricultural production, processing raw materials locally, or developing domestic food production - all activities that might have promoted domestic economic linkages and brought the structure of demand and production into line.

As a result of the above structural constraints, most ACP countries, particularly sub-Saharan African countries, failed to diversify their exports into non-traditional products. The few countries that have made modest efforts towards diversifying into garments, fresh fruit, flowers and vegetables are finding the going difficult. The market niches for non-traditional exports are highly competitive. They require connections to complex international commodity networks, which continually draw new entries from countries worldwide. Moreover, products for new market niches are highly perishable. Because they require expensive transportation and are subject to wide-ranging price fluctuations, they do, indeed, entail high risks for producers. The vast majority of traditional agricultural exports are native to temperate rather than tropical climates. This disadvantages most African entrepreneurs, whose knowledge is essentially of local tropical crops. The above features, combined with the need for large capital investments, contribute to the dominance of large foreign firms, for which local people serve as low-wage laborers (Klak, 1998).

Above all, most African economies have failed to become competitive in the E.U. market. Some observers have concluded that the preferential treatment enjoyed by ACP countries has not been sufficient to develop their trade. Indeed, the structural factors inherent in Euro-African relations appear to have limited the intended effects of preferences. As noted earlier, there is mounting evidence to suggest that the developments in science and biotechnology that are taking place in Europe are swiftly eroding Africa's traditional, comparative advantage in the current international division of labor. Already, key agricultural crops such as sugar, cocoa, cotton, and timber are competing with the E.U.'s bio-technologically engineered substitutes, which are often stronger, more versatile, and easier to work with. All these primary commodities can be switched and substituted whenever either the supply of one commodity fails or the price rises. Therefore, one can safely argue that the on-going technological transformations in the global economy are likely to reduce African economies to a position of near structural irrelevance (Clark, 1990).

Similarly, the agriculture and textile sectors, in which poor African countries are most competitive, are subject to a prohibitive array of high and escalating tariffs, quotas, producer price supports, export subsidies and seasonal restrictions. The world trade in textiles and clothing stood at $248 billion in 1998. If there were a genuinely free global market, then the countries of the South, including China, would be the natural clothiers of the rest of the world. For well over 30 years the Multi-Fiber Arrangement has provided domestic protection to Northern producers of textiles and clothing. This agreement is expected to remain in place until possibly after January 2005. However, the Uruguay Round smuggled in safeguards to continue protecting industrialized countries! By failing to level down escalated tariffs, the Uruguay Round deliberately gave an unmistakable signal to the South that it was not particularly keen to allow the South to compete with the North. This is a clear example of how most powerful countries suspend their belief in the law of comparative advantage when it suits their interests (Finger and Schuler, 2000; Harrison *et. al.*, 1999). Ultimately, Africa is once again the greatest loser.

A careful reading of the Uruguay Round Agreement reveals that non-tariff barriers have clandestinely replaced tariff barriers, with the former being far less transparent than the latter. Perhaps the most egregious of these barriers are anti-dumping and countervailing duties. Whereas the current WTO rules on agriculture require poor countries to liberalize their markets, they allow industrialized countries to subsidize and dump their agricultural exports on Africa. In West Africa, for example, a flood of cheap European tomato concentrates and meat has seriously undermined the local tomato and meat industries. This is hypocrisy of the most absurd order. Although the powerful preach the virtues of openness, too often in areas where they lack comparative advantage, they engage in strong protectionist measures. This is one area where globalization is dymystified. At the same time, while most African countries are making increasing use of anti-dumping measures, they are often unable to mount cases in the WTO's dispute-settlement system and have difficulty contesting anti-dumping and countervailing duty actions (Oxfam, 2002; 2000).

Worse still, the protective 'Rules of Origin' in the E.U. have equally undermined Africa's prospects for industrialization. They have been particularly problematic because they stipulate that ACP exports must have 50 percent of their value-added originating in ACP states and/or the E.U. Given the very low level of industrialization in most African states, a requirement of 50 percent value-added is highly restrictive and particularly onerous. Most of Africa's processed and manufactured products do not benefit from the Lomé Convention's free access provision because they have only between 20 and 48 percent value-added as a proportion of their gross value (Twitchett, 1978:475). Indeed, some observers consider the Rules of Origin as one of the major disincentives to Africa's economic diversification and industrialization (Ravenhill, 1985; Lister, 1998; 1999).

Other critics also point to the existence of a 'Safeguard Clause,' which allows E.U. member-states to make derogations from the guarantees of free access if products from Africa threaten their markets. The presence of this clause introduced considerable uncertainty into the Euro-African trade relationship. Trevor Parfitt (1996) notes that the United Kingdom invoked the Safeguard Clause in 1979 to force Mauritius to conclude a voluntary export restraint against its textile exports to the Community. The implications of this decision went beyond this one sector, since no potential investor in the ACP countries could be certain of access for future production and export to the European market if there were a possibility that such exports might adversely affect European interests. This is quite clearly unjust.

In a similar protectionist stance, the E.U. has put in place an upward harmonization of Europe-wide technical standards for imports. Public concern about the health risks of food and appropriate sanitary standards has been on the rise in the industrial countries of the North. In fact, previously, the E.U. had constantly invoked sanitary and phyto-sanitary measures to bar African products, such as fish and meat products. The use of import bans and regulatory interventions by the European Commission, for example, is increasingly justified, in part, under the precautionary principle which seeks to mitigate against risks even under conditions in which science has not established a direct causal relationship. In addition, fast technological changes have enhanced inspection capabilities and allowed these economies to adopt progressively more restrictive sanitary and phyto-sanitary standards. African countries are likely to be vulnerable to such stringent regulatory standards. Compliance requirements are likely to impose huge costs in terms of upgrading production systems, processing and storage equipment, and quality control stations (Henson *et. al.*, 2000).

Most recently, the European Commission proposed harmonization of aflatoxin standards. Aflatoxins are a group of structurally related, naturally occurring toxic compounds which contaminate certain foods (e.g. in peanuts and corn) and result in the production of acute liver carcinogens in the human body. This policy move has the potential to exclude most of Africa's exports. One study by World Bank researchers examined the effects of a European regulations limiting the amount of aflatoxins in imported food. The regulation insists on a higher standard than that recommended by CODEX, which sets international food standards, or by the WHO and the U.S. Food and Drug Administration. The study calculated that this new E.U. standard would reduce exports to Europe for cereal, dried fruit and nuts from nine African countries by 64 percent or $700 million. It concluded that the E.U.'s sampling method would further reduce African exports (Otsuki et al., 2001). Similarly, Michael Finger and Philip Schuler (2000:1) have noted that WTO obligations reflect little awareness of development problems and little appreciation of the capacities of poor developing countries. In most cases, standards have been developed with little input from the least developed countries, thus undermining their sense of ownership. More fundamentally, it is not clear that all these standards are appropriate for the least developed countries and there is an ever-present danger that they will be used to protect E.U. markets. In a nutshell, the use of health and environmental standards, important and desirable as indeed they are, intrinsically threatens to further restrict developing countries' access to international markets. Most African countries often lack the resources and capability to implement these standards. All in all, the discussion above demonstrates how heavy dependence on a few markets can increase the vulnerability of export earnings to political expidiency and to fluctuations in demand in the importing countries.

A new round of multilateral trade negotiations that transformed GATT into the World Trade Organization (WTO) broadened the agenda of trade negotiations to include services, intellectual property rights (IPRs), investment measures and competition policy. As knowledge becomes much more important in the modern economy, the 'knowledge gap' within and between countries is rapidly growing. WTO agreements on intellectual property rights significantly increase the length and scope of patent protection for many countries. Its rules grant corporations a 20-year monopoly on knowledge, far beyond the useful life of most new technologies, thus creating unfair barriers to new competitors from poor countries. Under the Uruguay Round concluded in 1994, the protocols relating to the so-called 'trade related investment measures' (TRIMs) and 'trade related intellectual property rights' (TRIPs) have severely circumscribed the sovereign rights of states. As pointed out earlier, developing countries can no longer regulate the activities of multinational corporations in order to foster their perceived vital development needs. The TRIMs protocol ties the hands of governments in developing countries, preventing them from requiring foreign investors to abide by specific local content requirements, domestic sales, trade balancing tests, or remittance and exchange restrictions (UNCTAD, 2000).

By the same token, investment liberalization is likely to strengthen the power of financial markets over national economies. The birth and expansion of a euro-currency market, the adoption of flexible exchange rates since the early 1970s and the creation of derivatives in the 1980s have all given rise to growing and devastating speculative pressure on commodity prices, as well as on interest and exchange rates. The Asian monetary and financial crisis is testimony to this speculative trend. Under intense international pressure, East Asian economies were forced to liberalize their financial and capital markets in the mid-1990s. These changes facilitated a flood of short-term capital, that is, the kind of capital that looks for the highest return in the next few days or months. Just as suddenly as capital flowed in, it flowed out. In the case of these East Asian economies, all investors tried to pull their money out at the same time, it caused an unprecedented economic crisis.

The TRIPs agreement seeks to consolidate, universalize, and strengthen previous international agreements, and makes them legally enforceable through the WTO dispute-settlement mechanism. Furthermore, the TRIPS agreement is designed to protect patents, copyrights, industrial designs and other forms of intellectual property dominated by multinational enterprises. This entire array of international regulations is likely to eliminate the prospects of copy-technology (reverse engineering) and these regulations force potential users of foreign technology into licensing agreements and royalty payments. Undoubtedly, such developments are likely to have adverse consequences on technological upgrading and adaptation by African economies. As UNCTAD observes:

> It is undeniable that the global economy is currently going through significant changes. The new trading regime under the WTO has reduced the scope for using measures which call for trad-related subsidies, lax enforcement of intellectual property rights, and strategic conditions imposed on foreign investments, which were an integral part of the East Asian development strategy. Certainly, the more generalized protection, which provided a backdrop for targeted policies in East Asia, no longer appears too permissible. It may also be true that the changes will reduce the scope for policy maneuver for the developing countries which wish to pursue a strategy involving vigorous infant industry protection and export subsidies (UNCTAD, 1996:25).

Finally, tight intellectual property rights will raise the cost of technology transfer for African countries and will risk blocking innovations in these countries. In turn, this will undermine Africa's capacity to compete in the increasingly knowledge-based global economy. Tighter controls of innovation in the hands of TNCs will invariably place corporate interests above the wider development interests of poor people and thus accentuate the unequal patterns of globalization. African states and international civil organizations can effectively challenge, and even help to write the rules and norms of the international trade regime only when they act collectively in the WTO. We should hasten to add that this would only be possible if Africans were to be effectively represented in Geneva. As the Oxfam Report (Oxfam, 2002:252) pointed out, 19 out of 42 sub-Saharan African WTO members do not have trade representatives at the WTO headquarters. Such severe under-representation almost automatically constrains the capacity of Africa to defend national and regional interests at this important decision-making institution. Unequal representation in Geneva is only an obvious manifestation of Africa's marginalization and its structural incapacity to exert adequate influence on the possible reform of the unjust international economic system. It is also symptomatic of Africa's under-representation in the overall regime of contemporary international labor migration.

International Migration and Africa's Exclusion

Besides unfavorable terms of trade, technology and investment, African countries suffer unfavorable terms in the flow of people. The General Agreement on Trade and Services (GATS) "Mode 4" provision is restricted to the temporary movement of service providers and covers only a tiny fruction of the cross-border movement of labor. This is yet another case of injustice. While migratory flows are as old as history itself, the dimensions of the contemporary upsurge are staggering.[22] In 1995, UNDP estimated that there were at least 125 million international migrants living outside the countries in which they were born. Yet the international market for labor is one of the most restricted markets (UNDP, 1995). Historians argue that migration was more common during the 19th century, when as much as 10 percent of the world's population moved. However, the bulk of that migration was from European countries into areas of new settlements by European emigrants like America and Australia. Today, much of the migration is from the poor countries of the South to the rich industrial countries of the North.

The free movement of the factors of production in liberal economic practice does not extend to labor. It is strictly regulated by governments. The practice is at variance with one of the basic tenets of neo-classical economic theory on 'factor price equalization.' Goods, people and capital moving across national borders should, in principle, tend to equalize prices between countries. Labor should travel from low-wage to high-wage economies and capital should move in the other direction. This movement would tend to depress wages in the migration destination countries, while raising them in the sending countries. Eventually, so the argument goes, some kind of equilibrium would be reached when the remaining wage gap would represent just the cost of migration between the two countries. As a result, migration should stop. However, this equalization does not happen in practice. This is yet another feature of the current process of globalization. It is also another example of the existent to which the supposed universal benefits of globalization are a myth.

As pointed out earlier, much of the contemporary immigration is from the poor to the rich countries. It consists, first, of unskilled people, often migrating illegally, and, second, of skilled (and legal) migrants. Governments in industrial countries are busy changing their immigration policies to weight them in favor of skilled migrants and restrict the inflow of the unskilled. This migration pattern has led to a peculiar asymmetry. The supply of unskilled immigrants currently exceeds demand in the North. By contrast, the demand for skilled immigrants exceeds supply. Consequently, the flood of illegal unskilled migrants into rich countries and the 'brain drain' of skilled citizens from the poor countries are two of the most critical issues of contemporary international migration. In a fast globalizing world, migration issues are a central policy issue for many countries. The immigration laws and consular practices in the North block the free flow of labor from the South (Dearden, 1999).

It is not altogether surprising that regional free trade arrangements such as NAFTA coincided with massive expenditure in the U.S. on border patrols, surveillance equipment and anti-personnel devices to prevent the movement of poor and uneducated Mexicans into the U.S. In the words of Peter Andreas (2000:x), "the result has been the construction of both a borderless economy and a barricaded border." Free trade is the mantra but, in practice it has been selectively applied, controlled and mixed with a raft of coercive state policies. This apparent policy contradiction is compellingly captured by Stephen Gill's phrase of 'disciplinary neo-liberalism' (Gill, 1995).

In the host countries, public opposition to international migration is exacerbated by domestic unemployment difficulties not necessarily of the migrants' causing. This has, in turn, purportedly encouraged a growth of racial intolerance in society at large in the North. Racism has been quite plain in immigration controls against people of color in the so-called 'open' world economy. It is feared that more immigrants can only erode the political hegemony of the native population, just as it is believed that more immigrants could undermine social cohesion and cultural solidarity. Above all, there are perceptions - often exploited by xenophobic politicians - that more immigrants are likely to displace citizens from jobs or become a burden in terms of social expenditure.

There has also been considerable discrimination against migrant workers, not just in employment but also in housing and welfare. For example, a 1993 public opinion survey by the E.U. found that about 52 percent of respondents felt that there were too many immigrants; a 1993 New York/CBS national telephone survey reported that 61 percent of Americans favored a decrease in the number of immigrants, compared with 42 percent in a 1977 Gallup Poll (Wienner, 1995:3). This sensationalism is least surprising precisely because the proportion of foreign citizens to resident population in the United States ranges between 1 percent of the population to over 15 percent, with the average around 8 percent (UNDP, 1995). Whether in Birmingham, Frankfurt or Paris, Southerners in general, and African migrants in particular, have become targets of simmering xenophobia and occasional racist attacks, with some ultra-nationalist groups even trying to court popularity by demanding that poor foreigners be forcibly repatriated.

In Europe as in North America, the issue of immigration is being perceived as a post-Cold War national security issue and this has resulted in the introduction of wide-ranging policy measures to curtail the flow of immigrants from Africa and other regions designated as 'security threats.' When conditions of high unemployment combine with the threat of transnational terrorism and medical scourges such as HIV/AIDS and the Ebola virus, European and American governments are less and less inclined to absorb the increasing number of refugees and displaced persons suspected to be allegedly carrying deadly viruses from Africa. According to estimates from the Joint United Nations Program on HIV/AIDS (UNAIDS) and the World Health Organization (WHO), Worldwide HIV and AIDS Epidemic Statistics (UNAIDS, 2001), there are 36.1 million adults and 1.4 million children with HIV/AIDS worldwide. The overwhelming majority of people with HIV, some 95 percent of the global total, live in the South. According to the same report, that proportion is set to grow even further as infection rates continue to rise in countries where poverty, poor health systems and limited resources for prevention and care continue to fuel the spread of the virus. It is little wonder that the HIV/AIDS and Ebola scares have exacerbated further racial hatred and xenophobia, and thus politicized immigration policies in most countries in the North.

Despite these negative attitudes, the political implications of immigration are subtle and complex, with various countervailing tendencies. For example, the market demand for certain types of foreign workers sometimes makes it difficult to put in place a hard-and-fast policy instrument to limit migration. Skilled workers already operate in a largely borderless world. These are people with high levels of education, experience and qualifications, whose skills are in demand everywhere and who can move from country to country, temporarily or permanently, as immigration laws are not restrictive for them. Many of them are employed by transnational corporations. But some of them circulate in their professional capacities or through systems of education and research. More than one-third of the workforce in the United States' Silicon Valley originates from the Indian sub-continent. Furthermore, in 1998, for example, the U.S. Senate voted to increase the number of foreign workers to fill thousands of short-term computer programming jobs. In the case of Africa, surveys have shown that one-third of the population who have completed a tertiary education live outside their country of birth. Moreover, newly naturalized immigrants can also form an important voting constituency. President Bill Clinton's administration adopted a 'Citizenship USA' plan in 1996, under which well over one million people became citizens. These new citizens provided him with an important source of votes for his re-election. Similarly, the state of California accepted the demands of the Hispanic community to allow illegal immigrants, who are largely Mexican, to get driving licenses, a political decision dictated by ethnic politics (Wienner, 1995; Andreas, 2000).

The E.U. has put in place an immigration regime that is sharply restrictive even to its ethnic cousins from Eastern and Southern Europe. In fact, unwanted would-be immigrants traveling from or through states sharing borders with the E.U. are increasingly faced with the so-called 'cordon sanitaire' created along the outer limits of the Union. To the South, the E.U. is contracting a fence via the Euro-Mediterranean Partnership Agreement concluded in Barcelona in late 1995, which includes readmission agreements, border control cooperation and aid. To the east, the Central and Eastern European countries (Poland, Czech Republic, Slovakia, Hungary, Slovenia, Romania, Bulgaria and the Baltic states) have also signed readmission agreements with the E.U., incorporated into the European Agreement. In exchange, Western states assist their neighbors both technically and financially to cope with the consequences of this policy. The results of the policy are rapidly becoming visible. The number of asylum applicants in the countries of the Union has fallen sharply since 1992 (Overbeek, 2000).

Strict immigration laws deny workers from the South the right to equalize the global supply and demand for labor, to move where they could best earn a living. Unlike their skilled counterparts, unskilled workers are subject to stringent controls. Coupled with the grinding poverty and political instability experienced by large sections of the world's population, these controls are stimulating a fast growing area of trade, namely, the illegal trafficking in people. There are organized brokers and criminal gangs in both labor exporting and importing countries who engage in human trafficking. Traffickers exploit the aspirations of those living in poverty and seeking better lives. They use the dramatic improvements in transport and communications to sell men, women and children into situations of forced labor and sexual slavery with virtually no risk of prosecution. Social networks of migrants in labor-importing countries reinforce these market institutions. Such networks provide their compatriots with information on immigration procedures and employment possibilities, providing temporary homes as well as financial support to new arrivals.

The U.S. Department of State estimates indicate that trafficking in persons generates $7 billion to $10 billion annually for traffickers, the third largest profits in illicit activities behind arms dealings and narcotics trafficking (U.S. Department of State, 2002). More specifically, the financial return to an unskilled Mexican successfully entering the job market in the United States is a nine-fold salary increase. Such rewards encourage high risk-taking, sometimes with fatal consequences. Estimates suggest that more than $9 billion is spent annually by people seeking to circumvent immigration controls in Mexico (Bloom and Murshed, 2001; Nayyar, 2002).

It has to be said that from the standpoint of the national interest of some poor countries in the South, remittances can be a significant source of foreign exchange, while returning migrants may bring capital and skills to foster economic growth. International migration also generates a diaspora that can provide valuable networks of finance, business contacts and skill transfers for the home country. In the mid-1990s, worldwide migrants' remittances were in the range of $75 billion per annum. Of these, remittances to developing countries were about $45 billion per annum, compared with inflows of foreign direct investment of $100 billion per year and foreign portfolio investment of about $63 billion (World Bank, 1999; UNCTAD, 1998). One UNDP study (1999:89) notes that Egypt received $4.7 billion in remittances in 1995, close to the $6 billion earned from the Egypt's Suez Canal receipts, oil exports and tourism combined. The Philippines received $7 billion in remittances in 1996, and these are only the official ones. Workers often send money clandestinely, because they are working illegally in the first place. But they may also find it advantageous to avoid official channels if there is a black market exchange rate much higher than the official one. These individual payments by citizens of developing countries amount to a much greater transfer of resources to their home countries than everything done by the countries of the North, NGOs and international organizations together, although this fact is hardly acknowledged in the development studies discourse.

In order to restrict what authorities consider floods of unwanted immigrants like the United States does, E.U. countries, have been setting higher and higher levels of entry qualifications. They admit migrants selectively, using instruments ranging from visa restrictions and border controls to legislated criteria for admission (age, wealth, education, national origin, or family ties). Host countries tend to give preference to those who are highly skilled, a flow that continues to cause a 'brain drain' from developing countries. This is detrimental to the economic growth of the poor countries of Africa. It has been estimated that between 1960 and 1987, Africa lost 70,000 of its highly skilled people, mostly to the European Union (Adepoju, 1995). Furthermore, while increasingly restrictive in admitting refugees, Northern countries welcome those who arrive with large amounts of capital. For quite some time now, Canada has had a very methodical migration system that awards points for education and skills. It also admits virtually anyone who will invest at least $250,000 in a Canadian business (Stalker, 2000:108). In this regard, one of the challenges for African states is to negotiate for a much fairer and broad-based free flow of labor with greater benefits for the continent.

The nagging migration problems have highlighted a gaping hole in the international institutional architecture. Despite the growing bilateral and regional treaties, there is no acceptable international regime to govern the international movement of people. There are only fragmented sets of institutions that deal with flows of humanity. The International Labor Organization looks after workers' rights. The United Nations High Commission for Refugees deals with forced migrations. The World Trade Organization, under its services agreement, manages temporary access of professional and semi-professional workers. The International Organization of Migration is a cross between a consulting body and an altruistic group. As noted above, the norms, values and interests of these institutions are heavily tilted against the interests of the poor and of weak actors in the international system.

At this point one is forced to ask: does Africa have any future? Given Africa's constantly declining influence in international politics and security affairs, falling share of world trade and investment, the restrictive movement of labor and technology, weak diffusion of information technology, fragile educational and scientific base (as well as the declining foreign aid and debt crisis), there can be no early end to Africa's marginalization and exclusion. Nor are the key norms and principles of the neo-liberal international governance paradigm showing any discernible signs of transformation. In fact, the more they change, the more they remain the same. In the context of all the observations above, it is now necessary to dispel any unintended evocation of a sense of unmitigated cynicism by discussing the different possible development futures for Africa.

CHAPTER 4

AFRICA: POSSIBLE DEVELOPMENT FUTURES

Introduction and Scenario Assumptions

The continued marginalization of Africa from the globalization process and the social exclusion of the vast majority of its people constitute a serious threat to global stability...In the absence of fair and just rules, globalization has increased the ability of the strong to advance their interests to the detriment of the weak, especially in the areas of trade, finance and technology...Africa's inability to harness the process of globalization is a result of structural impediments to growth and development in the form of resource flows and unfavorable terms of trade...The increasing polarization of wealth and poverty is one of a number of processes that have accompanied globalization, and which threaten its sustainability (New Partnership for Africa's Development, 2001: para 28, 40,52).

As was noted in Chapter One, any attempt to address possible development futures for Africa is rife with pitfalls. Even though substantial techniques and instruments have been developed, the future is, predictably uncertain. The art of prediction is largely dependent on the assumption that most key variables will remain constant, but in today's rapidly changing world, this is unlikely. Nonetheless, in an attempt to construct and predict Africa's possible futures, several assumptions are in order. We start with the assumption that the development pattern in the global political economy will be increasingly influenced by the neo-liberal economic management doctrine. In this regard, development patterns will continue to be based on the blind pursuit of liberalization, deregulation and privatization. Adherence to SAPs will become a condition for access to private and public loans and other types of economic assistance. The role of the World Bank, IMF and WTO as well as that of the Group of Eight (G8), the Trilateral Commission (TC) and the World Economic Forum (WEF) will grow immensely in determining the future agenda for Africa. They will exercise decisive influence over capital and labor movements, trade and product markets.

It is also assumed that, despite considerable diversification of economic links by African states in the three decades since independence, the European Union will remain the most significant economic partner for most African economies. At the same time, Europe will strive to multilateralize its relations with Africa largely through the WTO. To this end, African countries will not formally belong to any of the three major economic and security blocs. However, singly and/or collectively, they will be vertically integrated into the E.U. and NAFTA markets through the Cotonou Agreement and the Africa Growth and Opportunity Act (AGOA). As relatively weak and defenseless actors in the prevailing international economic and political systems, the major policies of most African states are likely to remain largely reactive rather than proactive.

The radical policy shift from aid to trade as an instrument of E.U.-Africa international development cooperation would decisively undermine the benign paternalism of the Lomé period. The subordination of the Lomé spirit to the dictates of the WTO is likely to engender further marginalization of African economies, as the introduction of reciprocity in trade between substantially unequal economic and political partners will be a license to annihilation. Already, the WTO Dispute Settlements Body has ruled that the Lomé Convention provided unfair preferences to the banana exports of the Caribbean countries. Moreover, the new E.U.-ACP economic partnership agreements (EPAs) propose a new basis for organizing individual countries or groups of African countries into separate free-trade arrangements with the E.U.. The proposed EPAs are likely, in many different ways, to fragment rather than strengthen integration arrangements in the ACP countries. This is largely because the prospective regional groupings do not conform to the existing realities of most ACP economic groupings. It is also partly because 31 of the ACP countries would be expected to negotiate individual economic partnership agreements with the E.U. The ultimate effect of these developments is likely to undermine the existing economic groupings, which African countries regard as building blocks for their economic integration (Cheru, 2001: 137; Rugumamu, 2000:58-59; Rugumamu, 2001b: 50-60).

Moreover, the potential benefits accruing from South-South cooperation in the emerging global economic and political configurations are likely to have a negligible impact on Africa's economic relations. The current first and second tier of NICs can be expected to continue to enjoy relatively high rates of growth, while a small number of countries in the South, for example, China, Brazil, Venezuela and India, might graduate to the NIC status.

However, economic relations with the NICs have already demonstrated that they are not likely to be any more charitable toward the less fortunate African countries than the advanced countries of the OECD have been. The same logic of capitalist accumulation will apply. There is little to suggest that these countries will willingly open their markets to labor-intensive manufactures should some few African countries decide to industrialize aggressively. Nor are they likely to have any significant interest in Africa's tropical agricultural products. With the exception of cheap petroleum and other critical minerals, most African primary exports are likely to continue to increasingly experience low demand from the North. As already pointed out, the recommendation by the World Bank to increase Africa's output and diversify into new non-traditional primary commodities is, to say the least, bad economics (World Bank, 1989:132). Such policy initiatives will lead Africa deeper into economic stagnation and self-reinforcing systemic risks, as well as speeding up the process of its marginalization, as flooded markets in the North will mean low prices. If these assumptions hold, then Africa is likely to experience a nightmare scenario as elaborated below.

Scenario One: Muddling Through the *Status Quo*
In this scenario, no major structural, institutional or policy reforms are envisaged. The present global arrangements will be sustained and even reinforced. In those circumstances, therefore, Africa is likely to be exposed to more explicit and intensive domination by the North, led and controlled by the U.S., the E.U. and the multilateral financial and trading institutions. Those international agencies that presently promote the interests of the South, such as UNCTAD, UNICEF, UNIDO and UNESCO, will be deliberately weakened in order to entrench the *status quo* and the privileged position of the North in the global division of labor, wealth and power. Moreover, South-South solidarity arrangements will remain loose and non-functional, as individual countries will be absorbed into the various spheres of influence of stronger regional powers. In the process, their aspiration for real political and economic independence will also be sacrificed and in some cases undermined. In the coming years, therefore, much of Africa will invariably struggle from crisis to crisis.

In this regard, most African political economies will slowly but inexorably decline in relevance to the E.U., their traditional economic and security partner, so that the latter will lose any real interest in maintaining the special relationship. The E.U. will also come under increased pressure from the WTO to gradually phase out the trade preferences that African countries have enjoyed over the last three decades under the Lomé Convention and its successor, the Cotonou Agreement. Its array of free and competitive trade regulations will undermine the Cotonou convention's multiple privileges and preferences that allowed African countries unfettered access to European markets. In the Cotonou Agreement, the E.U. has liberally interpreted free trade requirements to mean that at least 90 percent of imports on both sides should be free of tariffs and that no sector should be completely excluded. Thus, African economies will be allowed to retain, for a while, their current preferential access to the E.U. market but in return they will have to progressively open up their own markets to E.U. imports. This transition process is to be completed within ten years of the Agreement. After the transition period, African economies will be expected to compete with the E.U. in the liberalized sectors, and over products, on the basis of productivity, product quality, timely delivery of orders and the like (Yeats, 1995; Lister, 1998). The unregulated openness will undermine economic diversification efforts by destroying most of the remaining industries which will not be ready to compete globally, destroying informal sectors whose vibrancy depends on internally coordinated exchanges, and creating unfair and unhealthy competition for the attraction of FDI.

The very idea of a transition period of ten to fifteen years proposed in the Cotonou Agreement, by which time African economies are expected to have advanced to the level on which European and American firms compete, is totally unrealistic. The notion negates both logic and history and it counters the very spirit behind the special and differential treatment previously provided under GATT. Evidence from the 1997 UNDP indicates that, if anything, the technological gap between rich and poor nations is widening, not narrowing. The world is characterized not by a spreading of wealth, knowledge, and well-being but by a growing concentration of wealth and power among a minority, as well as growing polarization between rich and poor countries and between people within countries and within the global human family as a whole (UNDP, 1997).[23]

It is difficult to escape the conclusion that such relatively short transition periods are a clear indication of the E.U.'s lack of interest in the African continent. Secondly, this new thinking reflects the E.U.'s desire to downplay foreign aid in favor of market access in its future partnership with developing countries – a typical *quid pro quo* argument between relatively equal actors! Thirdly, and as noted earlier, with the decreased geopolitical, ideological, and security significance of African countries to Europe as a result of the conclusion of the Cold War, and with the enlargement of E.U. membership to include countries with low or no colonial links with Africa, the traditional arguments for non-reciprocity and the protection of 'infant industries' will no longer be compelling or soothing. Predictably, most of Africa will be delinked from the most economically developed and dynamic countries and regions of the world.

Whereas Africa used to account for the largest share of E.U. aid disbursements, in recent years, it has experienced a sharp decline as a proportion of total E.U. aid from 70 percent at the beginning of the 1970s to less than 40 percent by the mid-1990s. The situation is expected to grow worse. In addition, in more recent years, OECD countries have been parading the argument that the shortfalls in official capital flows will be compensated for by private capital flows. But as pointed out earlier, beginning in the early 1980s, there has been a significant decline in the growth of international bank loans destined for the continent. For most foreign business people, Africa is being portrayed as an abysmal sinkhole that swallows money with little or no longer-term returns. Not surprisingly, during the 1980s, for example, 43 out of 139 British firms with industrial investment in Africa withdrew their holdings, mostly from Nigeria, Kenya and Zimbabwe. Some observers have predicted that this trend is likely to continue in the future if Africa's investment climate does not improve appreciably (Callaghy, 2000:47). Indeed, in that inauspicious environment, African countries would compete intensely with each other to see who could be the most subservient and offer the economic conditions most disadvantageous to themselves.

Colin Leys projects Africa's future in a similarly pessimistic vein. For him, by 2025, countries with initial conditions that make them less suited to take advantage of globalization will lose out and become more marginalized in relation to other countries. More specifically, he argues that most states in Africa – those that are small, poor, insular, land-locked, disadvantaged, highly indebted, and either racked by civil wars or with neighbors that are racked by civil conflicts – are not likely to participate productively in the increasingly sophisticated and regionally integrated global economy. He adds:

> Most observers accept that significant parts of the former Third World, including most of sub-Saharan Africa, are more likely to regress than to advance in the new global economy; it is in the nature of unregulated competitive systems that this will happen. Not every country has the capacity to compete in the market; a few will succeed, while others will decline and some will collapse into civil wars or anarchy, as Uganda, Angola, Mozambique, Liberia and Rwanda already have in Africa, at different times (Leys, 1996:42).

In this nightmare scenario, current international economic relations will remain essentially unchanged for the next three decades or so. Africa will cease to matter, if it ever did. Of course, it would be naïve to assume that states, transnational banks and corporations, and various local social forces that benefit directly from the present liberal world order would readily consent to its effective reform, let alone its transformation. They will come up with various justifications to rationalize the existing international system. Most of Africa will continue to find itself marginalized and excluded from major currents of the world economy, yet highly dependent on it. As already pointed out, under the economic regime of globalization and liberalization, Africa will have limited capacity to respond flexibly to fierce and often unfair external competition, and there will be diminished demand for traditional exports. The individual and collective capacity of most poor African countries to effectively participate in multilateral economic negotiations that regulate the global economy will erode completely. Their continued embrace of SAPs would only speed up the process toward increased impoverishment and marginalization. SAPs will not result in any significant recovery of economic growth nor in regional cooperation and integration. On the contrary, they will lead to disinvestment and the dismantling of the few remaining industries without creating conditions for dynamic national and regional economic growth. The balanced budgets and external balances so dogmatically pursued will not only become a mirage but, more importantly, they will cause only marginal tinkering with the foundations of national economies. The formal sectors of the economy will deteriorate rapidly and most of the population will rely predominantly on the informal and criminal economy for mere survival: subsistence peasants, drug peddlers, money launders, sex workers and slave workers.

Gripped by the ongoing global slowdown, the E.U., the United States and Japan will be less inclined to open their markets to any processed or semi-processed products from the few resilient economic enclaves of Africa. Cities, regions and countries of the most techno-scientifically developed world will evolve in such a way that they minimize their dependency on traditional agricultural commodities and minerals from Africa. The North will follow its own development patterns and maintain weaker and looser links with most of the South, which will be faced with poverty, disease, inadequate and outdated infrastructure, and an increase in local ethnic, religious and inter-state wars. In a similar vein, migrations of people from the South seeking jobs or running away from conflict, famine or disease will increase but will be energetically controlled by the governments of the North.

In short, the gradual delinking by the North will be strategically based on the increasing role of sophisticated knowledge and technology incorporated into the production processes, products and services. The exclusive interests of the North will drive the global science and technology policy agenda to a significant extent. Priority areas will be identified in terms of their expected contribution to the industrial and economic competitiveness of their economies. Africa will become irrelevant economically, politically and strategically. The resulting abject poverty and misery will give rise to a culture of desperation and violence among the disgruntled poor, the petty drug dealers and other alienated sections of society. As poverty increases, the North/South conflict will deepen, while the affluent North, through various mechanisms including NATO, OECD and the World Bank, will strive to impose various forms of containment to consolidate its power and privilege and secure its borders and economic fortunes.

Within this nightmare scenario, a possible collusion of most, if not all states in the North against states in the South is envisaged by 2025, in which the United States will closely coordinate and preserve the security interests of the North and its allies. Following a series of setbacks, American and European powers will gradually withdraw from regional peacekeeping and humanitarian assistance in Africa. As a result, war, famine, disease, drought and the collapse of state services will drive more and more people to a few crowded and insecure cities. In tandem with this, Africa's various sub-regional security arrangements, such as SADC's Organ on Politics, Defense and Security or the ECOWAS Monitoring Group, will become hollow shells. With the erosion of the legitimacy, sovereignty and moral authority of the African state, the continent is likely to be exposed to more explicit and extensive domination by the Northern powers. Behind the cover of 'war against terrorism,' 'war against drugs' 'clash of civilization,' 'regime change of rogue states,'[24] 'containment of proliferation of nuclear weapons' or any other pretext, the North, under the leadership of the United Sates, will intervene indiscriminately in the internal affairs of African countries and seek to impose their preferred 'social order and democracy'. In fact, the *2002 US Homeland Security Strategy* argues that America deserves the right to take pre-emptive strikes to deal with any major security threats anywhere and at any time (US Homeland Security, 2002). As would be expected, Africans will live in the harrowing grip of constant fear and insecurity, as much from the unrestrained imperial states of the North as from internal rogue states.

In the realm of international economic relations, Africa's role and importance will continue to be eroded. Post-Lomé E.U.-African relations have undergone a radical change. This period has witnessed a marked shift from aid to trade as the main instrument of cooperation. The future focus will be on strengthening commercial links that are motivated by purely economic interests. The Japanese and European Union's tariffs and non-tariff barriers on textiles, clothing, and other products of particular importance to developing countries in general and to African economies in particular, are not likely to come down as quickly as might have been hoped. Important sectional lobbyists in the industrial economies are likely to prolong their protection for many years to come. It is also anticipated that new kinds of non-tariff barriers to trade, such as anti-dumping and countervailing duty actions, export restraint agreements such as the Multi-Fiber Agreement, and direct subsidies, will not go away quickly (Rugumamu, 2000; 1999b). In short, whatever gains some African countries may expect to derive from their relations with the North, they are likely to be not only marginal but also short-lived. In a world economy of cutthroat competition, the weak are likely to die before their time!

Some have sought to argue that even the African Growth and Opportunity Act of the U.S. (AGOA) will not offer any tangible promise of hope. The AGOA trade initiative seeks to reduce or eliminate tariffs and quotas on more than 1,800 products. Although the range of products is large, ranging from umbrella and steel to tobacco and fresh yarms, clothing exports tend to dominate with weak rules of origin. However, other attached economic and political conditionalities smack of imperialism *par excellence*. As Julius Nyang'oro (2000:45) poignantly notes, "because of the tremendous economic difficulties in most countries, African governments are willing to try anything that may give them an opportunity to tap into the most vigorous market...however unrealistic that hope may be." Worst of all, only 'non-sensitive products' qualify and these face strict conditions.

Unlike the Cotonou Agreement between the European Union and the African, Caribbean and Pacific countries, which is largely based on preferential trade, the AGOA seeks to promote globalization of the world economy through unrestrained trade liberalization and privatization. Most importantly, it is a strategy aimed at creating markets for U.S. corporations on a bilateral basis. Section 104 of AGOA, for example, outlines eligibility requirements and conditionalities for countries to access U.S. trade benefits. They are extremely harsh conditions. While the Act grants extensive rights and benefits to American firms intending to operate in sub-Saharan Africa, it is almost silent on direct benefits to be accrued by African workers and entrepreneurs. In fact, the Act does not make any provisions for effective transfer of appropriate technologies by the U.S. corporations, a vital instrument to foster trade and development. Instead, it requires beneficiaries to guarantee intellectual property rights, protect foreign investment, and ensure internationally recognized workers' rights as well as adhering to a U.S.-style democratic governance. Nor does it stipulate deliberate mechanisms for controlling potentially predatory business practices of transnational corporations emanating from the United States. Above all, the bilateral character of the AGOA is likely to destroy one of the fundamental principles of the African Union, that of building and consolidating sub-regional economic blocs, and promoting its collective bargaining strategy with the North. In short, the AGOA is yet another retrogressive policy initiative of the United States that aims at disempowering Africans. Its eligibility requirements and conditionalities go far beyond those stipulated through the WTO/TRIPs and other international trade agreements. It is providing neither growth nor opportunity for African economies. It should be renegotiated or simply rejected.

As if the above cross-conditionalities were not enough, the Act includes riders, such as the requirement that clothing exports to the United States would have to include vast components of U.S.-sourced raw materials. This is harsh because cotton is one of Africa's major exports. Section 112 of the Act states that preferential treatment shall apply only to:

> ...Apparel articles assembled in one or more beneficiary sub- Saharan countries from fabrics wholly formed and cut in the United States, and yarns wholly formed in the United States (including fabrics not formed from yarns, if such fabrics are classifiable under headings 5602 or 5603 of the Harmonized Tariff Schedule of the United States and are wholly formed and cut in the United States.

Given this doom and gloom scenario, development prospects for the non-oil producing countries are dismal, especially for aid-dependent and debt-ridden African countries, suggesting a lack of growth possibilities, development or choice. The simultaneous processes of globalization, exclusion, and dependence are likely to continue and will probably further accelerate the marginalization and exclusion of the continent. Dependence on primary commodity exports offers an almost automatic route to a diminishing share of world exports and world income, with its attendant implications for living standards. The negative impact of the deteriorating terms of trade will be particularly severe for poor African countries, partly due to their higher dependence on price-volatile primary products and partly due to their relatively low level of access to timely liquidity to help them ride out these reverse shocks (Helleiner, 1993).

Furthermore, given the current trends in external financial transfers, the losses from deteriorating terms of trade are not likely to be offset in the future by either aid or loan transfers from the North. At the same time, one could safely speculate that the global trade in toxic waste from the North will not only become the norm but, will gradually dominate the structure and composition of traditional North–South trade. In order to stay healthy, the North will need Africa largely as a dumping ground for disposal of its garbage, such as toxic waste, low quality porn material, kitsch art, outdated and polluting technologies, surplus food stocks and dubious business people. Some firms from the North, especially producers of toxic substances like pesticides and heavy metals like zinc, are likely to relocate their plants to sites in the South where environmental regulations are less stringent. Above all, under the draconian policies of the IMF and World Bank, most African states will be forced to abandon the enforcement of environmental laws and regulations in order to achieve the fiscal targets of SAPs by turning their countries into dumping sites for toxic waste. The resultant environmental consequences for the people are too devastating to contemplate.

By the early 1990s about 20 percent of hazardous waste generated and exported by the industrial North was shipped to the South, and particularly to African countries. The incentives for dumping of toxic wastes in these poor countries range from direct payment to proposals to process imported waste for energy generation and various other developmental applications. In some instances, transnational firms dumped such waste without the knowledge of either the people or their governments. In other cases, however, private individuals and governments were paid handsomely to accept waste, especially in countries where the economic crunch had created a desperate need for foreign exchange. Several countries in West Africa were reported to be victims of hazardous waste dumping. Nigeria discovered 4,000 tons of illegally shipped toxic waste from Italy in its territory in 1988. In Sierra Leone, 625 bags of hazardous wastes originating from the United Kingdom were abandoned in the capital city's garbage dump. Cases of attempted dumping involving a British company in Liberia, an American firm in Guinea Bissau, and a Belgian firm in Sierra Leone have also been reported. In Guinea, toxic dumping by a Norwegian shipping company in a coastal town ruined the local fishing economy[25] and brought the tourist industry to a halt (Transnationals, 1994:4).

Unremitting marginalization and exclusion will further compound the problems of the African continent in terms of trade and investment. The related decrease in aid flows, euphemistically described as 'aid fatigue,' and the new economic, financial and sociopolitical strings attached to bilateral and multilateral transfers as well as to debt relief, mean that there will be increasingly tight prescriptions for Africa states in the future. Highly dependent on these resources, most African states will be left with fewer opportunities to avoid the rigid external tutelage and stiff conditionalities of the IMF, World Bank and creditor nations. The perpetuation or even intensification of dependence on Northern institutions and economic systems is likely to pose considerable problems for decision makers in the future. The claims of the final triumph of market rationality and the end of history do not portend tolerance of alternative pathways to social development. Donors, no longer preoccupied with security considerations, are likely to push aggressively for a particular form of democracy. The demand of political conditionality may well pre-empt any distinctive local forms of democracy.

By the year 2025, prospects for South-South economic cooperation will have inexorably diminished. Most African economies will lack the necessary capacity and willingness to engage meaningfully with would-be external economic actors. The struggle for political survival of weak states will override all other important national concerns. At the same time, the more developed economies of the South, particularly the NICs and oil-producing countries, will seek lesser cooperation with an economically decaying Africa, and instead will consolidate links with the vibrant economies in the North. It bears remembering that the petro-dollars of the mid-1970s were securely invested in banks in the North, suggesting that the adoption of 'Islamic economics' and South-South cooperation and solidarity were not perceived as entirely profitable! In this regard, the little South-South cooperation that will endure will essentially reflect a core-periphery relation – periphery Africa supplying mineral and agricultural exports and importing manufactures from semi-periphery NIC economies. Although South-South trade has increased over the past two decades, the growth of trade links between developing countries will continue to be severely constrained by import restrictions. As one World Bank study observes, the average tariff restrictions applied by developing countries to other developing countries' exports of manufactures is more than three times higher than the average tariffs imposed by rich countries. Developing-country tariffs on agricultural exports from other developing countries are also higher (World Bank, 2001).

Moreover, the opening up of democratic space in most African countries under these inauspicious economic conditions will have a catalytic effect on expressions of self-identity, and ethno-regional or religious demands. These forces will challenge the weak incumbent regimes as violently as will the concepts of citizenship and territoriality. Vicious struggles will quickly become manifest in countries such as Rwanda, Burundi, Nigeria, Uganda and Kenya that have historically politicized ethnic and religious identities. Dense networks based on so-called 'primordial attachments' will likely emerge as a response to the decay of state capacities, not least with respect to the preservation of civil peace and individual security. Most distinctively, structural forces such as predatory economic strategies and inequitable distribution of resources (as engendered by liberalization and privatization), will further generate and feed the spiral of violence. When all this happens, catastrophe theorists, conjuring up world political horror scenarios will become fashionable. Africa will become the main laboratory of such researchers (Abrahamsen, 2000).

However, we should hasten to add that the trajectory of development or disintegration of individual countries would be directly affected by the nature of their internal political and economic configurations. More than any other actor, the role of the state will be paramount. As William Munro (1996:113) has phrased it, "the state is pivotal to the political future of African countries. Even in the most abject cases of political chaos in Africa, some institutional form of political and administrative organization exists which calls itself, and is recognized as the state." Its overall capacity – the technical, regulatory, extractive and administrative capabilities – to provide essential political and economic infrastructure, as well as to formulate and implement requisite policies to manage peace and security, will be critical. These technical capacities, together with ideological clarity, will be decisive in facilitating the positioning of respective countries in the international political economy.

States will also be critical in influencing a country's effectiveness in bargaining and interacting with all types of actors e.g. private business groups, states, the international institutions and NGOs. It is therefore predicted that the only African countries that are likely to reap any significant benefits from the emerging global economy are those that develop and nurture strong institutional capacities, promote peace and security, seek to keep pace with technological developments, create and sustain efficient and competitive production structures, improve labor productivity, and respond flexibly and imaginatively to changing tastes and trends in global demand. But such economies and states are likely to be few.

On the economic front, the globalization of production will have differing impacts on the South depending on the level of each country's manufacturing capability and resource endowment. Relatively more diversified economies with adequate transport and communications infrastructure will compete for the production of low-tech, labor intensive and highly polluting manufactures. In the process of the globalization of production, multinational enterprises will continue to relocate segments of their integrated processes to some African countries. There is a real danger that more and more African states will strive to take part in a race to the bottom by lowering their environmental standards and their wages, and by introducing attractive tax breaks in the contest to attract a few willing foreign investors to establish sweatshops and provide a pollution haven for dirty industries. In addition, a few relatively dynamic political economies, such as Botswana, South Africa, Mauritius, Senegal, Tunisia and, perhaps, Egypt, are likely to become specialized locations for one segment of an industry, such as engines in automobiles, semi-conductors in electronics, or data entry. These economies may become significant players in that industry. Sources of comparative advantage - capital, know-how, experience, and technology, for example - will thus be transferred across borders in greater quantities as more and more sectors of these economies participate in various stages of the value-adding process of an industry (UNCTAD, 1992:104).

Aside from the South African-EU Free Trade Area Agreement, few other relatively dynamic African economies will negotiate individual economic cooperation agreements with major regional economic blocs. To remain competitive, these few will have to engage in competitive deregulation to maintain their economic position. Above all, their wage levels will have to be depressed and abysmal working conditions will have to be sustained within individual enterprises and sectors in order to attract the physical relocation of foreign firms. It is not often stressed enough that the system of flexible accumulation and subcontracting tends to be particularly negative for women and minority populations, because both groups tend to be the last hired during times of economic expansion and the first fired in times of economic recession. Some feminists claim that women tend to provide an optimal labor force for contemporary capitalism because they are defined as housewives rather than as workers and therefore can be paid lower wages on the assumption that these wages merely supplement their family income. Additionally, because of expectations associated with traditional gender roles, there is often a mistaken view of what is meant by femininity and masculinity.

Profit-hungry firms in subcontracting businesses tend to favor hiring young unmarried women who can achieve a high level of productivity at lower wages, work for longer working hours, have weak protection in the workplace, provide a docile workforce, have weak trade union rights, and can be fired easily once they are married or pregnant! As C. Enloe (1989) points out, globalization benefits from a measure of dominance of traditional and sexist ideas about women. These are beliefs that hold that women 'naturally' possess nimble fingers; they have patience for tedious jobs and sew naturally. It has been estimated that, in the sweatshops of the export processing zones (EPZs) in Asia, Latin America and Africa, well over 70 percent of the workforce is made up of women. China's phenomenal export growth has been driven increasingly by a workforce numerically dominated by women, with an estimated 24 million female assembly workers located in the special economic zones alone (Oxfam, 2002).

Various studies have demonstrated that the system of flexible accumulation has high social costs for countries in the South. TNCs will be attracted to the South if they are offered cheaper and submissive labor, cheaper raw materials and fewer environmental regulations. Since the late 1980s, foreign direct investment has been a central part of the national development strategy for countries such as China, Mexico, Indonesia, Bangladesh, and Malaysia. In Mexico, the maquiladora assembly plants along the Mexican side of the Mexico-U.S. border provide jobs and industry for Mexico, but at a prohibitive social cost. This border region, including the Rio Grande River, is one of the most heavily polluted zones in North America. But the system of flexible capitalist accumulation enables TNCs to evade responsibility for many of the destructive consequences of their global expansion and exploitation. By contracting out the production of commodities, corporations often claim that they are not responsible for the repression of trade union policies or the environmentally destructive practices of the local producers that they buy from. If questions are raised, then TNCs are likely to shift their contract to another producer in another country (Castells and Tyson, 1989; Mortimore, 1998). This is a daily reality that globalization offers Africa.

While vertical integration of production will ensure export growth in a few African countries just as in Latin America and Asia, it will be largely based on simple low-cost assembly operations. Dynamic linkages with the local economy will remain organically disjointed and exceptionally weak. Various studies in Latin America have amply demonstrated that these so-called booming export economies obtain virtually all their production inputs from the country of origin of the partner TNC and export their finished products to the United States. This skewed mode of integration into the global economy has compromised the development of nationally integrated and self-sustaining economies by restricting value addition, limiting product diversification, and constraining the local sourcing of inputs. Admittedly, such perverse industrialization strategies would generate little demand for Africa's industry, and hence little employment and investment outside a few participating firms (UNCTAD, 1998; ECLA; 1999). From this development platform, it will become increasingly difficult for Africa to create the necessary foundation for self-sustaining economies and for successful integration into the world economy. Ferdinando Cardoso, former President of Brazil, provides the following counsel:

> Therefore, we are no longer talking about the South that was on the periphery of the capitalist core and was tied to it in a classical relationship of dependence. Nor are we speaking of the phenomenon, described some twenty-five years ago by Enzo Faletto and myself in our book, *Dependency and Development in Latin America*, where multinational companies transfer parts of the production system and the local producers are tied to foreign capital in the 'dependent-associated' development model. We are dealing, in truth, with a crueler phenomenon: either the South (or a portion of it) enters the democratic-technological-science race, invests heavily in R &D, and endures the 'information economy'... or it becomes unimportant, unexploited, and unexploitable (Cardoso, 1993:156).

After looking at what was taking place in West Africa, Robert Kaplan's sensational 1994 article in the *Atlantic Monthly* portrayed the entire continent as a 'prototype of the coming anarchy.' He described a continent "mired in endemic political chaos and collapsed states, filth and new epidemics, population explosion and massive slums, 'unprovoked crime' and lawlessness." All this, he added, without caring to explain the historical and contemporary causes of economic decline and social decay, will rise from a degenerative African political culture, one festering in the crucible of a life and death struggle by a mushrooming population that fights over a shrinking natural resource base and that causes massive environmental degradation. Kaplan predicted that, "Africa's immediate future could be very bad. The coming upheaval, in which embassies are shut down, states collapse, and the contact with the outside world takes place through dangerous, disease-ridden coastal trading posts, will loom large in the century we are entering" (Kaplan, 1994:110-116).

Bizarre as it sounds at first reading, Kaplan's predictions seem to be close to an apocalyptic vision of post-Cold War Africa. Achille Mbembe's (1995:28-30) vision of the most likely African future is an equally bleak one. He projects the further deepening of the criminalization of the state and the privatization of violence, the material devastation to be experienced by the masses of the people, and the steady erosion of the capacity of the state to effect its own policies under the onslaught of externally imposed austerity programs. Conflict, insecurity and underdevelopment seem to define Africa's present and its near future. One may easily consider, in particular, two major regional wars that have affected the African continent for about a decade. One, centered on the DRC, involves ten countries and, the other, on the axis from southern Senegal to the Liberian border, involves five additional countries. These protracted conflicts will undoubtedly leave behind a legacy of violence, misrule, corruption, state erosion and economic decay. The consequences of civil conflicts invariably spread beyond a country's borders. Regional security is undermined, flows of refugees are created, small weapons proliferate, communities and trade are interrupted, especially where sanctions are imposed and where such conflicts result in environmental damage. Most tellingly, approximately 8.1 million of the world's 22 million cross-border refugees live in Africa, with many millions more having been displaced within their own countries (UNHCR, 1997). As pointed out earlier, neither the U.N. nor the A.U. is likely to deal effectively with the conflicts wracking African countries in the near future. The Hobbesian political logic of 'war of all against all' is the most likely scenario in a good number of African countries (Chabal and Daloz, 1999).

Meanwhile, the problems of state-society conflict in Africa continue unabated. Low intensity conflicts will continue to simmer in Burundi, Rwanda, Chad, Djibouti, Uganda, Côte d'Ivoire and Congo Brazzaville. Besides violent conflicts, an overwhelming number of states in Africa face a high degree of political instability and a real risk of state collapse. In these states, legitimacy is constantly under a heavy cloud of suspicion. For most of the time, the state machinery is preoccupied with the survival of the regime in power. Some of these states, including Botswana, Tanzania and South Africa, have had periods of relative stability and political tolerance and they could overcome their present difficulties with creative leadership. However, the pull towards instability and violence is strong because the overall institutional environment of democracy, peace and stability remains highly elusive. These countries and others are likely to drift further and further into various forms of intolerance, authoritarianism, nihilism, fundamentalism and the other recurrent predicaments engendered by globalization in the marginalized societies of the capitalist system.

Kaplan's sensational predictions are captured well not only by the challenges posed by the gradual slide into chaos in Africa and flourishing criminal business enterprises but most importantly by the intensification in the spread of HIV/AIDS and the mass movement of refugees. Already about 90 percent of the estimated 36 million people infected with HIV by December, 2000 lived in the South, where drugs designed to mitigate the effects of the disease and where prophylaxes to prevent its spread are too costly for all but the wealthiest few. However, nowhere is the picture as bleak as in sub-Saharan Africa: here, more than 25 million Africans infected with HIV/AIDS (70 percent of the world's cases) and 17 million are already dead. On its current trajectory, by 2010, the disease will decrease life expectancy on the continent to levels found at the beginning of the last century. The December 2000 report *AIDS Epidemic Update* by the United Nations AIDS Fund/World Health Organization described it as 'Africa's human tragedy' (UNAIDS and World Bank, 2001). The devastation associated with the pandemic prompted the Bush and Clinton administrations to treat the AIDS pandemic as a national security issue with the potential to threaten the United States itself and American interests worldwide.

Some recent studies indicate that HIV-induced declines in gross domestic product levels in sub-Saharan Africa are severely undermining poverty reduction efforts in the relevant countries. In fact, it is widely believed that AIDS is the single biggest threat to economic development in sub-Saharan Africa. The macroeconomic costs of AIDS and other associated infectious diseases pose an extra burden on societies. As sickness strikes at the labor force, it takes a toll on productivity, profitability, and foreign investment in the future. The pandemic is shaving off up to 2 percent of annual economic growth in the worst affected countries (UNAIDS and World Bank, 2001). Another study by Price-Smith argues that there is a linkage between AIDS-related deaths among fifteen to forty-five year-olds, the commensurate loss of human capital, and the resultant falling GDP levels in Africa. He reasons that, as AIDS skims off doctors, teachers, lawyers, entrepreneurs, judges and policy-makers, it leads to institutional and societal fragility. The net effect of an AIDS-depleted society is a hollowing out of the state and social networks that are already under pressure from poverty and sundry other variables. Finally, power struggles over limited resources increase the likelihood of violent conflicts (Price-Smith, 2001).

Africa's future is threatened by violent political insecurity as much as it is threatened by the spread of HIV/AIDS and collapsing states. Not surprisingly, Kaplan's portrayals of anarchy in Africa are best reflected in the traumatic episodes of collapsed and collapsing states on the continent. The post-Cold War decade, which held out the promise of an African Renaissance, deteriorated rapidly into severe instability across the continent that shows little signs of abating. The recent phenomenon of collapsed states includes situations where the structure of the state, authority (legitimate power), law and political order have fallen apart and must be reconstituted in some form. The entire nation tends to slide gradually into chaos, and state control is virtually conceded to an assortment of belligerent warlords. Recent examples include Somalia, Rwanda, the DRC, Liberia and Sierra Leone. Imminent political, religious, or ethno-political hatred and divisions that could dramatically erupt into violent conflict at any time threaten several other African countries. These are countries and sub-regions where criminal business enterprises could be launched, places that would traffic in human beings and narcotics without any restraint, and places where terrorist networks would be likely to proliferate. In economic terms, not only will these collapsed states disrupt the growth process, they will also result in the deterioration of human and physical capital as well as in the curtailment of prospects for future investments. War-torn states will have harmful spillover effects on neighboring countries. The overflow of refugees, heightened ethnic tensions in some cases, and the resulting diplomatic conflicts will most likely engage substantial resources and efforts from the relatively stable countries that share borders with collapsed states.

One of the major challenges for Africa in the coming years relates to the management of violent conflicts between and within states, as well as the disruption of the cycle of state collapse. The 1990s witnessed a steady climb in violence across sub-Saharan Africa, with the number of states at war or with significant lethal conflicts doubling from eleven in 1989 to 22 in 2000. It should be remembered that the A.U. Mechanism for Conflict Prevention, Management and Resolution would have neither the organizational capacity nor the resources to contend with the anticipated widespread breakdown into anarchy, to provide emergency relief, or to set countries on a path to sustainable development. Failed states are most likely to be turned into lucrative drug plantations for competing warlords, havens for organized multinational crime syndicates and networks, and beachheads for fundamentalist terrorist groups. William Reno's study of Sierra Leone (1995) shows how advanced state decay accompanied by a growing involvement of the remnants of the state, and how factional elites can engage with impunity in international criminal activities and form partnerships with 'fly-by-night' foreign operators and speculators. This is a potentially big business. Drug trafficking and money laundering are two of the most widespread criminal activities – over $100 billion worth of drug money has been laundered annually in Europe and North America over the past decade (UNRISD, 1995:12). The competing warlords that will benefit from chaos and lack of political accountability will have little or no interest in stopping civil conflicts and negotiating peace. Until such time as Africa's development crisis is perceived as part of the impending global security crisis, the continent's social and economic decline will tend to continue unnoticed.

Although the distinct threat from the spreading chaos of one or two failed or collapsed states has often been understated, the implications are likely to be colossal for global peace and security if Africa's pandemonium becomes further entrenched and widespread. As pointed out earlier, when states fail, local and organized international gangs and criminal syndicates assume control in order to exploit the power vacuum for their own ends. Ray Takeyh and Nikolas Gvosdev (2002:98-101) note that failed states hold a number of attractions for terrorist organizations. In the first place, they provide the opportunity to acquire territory on a scale much larger than a collection of scattered safe houses; enough to accommodate entire training complexes, arms depots, and communication facilities. Osama Bin Laden's experience in Sudan and later in Afghanistan clearly demonstrates the true value of relocating operations from one failed state to another. Moreover, failed states enable terrorist groups and organized crime networks to establish trans-shipment points for the dispersal of drugs, weapons, dirty money and illegal migrants.

Under this scenario, the Northern states are likely to continue being largely consumed by their own, short-term self-interest security agenda. They will finally be devoting most of their attention to combating the symptoms, rather than the root causes of terrorism in the South. They will even invoke Chapter VII of the U.N. Security Council in order to intervene anywhere and at anytime to find and destroy terrorists, terrorist-sponsoring states, 'rogue states' producing, using and exporting weapons of mass destruction (WMD), drug traffickers, and those who support and harbor them. In fact, this overly paranoid security objective is one of the organizing principles of the 2002 US Homeland Security Act. As Noam Chomsky (2000) has aptly concluded, unrestrained big powers will behave exactly like the rogue states that they are trying to contain. In this regard, most of Africa will live in constant fear of external interventions by big powers from the North.[26]

Rather than erect a *cordon sanitaire* around Africa or resort to indiscriminate interventions in Africa, Ali Mazrui (1994) and William Pfaff (1995) have cynically gone as far as to suggest the institutionalization of a disinterested neo-colonialist dispensation for failed African states. In particular, Mazrui, claims "some dysfunctional states will need to submit to trusteeship and even tutelage for a while." According to this logic, the North can no longer afford to ignore the disorder beyond its borders. Global security demands, so the argument goes, under this doom and gloom scenario, a new 'benign' imperialism in order to rebuild collapsed states. Should the U.N. decide to ignore developments in Africa, Mazrui further proposes a regional organization that would have the authority and resources needed to help bring about and orchestrate the restructuring of Africa's state-society relations. Mazrui is careful to specify the form of colonialism he has in mind: "A trusteeship system, like that of the United Nations over Congo in 1960...could be established that is more genuinely international and less Western than the old guise. The administrative powers of the trusteeship territories could come from Africa or Asia, as well as from the rest of the U.N. membership. The white man's burden would, in a sense, be replaced by humanity's shared burden" (Mazrui, 1994:36).

Other recolonization proponents, such as William Pfaff, dismiss a United Nations-based proposal as simply impracticable: "an internationalist U.N. trusteeship," as Mazrui advocates, "seems...unlikely." He contends, "the U.N...is overburdened. It has a great difficulty finding peacekeeping troops. It is all but bankrupt.... It has no apparatus for actually governing a country, and the politicking of its membership makes it all but impossible to acquire one" (Pfaff, 1995). He calls for Europe, perhaps led by France, to take the responsibility for post-colonial state building in Africa.

These and similar proposals have been roundly dismissed as socially unacceptable and politically unfeasible (Sisk, 1995). As will be argued, the situation of failed states requires an objective understanding of genuine nation-building by focusing on existing conditions in every society and working to rebuild and reconstruct viable political institutions and social infrastructure. We shall return to this subject in the concluding Chapter.

Viability of the Scenario

Although the nightmare scenario would be the least preferable, in the short and medium terms, it is the most likely future for the African continent for a number of reasons. Firstly, both the local ruling classes, who have been responsible for the rape and pillage of the continent, and the international financial oligarchy will remain religiously committed to pursuing IMF/World Bank SAP policies and programs and are unlikely to accept any substantive systemic change. Of course one can argue, as the neo-liberal gatekeepers do in defending their structural adjustment programs, that without SAP initiatives things would have been much worse than they are. This is a counterfactual proposition that is impossible to confirm or deny conclusively. However, to some prophets of doom and gloom, the likely consequences of doing more of the same are written boldly on the wall.

Secondly, the forces of opposition and resistance against capital in the South in general, and in Africa in particular, are too weak and poorly coordinated to mount any meaningful challenge, while imaginative visions of an alternative future also remain only vaguely problematized and articulated. The class and social strate of the exploited, oppressed and marginalized is too weak to challenge the hegemony of the financial oligarchy. They lack both the necessary revolutionary consciousness and the visionary leadership to transform the discontent of their daily lives into a political program for revolutionary action, resistance and revolution. They need to be mobilized, organized and provided with channels of deliberation, consultation and democratic decision-making. Because such revolutionary consciousness and leadership are conspicuously missing in most African countries, the historical possibility of transforming the economic, cultural and political predicament of poor Africans seems illusory. Worst of all, the emerging home-grown visions of development, namely the Abuja Treaty and NEPAD, are rooted in the same reactionary neo-liberal mode of thinking.

As conditions move from bad to worse, the gatekeepers of the world economy will continue to promise, bribe and manipulate African leaders and their advisors in order to remain on current course. Non-conventional development models and strategies that seek a more just social and economic order will be vehemently resisted. The World Bank, IMF, WTO and the leading governments of the North will come up with renewed but empty promises and advice on how best the South in general, and Africa in particular, can exploit the various opportunities which are claimed to be proffered by globalization. The protagonists of globalization will seek to perpetuate myths like the one about poor countries catching up with the rich, the growing convergence of rich and poor, and the benevolence of the capitalist system towards the less fortunate. They will even promise new rounds of talks to eliminate the remaining trade barriers, improve commodity prices, transfer old industries to the South, increase foreign assistance, regulate the predatory activities of TNCs, reduce debt and encourage foreign direct investment (e.g. the World Commission on the Social Dimesion of Globalization, Blair's Commission for Africa, etc.). They may go as far as proposing that one African country be allowed to sit on the U.N. Security Council as a permanent member. However, in the entire scheme and logic of the system, the North will firmly resist any realistic changes that seek to alter the fundamentals of the world economy, or of power and privilege. As pointed out earlier, marginal, cosmetic and disjointed changes in the *status quo* will hardly make any dent in the structural foundations of distorted African economies or the asymmetry of international relations.

It is also important to fully recognize that the consequences of failing and collapsed states in the South cannot be practically isolated with a *cordon sanitaire* as is often assumed. Indeed, territorial containment would be meaningless in the world of globalization. Diseases, weapons of mass destruction and economic migrants have somehow often been able to overcome man-made restraints on their cross-border movements. The narrow, short-term self-interest of the North will have to be balanced against the long-term collective self-interest of humanity in general. This primary concern derives from the imperative that grinding poverty and human misery, and the enormous waste of human potential that it causes, should not be tolerated in the midst of plenty. It also derives from purely economic considerations: all countries stand to benefit from the prosperity that economic development can create. In a similar vein, social and economic problems posed by poverty, despair and inequality in a globalized world tend not to respect national borders. The resulting conflicts, refugees, and the health problems that poverty creates are likely to be exported to other countries. And, as we have already witnessed in other parts of the world, as fighting and instability spread in Africa, so too does the growth of terrorist networks and international criminal organizations, the destruction of the environment, and the spread of diseases, refugees, poverty and ethnic strife. This critical argument points to the renewed need to focus on eradicating the root causes of human insecurity (Chege, 2002).

As some other observers of African political economies have noted, large-scale marginalization should not necessarily be interpreted exclusively in a negative way. Viewed dialectically, every tragedy creates opportunities. The exploitation, social exclusion and marginalization wrought by the forces of globalization will eventually sharpen and deepen people's understanding of their reality as well as heightening their revolutionary consciousness. Instead of screaming and raving about economic exploitation and social marginalization, Africa will seize the moment for a thorough collective introspection. Globalization is likely to offer an historic opportunity to end the scourge of underdevelopment and marginalization. The ongoing crisis will give rise to visionary leadership and release the creative energies of the people as they struggle to survive and respond to the multifaceted crises of their lives.

Moreover, the excruciating effects of globalization provide a compelling occasion to redefine African priorities away from compulsive global integration and to focus on national self-reliance and a new regionalism, to recognize informal economies, and to encourage informal politics, particularly political participation by the civil society. From the ashes of marginalization, radicalized social movements and political parties will struggle to undo predatory internal relations of power, politics, and production and exchange. The effectively mobilized and empowered citizenry will, in turn, map out alternative platforms to deal with global apartheid, restructure skewed power relations, and reform the unfair rules and regulations of international trade and investment, as well as strive for collective renegotiation and/or repudiation of foreign debts (Shaw, 1994; Ihonvebere, 2000; Aina, 1996). Claude Ake is even more forceful when he argues that:

> .... Perhaps marginalization, so often decried, is what Africa needs right now. For one thing, it will help the evolution of an endogenous development agenda, an agenda that expresses the aspiration of the people and can therefore elicit their support. Because of exogeneity, and its contradictions, Africa does not even at this stage have a development agenda (Ake, 1996).

As noted earlier, the emerging global political and economic realignments seem destined to bypass Africa in every major respect. The continent's exponential marginality will, in all likelihood, obliterate its ability to exert any significant leverage in the emerging political economy. In this regard, national self-reliance and regional cooperation and integration will present themselves as matters of necessity rather than choice. Africa should not let itself be taken by surprise. Maybe it is time Africa revisited the old-fashioned yet insightful development ideas of Friedrich List (1904), Alexander Hamilton

(1904), Alexander Gershenkron (1966) and Samir Amin (1976) about national self-reliance and structural transformation in backward societies. They demonstrated how free trade has historically tended to favor powerful actors over the relatively weak ones in the global economy. They regarded the policy of selective delinking as the external precondition for sustainable development. Historical experiences of capitalist and socialist development that resulted in dynamic and sustainable political economic structures demonstrate that, without a period of self-centeredness, i.e without a protection-motivated development policy, balanced development is hardly possible. These writers categorically rejected the prescription that least developed societies should lay themselves open to unfettered and unlimited free trade and investment. Recent successes in East Asia amply demonstrate how selective external opening can facilitate access to the benefits offered by global markets, international savings and technology transfers. These economies gradually and favorably integrated themselves into the world economy through a mixture of outward orientation and unorthodox policies - high tariffs and non-tariff barriers, public ownership of much of the banking sector, patent and copyright infringements, and restrictions on foreign capital flows, thus violating practically every conventional prescription of the orthodox IMF/World Bank structural adjustment model. Globalization, and the resulting marginalization and exclusion, seem to offer Africa the very conditions that the giants of political economy once preached and craved for.

The task of reducing dependence, increasing national and regional power and achieving the goal of equitable and sustainable development requires a people-centered approach that is need-oriented, self-reliant, indigenous and economically sound. A dynamic transformation depends on seeking to balance supply and demand by increasing the former without necessarily suppressing the latter. Research has shown, for example, that social measures promoting education, nutrition, equity, gender balance, social cohesion and empowerment generate high economic returns and a stable macro-economy. The journey is bound to be long, torturous and, at times, hazardous. It will also mean heavy losses in terms of the short-run cost-benefit assessment. These are perceived as inevitable learning costs à la Peter Senghaas (1985:217).

The immediate cost of self-reliance and greater economic independence and transformation will not necessarily be slower growth but less current consumption. Under a mass-based democratic regime, the burden of accumulation would be shouldered by most citizens in the form of higher taxes and high prices for relatively inferior domestic goods and services. But, this time around, the implied sacrifices would not be borne as much by the majority, whose consumption is already very modest. Rather, luxury consumption by the few would be deliberately curtailed. What this means is that international economic transactions would be continued but would be of a different kind. The composition of imports, for example, would change dramatically to reflect the emerging patterns of production, investment, and consumption. The engine of development and growth would be deeply anchored within national, regional and South-South axes.

In order for Africa to participate in the global economy on its own terms rather than merely be pulled into it, Africa will have to look inside itself for internal strength and carefully evaluate the opportunities offered by the international political economy. This brings us to the rationale for presenting two more scenarios whose prospects will largely depend on how decisively African societies and their respective states grapple with the fundamental political, economic and social questions raised in the the first dooms-day scenario.

Scenario Two: Reforms of the Global Agenda, Economy and Institutions
Although the assumptions in this scenario remain the same as those applying in the previous case, different policy, institutional strategies and values are proposed. This scenario revolves around the project of initiating gradual yet systemic reforms in the world economy, promoting enlightened development and human-centered cooperation agendas, and reforming key international institutions. The scenario presupposes the emergence of a politically revitalized South and an enlightened North. As in the first scenario, it assumes that global development dynamics will be influenced by the neo-liberal economic doctrine. Consequently, most African economies would then be likely to continue with the implementation of various brands of structural adjustment programs. It is further assumed that the role of the IMF and the World Bank in Africa's policy management will become further entrenched as the continent's economic crisis deepens and as the debt problem remains unresolved. Moreover, it is assumed that Africa's economic structures and patterns of trade will remain largely unchanged. However, a small but cohesive group of states supported by a diverse coalition of grassroots organizations will emerge in the South, galvanize itself around critical North-South issues and seek strategic alliances with progressive forces in the North

to fight for the reform of the skewed institutions of global governance, economic inequality and to work toward putting in place an environment that is capable of arresting or even reversing the processes of marginalization and exclusion.

The victorious powers defined the governance structure of the post-World War 11, centred on the U.N. and the Bretton Woods institutions - a system that constitute the core of global governance today. Since then, much has changed. Today there are over 190 member countries, compared to about 10 then. Over this period, a few countries in the South have joined the ranks of the high-income league, while middle-income and populous ones such as China, India and Brazil have emerged as significant players in the global economy. However, as noted earlier, the politics of the global system continue to be characterized by a lack of democracy and skewed representation. Membership in the Security Council, for example, is based on the situation that obtained in the period after the Second World War. Moreover, countries from the South are under-represented in the voting structure of the Bretton Woods institutions. Reforms of the membership and decision-making procedures in these institutions have become more urgent than ever before.

Genuine reforms of the key institutions of global governance, it is often argued, would facilitate the articulation of coherent policies and rules, as well as the promotion of the right environment for sustainable and equitable development, particularly that of the poor regions and poor sectors of society. Most importantly, reforms in global governance would seek to address reckless capitalist exploitation and mass poverty, under-representation of the interests of the majority, proliferation of weapons of mass destruction, environmental degradation, spread of deadly diseases, and the entrenchment of bourgeois social decadence, all of which threaten global security.

The need for and the possibility of implementing the envisaged reform of the global governance architecture is premised on three assumptions. First, reforms of the key institutions of global governance would provide an auspicious environment that would unlock Africa's economies from its asymmetrical relationships with the North. Second, pressures for enlightened policies and institutions would come from grassroots movements and would coalesce around commonly-agreed values and ethics of sustainable, equitable development and democracy for all. Third, the same pressures would give rise to the need to reconstitute the state and state-society relations. This is a kind of state in which social equity, social inclusion and democracy, national unity and respect for human rights would form the basis of national economic policy. This development strategy is what Richard Falk (1992) in |*Explorations at the Edge of Time* describes as 'globalization from below.'

In his examination of global citizenship, Falk makes a distinction between 'globalization from above' and 'globalization from below.' He defines the former in terms of the collaboration between leading states and the main agents of capitalism. The second type of globalization is characterized as both a reaction to these developments and a response to different influences that emanate from the concerns of grassroots movements and enlightened leaders of poor countries with new visions of a human community. For Falk, this kind of globalization from below inclines toward a 'one-world community premised on a politics of aspiration and desire' and 'rests upon the strengthening over time of the institutional forms and activities associated with global civil society.' Globalization from below closely relates to the question of social movements and the constitution of citizenship. If alternative visions of globalization are to gather weight, he argues, the connections of solidarity between social movements in different countries need to be given greater priority. Struggles around issues of, for example, the environment, human rights, decentralized forms of government, gender politics and indigenous communities express an increasingly common agenda, and in the South such struggles provide an emerging basis for new and alternative visions of justice and codes of ethics in a global context (Falk, 1992).

While Falk's view of the role of international civil society seems compelling at first sight, civil society organizations are only a section of the global opposition to the globalization process and are not ideologically homogeneous. Some of them, often shady, are out to support the entrenchment and consolidation of the *status quo*. They are "grassroots reactionaries who complement the work of the IMF by pushing privatization 'from below' and demobilizing popular movements, thus undermining resistance" (Petras and Veltmeyer, 2001:130). The double-edged character of civil society organizations presents a serious challenge that requires a critical analysis of their origins, structure and ideology.

There is already a growing consensus, even among the centers of power in the North, in favor of promoting the democratic managing, steering or shaping of world politics and economics. It is commonly agreed that the underlying processes of globalization involve more risks than even the privileged few actors in the North can afford. There are various calls for national and multinational actions to respond collectively to the fragmentation of economic and political systems and the transnational threats permeating borders. The growing need for global democratic governance is, in part, the product of the inevitable creeping acknowledgement that there are various forces of globalization that reduce the relevance and efficacy of the existing global management institutions, such as the Security Council, the World Bank, the IMF and the WTO, which are fundamentally undemocratic and non-transparent. As Jan Nederveen Pieterse (2001:14) argues, it is more compelling to treat global reforms primarily as a form of 'global risk management.' Inspite of the diverse and conflicting interests of the North and South, mutual interest and shared responsibilities ought to remain the guiding normative principles for wider concerns, such as those for the global environment and security, poverty, ecology and natural resources.[27]

Globalization, the changing nature of conflict since the end of the East-West conflict, and the emergence of new actors in regional conflict management, all have had a deep impact on the Security Council's ability to consistently address serious threats to international peace and security. Worries abound about the Council's legitimacy as presently constituted, and its overall effectiveness and arbitrariness in its decision-making procedures and practices. First, the Council's composition is largely perceived as lopsided. As long as Japan and Germany are excluded from permanent membership, as well as other major regional powers from Asia, Latin America and Africa, the Security Council cannot claim to be representative of the international community of nations. Second, there is a growing impression that the Council's decisions are arbitrary. When it comes to making decisions on intervention, for instance, there is a tendency for the Council to act rigorously in some cases, and to be very restrained or not act at all in others. Despite widespread conflicts in Africa, the continent is widely perceived as the region most neglected by the Security Council. Third and finally, the perennial poor delivery capability of the Council is yet another source of international concern. This inability is not only influenced by the general lack of political will to implement the Council's decisions but, most importantly, by the members' failure to delink their global responsibility from their vital national interests. Thus, the legitimacy and effectiveness of the United Nations and its Security Council could only be improved, not by tinkering at the margins of the organization, but by reforming its very structure, mandate and representation (Kuhne, 2001).

Once the majority of the key members lose confidence in the existing international management architecture, then a classic crisis of legitimacy will come to the fore. In Gramscian logic, 'the withdrawal of consent' is likely to spread to the core institutions and practices of global capitalism. Again, once the process of delegitimization takes hold, then a widening of the terrain of mutual interests and vulnerability may occur, as well as new opportunities for compromise. The brazen confidence of the system will have been shaken to its foundations. Then negotiations for a new order should begin in earnest. These are the organizing concerns of Scenario Two. However, what remains contentious are the fine details, the breadth and depth of possible compromises. The *1999 Human Development Report* (UNDP, 1999) proposed a new 'global architecture' that would have a number of interesting features:

♦ A global central bank to act as a lender of last resort to cash-strapped countries and to help regulate financial markets.

♦ A global investment trust to moderate flows of foreign capital in and out of the South and raise development funds by taxing global pollution or short-term investment.

♦ New rules for the WTO, including non-monopoly powers to enable it to keep global corporations from dominating indigenous industries.

♦ New rules on global patents that would keep the patent system from blocking the access of the South to development, knowledge, or healthcare.

♦ New talks on a global investment treaty that would include the South and respect local laws.

♦ More flexible monetary rules that would enable the South to improve capital controls to protect the environment.

♦ A global code of conduct, requiring multinational corporations to abide by labor and environmental laws that exist in the North.

Following the above UNDP logic, and given the fact that the current crisis of development is systemic, its solution inevitably requires profound institutional and policy reform at all levels. Single-issue and disconnected campaigns, important as they are, are not likely to foster sustainable development without concomitant reforms in the nature and structure of the current world economic and political system. By the same token, not only must the range of actors be broadened and areas of negotiation widened, but the agenda of global sustainable development must also be interactive and multidimensional: global governance must heed the global economy; global taxes must interact with policies regarding development; and ecology, population, gender and cultural questions must be closely linked. Simply put, global reforms must be grassroots-based and should seek to exploit inter-sectoral synergies.

In a similar vein, the Group of Lisbon study entitled *Limits to Competition* calls for a 'system of cooperative governance in order to negotiate global contracts.' The call involves linking a multitude of socio-economic networks at various territorial levels around visible targets and common objectives aimed at achieving social justice, economic efficiency, environmental sustainability, and political democracy to avoid the many possible sources of global implosion. It further posits that global governance initiatives should be informed by global democracy. This is a form of world governance which would be based on the democratic consent of the governed, designed to foster international peace and equal development, and adhering to some basic global environmental and economic standards (Group of Lisbon, 1995). These veritable struggles call for firm South-South solidarity and coordination. Strengthening the basis of Southern solidarity above and beyond rhetorical proclamations would significantly increase the political and strategic weight of the South *vis-à-vis* the North. The coordination and integration of development efforts would be a necessary condition for accumulating collective power. As Mahdi Elmandjra (1998:52) asks rhetorically, "can the North take the South seriously unless the South gives some tangible proofs of its commitment to minimum cohesion, coherence and solidarity?" Indeed, South-South cooperation would markedly enhance its bargaining power on a variety of important issues like global governance structure, international money and finance, technology transfer, trade, debt, aid and the environment.

Unquestionably, the arena of global environment would open a strategic window for the initial negotiations. It has become increasingly intertwined with the politics of international economic relations, international politics, and development policy in recent years. Trade and the environment, the financing of sustainable development, and consumption patterns were not on the international political agenda at all two decades ago. Moreover, several critical developments have converged: the growing influence of environmental consciousness on trade policies; the emergence of an environmental regime requiring major social and economic transactions in all societies; and the convening of history's first global negotiations encompassing both environmental and economic policies popularly known as the Earth Summit, in Rio de Janeiro in 1992. The idea of sustainable development underpinned the discourse at this Summit.

The thrust of the debates at the Earth Summit was to seek common ground that reconciled the environmental concerns of the North with the developmental preoccupations of the South. These policy concerns came to be popularly known as 'sustainable development.' The concept emphasizes the interdependencies and complementarities between social development and environmental protection. Its adherents attempt to provide an imaginative policy agenda to address intertwined developmental issues in a world of very uneven economic and social circumstances. The North was initially persuaded to accept the main burden of subsidizing adjustment costs in the South that were associated with environmental protection, if only for their long-term self-interest. The 1990 South Commission Report tersely captured the security argument:

> Were all humanity a single nation-state, the present North-South divide would make it an unviable, semi-feudal entity, split by internal conflict. Its small part is advanced, prosperous, and powerful; its much bigger part is underdeveloped, poor and powerless. A nation so divided within itself could be recognized as unstable. A world so divided within itself should likewise be recognized as inherently unstable. And the position is worsening, not improving (South Commission, 1990:1-2).

At first, sustainable development became the only song in town. It featured in all subsequent United Nations summit reports. A multi-billion dollar Global Environmental Facility was agreed upon and established to promote sustainable development in several main sectors of activity by facilitating North-South resource transfers. The North was prepared to consider some limitations on its affluent lifestyle and the South to forego short-term developmental opportunities offered by destroying their environment. However, it is important to emphasize the fact that the potency of the concept in framing the global debate on development is as valid now as when it was first enunciated by the Brundtland World Commission on the Environment and Development, published under the title *Our Common Future*. It contributed to the formation of a global consensus: the environmental crisis can be managed but only if states cooperate as never before on behalf of sustainable planetary interests, and this will happen only if pollution is understood to encompass poverty, thus placing the economic burdens of adjustment on the countries of the North and promising that development in the South will not be diminished by efforts at environmental protection. These arguments could not be sustained for long. Conflicting interests of the rich and poor nations quickly became manifest, and then sustainable and equitable development degenerated into an empty political slogan.

Most of the views on the global environment in the South have been shaped, to a considerable extent, by the preoccupation with economic growth, their fears of the high costs of environmental protection, and their general distrust of the policies of the industrial North. African countries, in particular, have always regarded the negotiation of global regimes on ozone depletion, climate change, biodiversity loss and the conservation of endangered species as a Northern agenda. Interestingly, most Northern countries are agreed that their consumption patterns are largely responsible for much of the current global environmental degradation. In fact, countries in the North use about two-thirds or more of the world's steel, aluminum, copper, lead, nickel, tin and zinc. They also generate most of the world's hazardous chemicals and almost 90 percent of the chlorofluorocarbons that destroy the ozone layer. And, over the past century, their economies have pumped out over two-thirds of the greenhouse gases that threaten the world's climate. Today, the United States alone emits more carbon dioxide than Asia, Africa and Latin America put together. How sustainable development should be paid for sharply divides the North from the South on almost every key issue of negotiation (Worldwatch Institute, 1991:156).

In order for it to remain politically relevant in the emerging political and economic configurations, the threat to the global environment should give the South new bargaining leverage regarding its economic problems. Protecting the environment and combating poverty are now widely recognized to be interlinked priorities, a reality reflected in the decision to focus UNCED on both the environment and on development. Similarly, the 1994, United Nations International Conference on Population and Development in Cairo looked at the complex interconnections among population growth, deteriorating social conditions, gender inequality and environmental degradation. In short, it has become increasingly obvious that a sustainable future cannot be secured without an aggressive effort to combat poverty and meet basic social needs. In this regard, African countries must collectively struggle to imaginatively exploit the inextricable linkage between debt, poverty and marginalization on the one hand, and environmental degradation and global security on the other. Just as the organization called the Club of the Earth succinctly observed, the current environmental degradation is "a threat to civilization second only to the threat of thermonuclear war" (Ecology Editor, 1987:129).

The shared objective of human security seems to be the most powerful argument in favor of increased recognition of the central importance of sustainable development on the international agenda. The often-proposed linkage is disarmingly straightforward: unless the environment is collectively protected and conserved, the planet is in grave danger of suffering a catastrophe of unparalleled proportions. As for the South, pervasive economic marginalization, exclusion, and dependence, crushing foreign debt and frustration have led to the wanton destruction of its tropical forests and to the exploitation of their resources. One hastens to add that the North long ago depleted most of its natural forests. In this respect, therefore, unless the South demands handsome compensation to forego further commercial logging, ranching, and poaching, tropical forests will soon be wiped out at a large cost to all of humanity. The multilateral arrangements and joint actions required in this area will require an active, concerted diplomatic effort on the part of the South. Despite the doom and gloom scenario sketched earlier, Africa has a very important role to play with regard to the critical issue of the protection of the environment. Its vast and enviable resources include forests, the virtually carbon dioxide-free atmosphere above the continent, and the minimal presence of toxic effluents in the rivers and soils that interact with the Atlantic and Indian Oceans and the Mediterranean and Red Seas. This enormous resource base, therefore, serves as an incontrovertible negotiations chip to restructure the present inequitable global governance structures.

In his seminal 1968 essay, *The Tragedy of the Commons*, ecologist Garrett Hardin (1968) compares today's predicament with the medieval degradation of common grazing lands. He describes how individual cattle herders pursued short-term economic gains to the detriment of everyone's long-term future, knowing that an individual's efforts to conserve the resource base would be overwhelmed by the actions of others. He glibly concludes, "ruin is the destination toward which all men rush, each pursuing his interest in society, which believes in the freedom of commons. Freedom in commons brings ruin to us all." Similarly, today's environmental geopolitics is marked by a 'new world disorder' *à la* Christopher Flavian (1997:10). The current situation lacks strong leadership and most countries have mixed compliance records. Shifting alliances have marked recent negotiations on the climate and biodiversity. However, with the current awareness of global environmental degradation, and the size and sophistication of the worldwide network of citizens' movements especially among environmental and development

NGOs, the new millennium would be the right moment for the South to bring this critical issue once again to the diplomatic center stage. As emphasized earlier, serious attempts should be made to negotiate not only programs such as debt-for-nature swaps, and debt-for-development swaps, and to demand multilateral funding for the development of environmentally friendly intermediate technologies for the South, but also and most critically, to negotiate measures to reform institutions of global governance.

In an important study for the U.S. National Academy of Sciences, Norman Myers (1984) estimated that the area of global primary forests cleared or degraded every year was about 200,000 square kilometers. He further projected that, if the destruction continues unchecked, the world's virgin tropical forests would be extirpated within 50 years. Incidentally, the value of global trade in forest products has risen steadily over the last few decades, climbing from $47 billion in 1970 to $139 billion in 1998 (French, 1997:186). In addition to the loss of genetic resources, uncontrolled floods and creeping deserts, deforestation impacts the global climate negatively. The destruction of forests threatens not only to disrupt world rainfall patterns but, more seriously perhaps, to destabilize the delicate chemistry of the earth's inner atmosphere. It is common knowledge that forests absorb significant amounts of carbon dioxide, and therefore tend to offset some of the emissions that cause global warming.

The Worldwatch Institute of Washington DC produces annual updates on the global environment. In its 1999 issue, it reported that the rise in temperature that results from the increasing atmospheric concentration of carbon dioxide (CO_2) was already alarming. When the industrial revolution began two centuries ago, the CO_2 concentration was estimated at 280 parts per million (ppm). By 1959, when detailed measurement began, the CO_2 level was at 316 ppm, a rise of 13 percent over the two centuries. By 1998, it had reached 367 ppm, climbing 17 percent in just 39 years. The average global temperature for 1969-71 was 13.99 Celsius. By 1996-98, it was 14.43 Celsius, a gain of 0.44 degrees. This fast rise in temperatures will definitely alter every ecosystem on earth. Already the coral reefs are being affected in nearly all the world's oceans. Coral reefs, complex ecosystems that are sometimes referred to as the 'rainforests of the sea,' not only serve as the breeding grounds for many species of marine life, but also protect the coastlines from storms and storm surges (Brown, 1999:6).

The destabilization of the climate threatens more intense heatwaves, more serious droughts and floods, more destructive storms and more intensive fires. The related shifts in rainfall and temperature are likely to jeopardize food production, the earth's biological diversity and entire ecosystems, as well as threatening human health by expanding the range of tropical diseases. Unless concerted and enlightened international efforts to curb these shifts are mounted carbon emissions will continue to grow faster than the population over the next 50 years, driving the earth's climate system into uncharted territory. The Intergovernmental Panel on Climate Change estimated that an eventual two-thirds reduction in global emissions is needed to avoid precariously high levels of atmospheric carbon dioxide (Watson *et. al.*, 1996). It should be emphasized that the cost of climatic change will be most stricking in the poor countries of the South not only because of their geographical and climatic conditions but also because of their high dependence on natural resources and their limited capacity to adapt to climatic variability and extremes.

From the foregoing discussion, it is increasingly clear that environmental security opens a window of opportunity for a new focus on some critical North-South agenda. The new global agenda should be strategically linked to other internationally agreed-upon issues, as developed during UN-sponsored conferences in the 1990s, and as adopted by the Development Assistance Committee of the OECD (1996a) report, *Shaping the 21st Century: The Contribution of Development Co-operation.* For the first time in a long time, Northern governments committed themselves to various noble development cooperation ideals. These included, among others, debt relief and poverty reduction. They noted that, while the primary responsibility for establishing and implementing strategies for meeting social development targets lay with national governments, an enabling environment for development needed to be created by the international community. By the same token, in order to achieve a new world order with a human face, new initiatives must be accompanied by policies that guarantee the satisfaction of basic needs, permit adjustments for highly unequal ownership of assets, ensure representative global governance, income, and power distribution - policies that are needed to prevent the growth of insecurity and social exclusion.

With the dawn of the new century, heads of state gathered at the United Nations General Assembly in September, 2000 to further articulate their vision of the world. They adopted the United Nations Millennium Declaration, recognizing their "collective responsibility to uphold the principles of human dignity, equality and equity at a global level." More specifically, they confirmed the global community's readiness to support Africa's efforts to address the continent's underdevelopment and marginalization. The Declaration emphasized support for the prevention of conflict and the establishment of conditions of stability and democracy on the continent, as well as for the key challenges of eradicating poverty and disease. The Declaration further pointed to the global community's commitment to enhancing resource flows to Africa by improving aid, trade and debt relationships between Africa and the rest of the world. It is time these bold commitments were translated into reality.[28]

On the development cooperation policy front, the first order of business would be to seek to reform 'global apartheid' by demanding far-reaching institutional measures aimed at restructuring skewed power relations in the management of the world economy, alleviating the debt burden, reversing the trend toward a sharp decline of foreign aid, opening up markets in the North for products from the South, and transferring technology. In order to achieve the estimated 7 percent per annum growth rate needed to meet the international development goals, and most importantly to halve the incidence of poverty by the year 2015, Africa would need to fill an annual resource gap of about 12 percent of its GDP. As already noted, there is growing consensus that even under the best possible policy regimes, African countries cannot internally generate the resources needed to sustain satisfactory growth and development. Various estimates of external resource requirements made by UNCTAD, the World Bank and the ECA suggest that at least an additional $10 billion per annum would be required for a decade or so. All this would call for a serious re-examination of the debt question, the foreign aid regime, and foreign direct investment.

More tellingly, an enlightened development vision would recognize that losses on bad loans to Africa should not be borne by the debtors alone but should be shared by creditors as well. It is no longer a secret that much of Africa's accumulated debt is a result of ill-conceived, creditor-supported development projects and programs, flawed policies and strategies that originated from development cooperation agencies in exchange for Cold War support and, admittedly, short-sighted policy decisions by corrupt African leaders. In all fairness, therefore, Africa's unsustainable debt should be accepted as a shared responsibility of creditors and debtors alike.

Closely tied to financial resource transfers to Africa would be the negotiation of equitable and fair-trade relations between the North and South. It was observed in Chapter Three that some rules and practices governing international trade are geared toward the corporate and political interests of the North, resulting in a highly unequal distribution of the benefits of world trade. The new global agenda should seek to correct such rules and practices that are biased against the very countries that need a fair trading system for growth and development. At the WTO, support should be given to the work of the Cairns Group, a coalition of 18 agricultural exporting countries who account for about one-third of agricultural exports. These countries have endeavored to seek profound reforms of the international trading system and the elimination of all forms of trade-distorting subsidies. In the same vein, it would also be important for the world community to revisit the suggestion of treating the seabed resources of the high seas and other potential wealth in outer space as belonging to the common heritage of humankind, rather than being subject to appropriation by states with the requisite technological and entrepreneurial capabilities to exploit them. This would entail a re-examination of the contents of the Law of the Seas, which tends to be anchored to the operation of global market forces and to disregard the interests of the weak states. The original spirit of the common heritage principle in the 1960s and 1970s carried with it the possibility of a more equitable distribution of resources situated beyond the limits of territorial authority. As Richard Falk (2000:176) compellingly argues, the idea of a common heritage could also be used "to raise revenues for the U.N. system, thereby weakening the bondage of the Organization to the priorities of its most powerful members."

Equally important on the global agenda would be to bring to center stage the nature and structure of global governance. In fact, the institutions that were created after the end of World War II are not only faced with increasing burdens and challenges, just as the transnational flows they are attempting to regulate, facilitate or mitigate are becoming more difficult to control, but also and most fundamentally, it has become increasingly apparent almost everywhere in the world that they have partially or entirely lost their legitimacy. Most people do not seem to believe in them any more. The multilateral institutions that should evolve must reflect shared aims and should ensure that rules are enforced through the participatory and mutually recognized interests of all parties.

There have been strong and sustained initiatives from the South for reform of the network of international organizations established after World War II. Proposals for new institutions include recombining the Bretton Woods institutions and the U.N. system, with a view to realigning economic and financial regimes with social development. One such proposal is for the adjustment of voting systems; another is for an Economic Security Council

Africa: Possible Development Futures

that would take over the role of the international financial institutions under U.N. auspices. The issue of the reform of the U.N. Security Council is deeply embedded in the whole question of legitimacy. Given that the United Nations is comprised of 185 member states, the second proposal revolves around the perceived imbalance in representation on the Security Council. There appears to be an emerging consensus on the inclusion of Japan, Germany, and three representatives each from Africa, Latin America and Asia as permanent members. Yet nagging questions remain, particularly those surrounding the veto provision and the mechanism of regional choice (Commission on Global Governance, 1995).

Viability of the Scenario

Although the concept of sustainable development represents a significant conceptual and programmatic advance in development studies, like capitalist globalization, it conveys different and often contradictory meanings for the diverse groups promoting it. Different actors have widely varying perceptions whether certain processes of historical change are developmental or degenerative. Views tend to be chiefly influenced by how the changes are likely to affect the proponent's own society and their position within it. There is little consensus on what kinds of reforms are the most urgent, how such reforms should be managed, or by whom. It is therefore not surprising that in spite of the impressive international relations rhetoric promoting sustainable development, there is little positive impact on the ground. Indeed, in many respects, the situation has become worse. The data on the indirect environmental consequences of air and water pollution, deforestation and land degradation all point to worsening global conditions. Social conditions have not fared any better, but were indeed falling for the low-income majorities in much of Africa and Latin America during the 1990s. The World Bank estimates that the total number of people living on less than $1 per day worldwide, which was 1.5 billion in 1999, could be projected to increase by 2015 to 1.9 billion, compared with 1.2 billion in 1987 (World Bank, 1999:25).[29]

One should hasten to point out that the conditions for the realization of this scenario do not seem particularly rosy. The central question for any strategy of transformation is that of agency. Who are the actors, and who will most vigorously and effectively champion sustainable development and construct social progress? In the short and medium term, dominant classes and powerful states in the North are likely to manipulate the system in order to maintain their own privileges and power. They will continue to hold that international institutions should be structured in ways that reflect the global hierarchy of power among states and their respective national interests. They are likely to claim that the effectiveness of any multilateral arrangements will largely depend on the relative power and commitment of their more powerful members. Nor are the internal opposition forces against social inequalities perceived to be sufficiently threatening to warrant the reform of the system. Even before the Rio Summit began, George Bush (Senior), then President of the United States, famously announced that the "American standard of living was not negotiable." The negative American reaction to the whole agenda was the last nail in the coffin of sustainable development. The funds that were pledged to support sustainability were not only inadequate but quickly evaporated.

The sustainable development crusade lacks credible and committed leadership. The United States' progress toward sustainable development since the Rio Summit has been limited, at best. That country has no federal sustainable development strategy, no agreed indicators, declining levels of official development assistance and weak commitment to the Millennium Development Goals; it has made little progress on major international agreements, particularly on the 1997 Kyoto Protocol, which was almost immediately rejected by the incoming Republication administration of President George W. Bush (Junior). He signaled his determination to rely more on the market and on voluntary, efficiency-driven measures to control gas emissions than on legislation and mandated benchmarks. Moreover, the U.N. Biodiversity Convention, which was similarly rejected by President George Bush (Senior) a decade ago, has never been presented to Congress for ratification. And the United States' much-criticized patterns of consumption show little sign of moderating. In short, the United States has a sad tendency to pick and choose which international agreements and conventions it feels like adhering to, while expecting the rest of the world to stick by them all! In this regard, its assumed global leadership role is highly circumscribed by its overall stance and performance on the subject (Chomsky, 2000:1).

In the South, the elite classes that preside over the economy and politics are not likely to surrender their privilege in order to create access to resources for deprived groups. They are not likely to enthusiastically support radical changes that would adversely affect their life styles or consumption patterns. It seems, therefore, that there is neither the necessary political will nor the requisite leadership and strong mobilizing ideology either in the North or the South to provide the necessary vision and inspiration to press for global consensus on critical common development interests. Unlike the Cold War period, there are no commanding ideologies to mobilize the marginalized and excluded sections of society worldwide. Socialist ideas would appear to have been discredited and fallen out of favor as part of the end game in the Cold War. Above all, the unity of political purpose and shared vision among social and union movements nationally, regionally and globally are still in their embryonic stages. Even with the most favorable circumstances, more time, patience and organizational effort will be needed for progressive movements to coalesce around certain critical world order priorities and to forge strong ties between, for example, women's, environmental and peace movements. It will require more sharing of knowledge, better ideological refinements, more resources devoted to transnational affairs, better education for members and, in general, concrete practical steps directed toward strategies of coordination and common action. It cannot be stressed often enough that civil society organizations cover a wide array of groups and conflicting agendas.

Moreover, South-South synergy and cooperation seems unlikely as some countries in the South are absorbed into the sphere of influence of the regional powers. Their aspirations for real political and economic independence will be sacrificed, both in the short and medium term. Arguably, grand expectations for Africa's sustainable development seem to be out of the question in the immediate future. What would be immediately required are sober assessments of the continent's capabilities and vulnerabilities in order to confront the emerging global order. It would also require the identification of various factors that will be decisive in shaping Africa's future as well as a critical analysis of their impact. To accomplish the above, Africa has to look within the continent to marshal the necessary visionary leadership in order to exploit its resources and other potentialities, as well as to harness every bit of available international goodwill in order to stop and reverse the current trends of economic and social marginalization and exclusion. In sum, in the short and medium term, Scenario Two, though preferable, is not feasible.

Scenario Three: The Imperative of Mutual Cooperation and Integration

Not to draw lessons from (that) experience and to seek an alternative that will address the continent's fundamental economic malaise is to court further disaster in the years ahead. To refuse to seek a way out and to persist with what has not worked, and what independent studies have concluded will not work, as presently conceived and implemented, is to act contrary to the way reason points and enlightened self-interest suggests (Adedeji, 1989).

Scenario Three seeks to explore the extent to which some of the development visions that are currently in vogue can propel Africa out of poverty and underdevelopment, deepen democracy and economic governance and, more crucially, pioneer a new relationship and partnership with the North. Three major visions merit close attention in this regard. They include the Abuja Treaty that seeks to establish the African Economic Community in 2025, the African Union, and the New Partnership for Africa's Development. All three visions are predicated on continental cooperation and integration as the engine for economic growth, political development and meaningful participation in the world economy.

At the extraordinary summit of the Organization of African Unity in Sirte, Libya in September, 1999, African heads of state and government took an historic decision to establish an African Union in conformity with the ultimate objectives of the Charter of the O.A.U. and the provisions of the treaty establishing the African Economic Community. At its 37th Ordinary Session in Lusaka, in July 2001, the O.A.U. Assembly of Heads of State and Government adopted the New African Initiative (later renamed the New Partnership for Africa's Development). Both visions seek to reconfigure the continent's political and economic institutions in order to manage the forces of globalization and to stop the continent from sinking further into anarchy. As its core objectives, the African Union seeks to promote democratic principles, peace, security and stability, greater unity and solidarity between African countries and African peoples, and the acceleration of political and socio-economic integration. Through NEPAD, a new kind of partnership is envisaged with the North and various multilateral and multinational institutions.

Scenario Three adopts the same assumptions as Scenarios One and Two. However, unlike the earlier ones, Scenario Three explores different social and institutional forces that are likely to respond in bold and creative ways to the imperatives of global capitalism. As Bade Onimode (1992:153) poignantly put it, "the unfolding mega-trends of the world system have transformed African cooperation from a regional necessity into a continental imperative - the urgent strategic basis for the corporate survival of the African economy." If developed and large economies like those of the United States, Germany, Japan and France find it important to engage in regional integration and collective security arrangements, then the case for Africa's underdeveloped, mini-economies must be compelling indeed. They are too fragmented and too vulnerable to be economically viable. It is also emphasized that Africa's new cooperation arrangements with the North should not be limited simply to the so-called new global concerns of protecting the environment, drug control and population issues, important though these issues are. Rather, as the previous scenario has proposed, the united African nations should press for the restructuring of international political and economic institutions, trading regimes, technology transfer, finance and debt. As the last two scenarios have demonstrated, the emergence and development of regionalism on a global scale clearly indicates that individual states outside of the major economic and security blocs will find themselves slowly but inexorably cast aside. If Europe needs economic and political integration for strength and prosperity, Africa needs it for survival. Only through integration can the continent collectively and effectively respond to the multifaceted challenges posed by the processes of globalization.

As pointed out earlier, for the entire decade of the 1980s, the vision of the Lagos Plan of implementing collective self-reliance remained largely elusive. The African continent was held ransom by the IMF/World Bank policies of structural adjustment and debt restructuring. It was not until 1991 that the Abuja Treaty, the treaty establishing an African Economic Community was finally signed. Following its ratification by the required two-thirds of member-states, the Abuja Treaty came into force on May 12, 1994. Subsequently, various protocols have been prepared and adopted.[30] One of the primary and core objectives of the Treaty is to promote economic, social, political and cultural development, as well as the integration of African economies, in order to increase economic self-reliance, self-sustaining development and political stability. Indeed, for the first time in African history, the AEC Treaty not only provides the legal, institutional, economic and political framework for economic cooperation and integration, but also stipulates a comprehensive list of principles to guide the conduct of member-states. The pursuit of these principles is expected to create an enabling environment for regional cooperation and integration. Above all, the Treaty designates the General Secretariat of the A.U as the secretariat of the AEC. The AEC institutions include the Annual Conference of the Heads of State and Government, the Council of Ministers, the African Parliament, the Economic and Social Committee, the Court of Justice, the General Secretariat and the specialized technical committees.

Unlike the previous integration proposals of the 1960s and 1970s, the current African vision underscores the imperative for both microeconomic and macroeconomic harmonization and coordination in multi-sectoral programs encompassing production, infrastructure, and trade. It also stresses the importance of close political cooperation during the early stages of the integration process. Moreover, the new approach emphasizes the need for an equitable balance of the benefits in order to induce confidence among the least developed member-states. In very broad terms, the Abuja Treaty outlines various strategies for achieving its goals. Specifically, at the economic level, Article 6 provides for a flexible plan for the step-by-step establishment of the economic community in six stages of variable duration.

Stage one involves strengthening the institutional framework for the existing sub-regional groupings (and creating new ones where they do not exist) within five years after the Treaty comes into force. During the second stage, concerted regional action will be focused on the liberalization of intra-African trade, reinforcing sectoral integration, and coordinating and harmonizing the activities of different sub-regional communities within the ensuing eight years. The third stage, covering one decade, will be devoted to setting up a sub-regional customs union, to be merged in the following two years, during the fourth stage, into a regional customs union. By the end of the fourth stage, it is believed the time will be ripe for promoting the regional customs union to a regional economic market within a period of five years, constituting the fifth stage. The common market will involve common economic policies and liberalization of the movement of persons within its area. It is expected to develop automatically in the sixth stage, covering five years, into a pan-African economic community, wherein the economic sectors will be integrated, and an economic and monetary union will be established along with the African Monetary Fund, an African Central Bank and a common currency. In the last stage, the African Parliament is to be established (O.A.U., 1991).

However, as Teshome Mulat (1998a: 119) argues, the "path toward the AEC is neither clear and predictable nor devoid of twists and turns." It has a number of serious shortcomings. The first and rather obvious major weakness of the Treaty concerns setting a rigid timetable for a long-term development objective. The Treaty specifies the time frame of each phase up to the year 2025, which is totally impractical. The process of programming and planning a continental project is likely to be very difficult at best and almost impossible in the uncertain African context. In an environment of frequent civil wars, disintegration tendencies in many states and societies, persistent structural disequilibrium, pervasive poverty and crippling debt, rigid timetables are, to say the least, unrealistic. Going by past experience, the ambitious objectives of the Treaty seem to be far beyond the capabilities of the African continent. The requisite institutional capacities, as well as human and financial resources, are simply non-existent. In this regard, Ahmad Aly (1994:94-95) correctly observes that, "all these factors combined have the negative effect of blurring one's vision and thus making it extremely difficult to assess the continent's future accurately."

According to the implementation schedule of the Treaty, by 1999 the first stage was supposed to have given way to the second stage. However, without the courtesy and formality of a prior rigorous assessment of the progress already made, the African Heads of State meeting in Sirte, Libya in 1999, decided to establish the African Union (A.U.). More specifically, point 8 of the Sirte Declaration called for the stepping up of the implementation process of the Abuja Treaty through the reduction of the original timeframe of 34 years. It also called for the immediate establishment of all institutions provided for under the Treaty. The institutions in question were the African Central Bank, the African Monetary Fund, the Court of Justice, and the Pan-African Parliament. If almost all the Regional Economic Communities (RECs) are still standing on very shaky ground, it is difficult to see how the previous, already unrealistic, timeframe could be shortened. The political exigencies of the Sirte Declaration reflect no lessons from history. What is even more troubling is the fact that the intractable political and economic problems that were encountered while establishing sub-regional cooperation and integration arrangements in Africa in the last four decades have been simply assumed away. There are absolutely no shortcuts to an effective and dynamic African Economic Community, or to a robust African political union.

The Abuja Treaty recognizes the sub-regional economic communities as the pillars of the future continental community. Presently, there are six OAU designated RECs: the Arab Mahgreb Union (AMU), the Common Market for Eastern and Southern Africa (COMESA), the Economic Community of West African States (ECOWAS), the Economic Community of Central African States (ECCAS), the Inter-Governmental Authority on Development (IGAD), and the Southern African Development Community (SADC). The RECs are expected to restructure their organizations, rationalize and harmonize policies, and coordinate joint programs in such a way that they are in conformity with the objectives, principles and priorities of the AEC Treaty.

In practice, however, the process of establishing and consolidating the RECs as 'pillars of the continental community' is fraught with fundamental institutional, administrative and policy problems. At one extreme, there are a few regional economic communities that demonstrate laudable progress toward regional cooperation and integration. SADC and ECOWAS, for example, both have a relatively longer history than the rest, and have developed comprehensive protocols dealing with various aspects of cooperation and integration. Both communities have gone beyond looking at economic cooperation and integration merely as the liberalization of trade. They have long realized that only limited success could be realized from narrow trade liberalization, as most African countries do not have sufficient locally produced goods and services to participate in this trade on balanced terms. In both these RECs, there are a few countries which have the potential to benefit immediately from market integration and, therefore, to emerge as effective players in sub-regional integration. As a result, three simultaneous processes have been consciously implemented. First, concerted efforts by all member-states are being directed toward equitable development, integration and rationalization of productive structures throughout the sub-regional economic space, especially in the case of basic industries and agriculture. Second, various sub-regional efforts are being directed at developing comprehensive programs of physical infrastructure - roads, railways, port facilities, telecommunications and energy. Third, the process of trade liberalization has been going on for some time, through a progressive reduction and phasing out of tariffs and other barriers to internal trade, harmonizing external trade protection measures, and integrating isolated national markets into sub-regional common markets.

At the other extreme, there are several RECs that are either in the formative stages or are simply non-functional. IGAD, for example, which attained recognition as a REC only in 1996, is in the initial process of establishing the basic administrative infrastructure for effective economic cooperation and integration. ECCAS has been dormant, chiefly due to the political and economic destabilization of the region. At the same time, the O.A.U. faced enormous difficulties in working with the AMU because Morocco, where the AMU headquarters is located, left the O.A.U. in 1982 over the question of the independence of the Saharawi Arab Democratic Republic. In short, the move toward building and consolidating a continental community through sub-regional communities is not as easy or as straightforward as it may look.

Moreover, many African states seek concurrent membership of more than one REC. Thus, the majority of COMESA member-states are also members of SADC and the most IGAD members are also members of COMESA. Ultimately, multiple membership of RECs makes the task of horizontal coordination difficult, since the same country will be progressing toward economic cooperation and integration at different paces in the different RECs to which it belongs. Likewise, the cost of membership rises with the increase in the number of organizations that countries choose to join. Furthermore, financial and management difficulties increase with the number of regional organizations and with shifting membership, rendering the RECs unsustainable. These problems, together with the fact that the RECs are not moving toward the AEC at the pace envisaged by the Treaty, have created great uncertainty as to which specific path toward integration is being followed.

Another source of serious conflict within RECs is the variable geometry of regions. There are different patterns of relations between countries, some representing fairly high levels of integration. For example, South Africa, Botswana, Lesotho, Namibia, and Swaziland are members of the Southern African Customs Union (SACU) and all states, except Botswana, are members of the Common Monetary Area (CMA). Several SADC member-states are members of COMESA. Then there are bilateral trade agreements between Botswana and Zimbabwe, Malawi and Botswana, Malawi and Zimbabwe, Mozambique, Tanzania and Namibia, and between South Africa and separately, Malawi, Mozambique and Zimbabwe. In order to play fully the role of the uniting force, SADC, or any other REC on the continent, will have to grapple with establishing a *modus operandi* with various cooperation and integration arrangements within their respective economic spaces. This is important in order to create a coherent and rational linkage of policies and programs as well as to pursue a coordinated and harmonized utilization of the meager resources allocated to regional integration.

But, although the process of economic integration in Africa would appear to be complex and intractable, the difficulties involved are not insurmountable. Nor should they discourage ongoing reforms and progress toward cooperation and integration. The existence of many integration organizations, in itself, should not be perceived as constituting an impossible impediment to reform. They should be understood as initial moves toward an ideal goal of integration. They can all contribute, in various ways, to the implementation effort of the AEC Treaty, if carefully thought-out harmonization and coordination policies are undertaken along the way. In light of this, the AEC Summit in Harare, in June 1997, adopted the Protocol on the Relations between the African Economic Community and the Regional

Economic Communities. This protocol, which governs AEC-REC relations, has the objective of strengthening the RECs and harmonizing intra-REC relations, with a view to facilitating progress toward the AEC. It calls for the realignment of the broad macroeconomic policy and institutional framework. Understandably, such alignments are expected to manage economic, political and social tensions that may arise along the way (Mulat, 1998b).

In order for the above Protocol, and indeed for others that are coming on stream, to achieve their integration objectives, several observations and recommendations are in order. First, it should be quickly pointed out that a new theoretical and policy orientation should be adopted to inform the way in which cooperation and integration arrangements are conceived and implemented in Africa. Second, following the neo-functionalists David Mitrany's (1966) and Charles McCarthy's (1995; 1999) approaches, we propose that a modest function-based cooperation be seriously considered. Broadly defined, it would be a regional cooperation arrangement which was essentially minimalist and incremental in approach, which did not make unrealistic demands on the institutional, technical and political capacities of participating nation-states. It would seek to concentrate on a few carefully targeted and politically viable development projects or schemes within clearly defined sectors. Among the advantages of this integration strategy are its flexibility and pragmatism in circumventing the problems posed by nationalism, and equity in the distribution of costs and benefits. It is also better suited to deal with the many fiscal, physical and technological barriers to trade that cannot be addressed single handedly by trade policy.

In this regard, the initial cooperation and integration projects to be considered in various sub-regions should include cooperation in the development of transport and communications infrastructure and electricity generation and distribution, the development and management of water resources, and cooperation in the provision of educational and research facilities. Many of these products and services require high-cost and indivisible investments and are likely to have lower unit costs when provided on a regional rather than a national scale. The targeted nature of this approach also serves as a practical means of inducing the cooperation, and thereby neutralizing the demands of domestic interest groups, and is suited to the creation of the infrastructure and production capacity necessary for growth and intra-regional trade, as well as successful entry into world markets. As cooperation proceeds and deepens, member-states' conception and evaluation of sovereignty is expected to change gradually and policy makers will feel less encumbered when making decisions in more controversial areas of high politics; this will almost inevitably contribute to a redefinition of regional identity apart from narrow national identities (Hurrell, 1995).

Closely related to the above argument is the idea that a program of credible but gradual state-guided liberalization that lasts for several years, if not decades, is likely to ease the economic transition by allowing less efficient regional and national enterprises and firms the time to become more competitive. Other interventions, such as transfer payments and broad-based social insurance, could compensate for the lower wages and the flexibility required for relatively backward economies to be competitive in international markets. Transfer payments to losers are likely to enable states to craft imaginative coalitions for growth-promoting reforms, and compensatory social spending is likely to ameliorate the costs of reform. Ultimately, social policies of deliberate redistribution have the potential to lessen income inequalities and to create poverty reduction (Graham, 1994).

The second essential prerequisite would be for states to transfer a certain degree of national sovereignty to elected supra-national bodies. Sovereignty is likely to be one of the areas of unmitigated dissention. As pointed out earlier, in theory, African states have hitherto claimed to retain total sovereign control of their territories and all aspects of decision-making, and have demonstrated a remarkable unwillingness to cede any part of this authority for the common good of the continent. The Abuja Treaty calls on member-states to relinquish some of their powers to the Union. This implies a willingness to sacrifice some control over national economic policy management that directly affects the populations of the participating countries. Indeed, this is the basic litmus test for genuine political will and commitment to any regional integration effort. The A.U. Constitutive Act remains ambiguous on this important subject. On the one hand, it seeks to defend the national sovereignty of member-states, while on the other, it proposes to appropriate the right to intervene in the internal affairs of member-states. This contradiction, if not properly handled, is likely to haunt future integration efforts in Africa.

In various previous integration attempts in Africa, political leaders jealously guarded their nations' sovereignty and were unwilling to transfer any of it to supra-national bodies. As a result, national political agents tended to determine the nature and the pace of their participation in the integration project. The transfer of some powers will not only provide sub-regional secretariats with the necessary legitimacy but, most importantly, will vest in these institutions the necessary authority to make tough policy decisions and to enforce coordinated action in critical areas of national policy management. These shifts in decision-making do not necessarily imply erosion of existing state power and authority. Rather, what will have changed is the way in which states use their power and authority; decision-making will be made in coordination with other member-states. Moreover, the transfer of authority to elected supra-national bodies will enhance their ability to plan, strategize, coordinate, monitor and evaluate the implementation of collective programs. In this context, sovereignty need no longer be thought of as a zero-sum game. Pooling it does not reduce sovereignty. Rather, the trade-offs of pooling sovereignty include security and stability, reduced anxiety and conflict, reduced military spending, and enhanced economic and technological cooperation (Rugumamu, 1999a; 2001b).

In the same spirit, the power of supra-national bodies to make policies, and design and supervise their implementation would require full support and compliance by the broad political, economic and social forces in each member-state. Ideally, the will and commitment to integration endeavors are affected, in the first instance, by expectations of gains and losses that member-states perceive would be derived from participation. If one of the main objectives of integration is balanced growth within the region, then efforts should be made to ensure that this objective is promoted and sustained at all cost. The Economic Community of West Africa (CEAO) seems to have done relatively better than most regional schemes precisely because the two relatively prosperous members, Côte d'Ivoire and Senegal, have been willing to shoulder a large compensatory burden. SACU, in turn, can credit its longevity as a customs union of unequal partners to compensatory payments that South Africa makes to smaller members of the Union (McCarthy, 1999:25). In short, the imperative of political will would constitute another important test of commitment to an integration project.[31]

Most successful regional cooperation and collective security initiatives in the world have thrived on the strong and willing leadership that Robert Keohane (1980), Charles Kindleberger (1981) and Robert Gilpin (1981) elegantly describe as 'the theory of hegemonic stability.'[32] Hegemony is a condition of dominance without resort to coercion, due to the dependence of the subordinate actors in the sub-system on the fortunes of the hegemon. As pointed out in Chapter One, a hegemonic dispensation is functionally necessary to institute and provide 'international collective goods' that make the international economy work better. The Dutch were hegemonic in the

European world economy of the 17th century. The British rose to hegemony in the 19th century, and the United States and the former Soviet Union emerged as the economic and military powers of the 20th century in the West and East blocs respectively. As a practical matter, equity among sovereign entities has always been a convenient international relations fiction. It has never been backed by reality because some powers have always been more dominant than others and, therefore, have been explicitly or implicitly charged with the responsibility of enforcing the agreed-upon norms of international behavior.

The theory posits that the leader or hegemon facilitates international cooperation and prevents defection from the rules of the dominant regime through the use of side payments, sanctions and/or other means, but can seldom, if ever, coerce reluctant states to obey the rules, norms and regulations of the regime. The presence of a regional nucleus has the capacity to serve as a positive force for developing and nurturing a viable economic cooperation arrangement, as well as for building a regional peace and security system. In order to lead, other member countries in the region would have, at a minimum, to accept such a benign hegemony and put sufficient effort into regionalization activities to gradually increase their own power and influence. As a maximum, benevolent leaders are expected to assume a disproportionate cost burden from the integration project, as well as to serve as paragons of compliance with the regime's rules, norms and procedures. It is not unusual in integration schemes to tax the wealthier member-states in order to aid the poorer. The hegemonic leader's economic strength and political stability, for example, would bolster the region's economic vitality and political stability. It should also champion the cause of cooperation and integration by pulling the less willing and the less able countries along, as it may not be possible for all countries to move at the same time and pace (Keohane, 1980).

The role of the United States in NAFTA, the emerging role of Germany in the European Union, and that of the Republic of South Africa in the Southern African Customs Union are excellent contemporary examples of hegemonic stability. In a much quoted study by Mancur Olson (1985), it is concluded that "thus the world works better when there is a hegemonic power - one that finds it in its own interest to see that various international collective goods are provided." Indeed, effective international regimes tend to rest on a political and economic base established through a strong and effective leadership that can persuade, induce, or force other countries to to behave in a given manner with the threat of consequences if they do not open up their economies.

While democratic and politically stable South Africa, Nigeria, Egypt and, possibly, Kenya have the capacity to play this strategic role in their respective sub-regions, the dominant position should be utilized in a constructive and benevolent way and guided by a long-term perspective, rather than merely short-sighted, national self-interest. By almost every measure, South Africa is the indisputable economic and military power in the Southern African sub-region, and will remain so for the foreseeable future. Its GDP was $130 billion in 1998. Its economy accounts for about three-quarters of the region's GDP and an estimated 57 percent if one includes the Common Market for Eastern and Southern Africa. The Zimbabwean economy, which comes in a distant second, was only $6 billion (Africa Confidential, 1995:7). With the fall of the apartheid system, commercial competitiveness has replaced its pariah destabilization campaigns. As a result, its shipping, port management, railways, road transporters, forwarding agents and air companies have further strengthened their dominant position in the region. As with the question of economic might, so with issues related to military superiority. The Republic of South Africa has no challenger in the region. It enjoys a marked supremacy on almost all counts: artillery, infantry, armored fighting vehicles, jet combat aircraft, helicopters and major warships. At least at the level of rhetoric, the present African National Congress government of South Africa has committed itself to linking its country's future to the future of the region as a whole. For a while, that is a reassuring posture.

Just as in the Southern African region, the role of Nigeria cannot be underestimated or ignored if one is to understand regionalization processes in West Africa. The economic and resource dominance of Nigeria is important in understanding the political economy of West Africa. It is by far the most populous country in Africa. With an estimated population of 126 million inhabitants, it dwarfs every other country in the region. Along with South Africa, Nigeria is a focal point of American foreign policy in sub-Saharan Africa. Moreover, its economic potential goes hand-in-hand with its population weight. Its GDP of roughly $30 billion is equivalent to more than half of the GDP of the West African region as a whole. Its industrial and military sectors are by far the largest and the most diversified. In terms of regional security, Nigeria has played an unparalleled role in finding solutions to internal conflicts in countries such as Liberia and Sierra Leone. Its banking and financial system is the most developed and its infrastructural base is the most extensive in the region. Nigeria has frequently sought to shape the region in order to suit its interests, but France and its Francophone allies have often counteracted it indirectly. However, with the end of the Cold

War and the gradual withdrawal of France from Africa, Nigeria, like South Africa, is likely to play a more decisive hegemonic role in its region. Egypt and Kenya display similar superiority in their respective sub-regions. The African Union should consider aggressively promoting the role of these potential hegemons in eachs sub-region.

Likewise, most of the arguments behind the failure of most previous integration schemes in Africa lie in both the scarcity of resources to finance projects and integration programs and in over-dependence on financial support from the donor community. At the same time, member-states were not always in a position to honor their obligations, given their fragile financial positions and their political will. Consequently, in the absence of adequate foreign investment, too much dependence on foreign aid rendered integration projects and programs unsustainable over time. In order to resolve the chronic financing problem, African economies will have to increase their levels of domestic savings and develop innovative capacities for domestic resource mobilization. Besides various forced savings schemes, governments must devise strategies to stop capital flight from the continent. For countries such as Nigeria and the DRC, with several tens of billions of dollars in private foreign bank accounts, any program that attracts back a significant portion of these funds could unleash the required momentum for growth in some sectors (Mkandawire and Soludo, 1999:115-116). Moreover, African economies will have to devise and operate innovative self-financing mechanisms as well as upgrade the capabilities of national and regional financial institutions. In this regard, in 1996, UEMOA presented its member-states with tax options and the formalization of revenue transfer to REC coffers. Surely, this is an exemplary practice.

In the same spirit, regional and sub-regional financial institutions, such as the African Development Bank, the African Development Fund and the Nigerian Trust Fund, will have to be strengthened and equipped in order to play a catalytic role in the mobilization of resources from the private sector, as well as from bilateral and multilateral development institutions. They should be scrupulous and publicly owned development finance institutions with tough financial sector regulations that would allow for effective circulation and reinvestment of the continent's financial resources. Admittedly, their previous combined record in promoting regional integration is not unblemished. Although the Statutes of the African Development Bank clearly define regional economic integration as one of its major functions, resources devoted to regional integration projects have not been rising in line with total loan commitments over the years(Otieno, 1990: 72-73).[33] As a practical and strategic concern, it should be emphasized that no serious national development endeavors, or indeed any integration programs in Africa should entertain excessive dependence on foreign assistance. These continental institutions should be the principal sources of development finance. As Ibbo Mandaza has counseled, a united Africa should develop a capacity to translate donor aid into programs and projects for self-reliant development, notwithstanding the dominance of international capital (Mandaza, 1990:151).

Ideally, these regional financial institutions should not only provide core development financing but, most importantly, serve as centers of excellence in offering development policy advice and technical assistance. Their research departments should respond to the policy management needs of the continent. They should, for instance, assist national and sub-regional economies to put in place sound macroeconomic policies. Through policy dialogue, the African Development Bank has succeeded recently in persuading most African countries to become members of the convention establishing multilateral investment guarantees (MIGA) and the Convention on the Settlement of Investment Disputes between states and nationals of other states. Moreover, on the basis of African Development Bank (ADB) advice, many African countries have established investment promotion agencies to combat their bad images as well as to facilitate investment. In the SADC sub-region, for example, all fourteen member-states have established such agencies. In addition investment promotion agencies from 25 African countries have joined the World Association of Investment Promotion Agencies (WAIPA) since 1995, in order to benefit from an exchange of information on best practices in investment promotion (ADB, 2000).

The prospects of easing the problems of financing regional programs have recently brightened through the adoption of new and flexible policies by the European Commission as well as by other bilateral and multilateral donors and creditors. Since the publication of its study, *Sub-Saharan Africa: From Crisis to Sustainable Development,* the World Bank (1987) has consistently emphasized regional cooperation and integration and shown greater interest in supporting regional integration projects. The E.U. is currently providing financial and technical assistance to RECs. This policy change reflects the changing views about regional integration:

> The objectives of the European Union, its view of development and the role of cooperation, will shape not only the content of the new agreement or agreements but also their geographic configuration. The creation of political and economic areas, which go beyond national boundaries, has been recognized as a necessary step for Europe and is so for the ACP states as well. The path of regional cooperation and integration seems

advisable not only because of the generally inadequate economic size of many ACP countries but also because such an option can encourage political leaders to adopt a more strategic approach to developing their economies. It is also likely to speed up socio-economic transformations, which are needed to develop a market economy and do away with clientelist structures often organized on a national basis (EC, 1997:26).

Of equal importance, in order to make Africans the genuine actors in the process of cooperation and integration and in order to facilitate cross-border dialogue toward the attainment of the pan-African ideal, the Abuja Treaty calls for the participation of the private sector and civil society. As pointed out earlier, there are important trends towards increased cooperative networking, knowledge and information sharing, joint pooling of resources and problem solving among a great variety of market and civil society actors engaged in regional cooperation efforts. These include informal cross-border traders and financiers, NGOs, think-tanks, social movements in important issue areas such as economic justice, debt cancellation, the environment, health and HIV/AIDS, as well as human rights activists and, not least, vibrant regional research and education networks. Promoting effective participation of such civil society organizations will be the most important way to build a broader base of support for regionalism. The fidelity with which each stakeholder represents the views and interests of its constituency will increase the effectiveness of the policy process as well as enhancing the consultation norm. Unquestionably, the process of cooperation and integration is too important to be left to state bureaucrats alone. This is what is meant by popular participation of the governed and public accountability of those in government. The people must not be taken as an unthinking bunch who, like minors, have to have their decisions made by on the behalf those in authority. The leaders for their part should be both responsible and responsive to the led.

By the same token, major cooperation and integration policies should be debated and discussed in various forums. This will necessitate the creation of new political and economic institutions to represent social interests operating on the regional level, thus going beyond the inter-state mechanisms that are in place now. To this end, African states may consider engaging the media to increase awareness of the African cooperation and integration project. In addition, in support of S. Asante, it would serve a good purpose to introduce a course on regional integration in all schools and universities in member countries, as well as to teach Kiswahili, Arabic, English, French Portuguese and other major regional African languages. All these efforts would help create a long-lasting intellectual foundation for the movement toward African unity among young people (Asante, 1990:132-133).

Several empirical studies have shown that countries that have a similar of gross national product and similar structures of manufacturing tend to be one another's best customers (Wannacott and Lutz, 1989; Maasdorp, 1992). This conclusion broadly reinforces the conventional view that economic integration has the best prospects if it occurs among countries which are at similar levels of industrial development, have competitive industrial sectors and have the potential to develop complementary industrial sectors. In most state-led African integration schemes, member-states differ widely in terms of size and capabilities. Understandably, they demonstrate dissimilar abilities to take advantage of specialization, economies of scale, augmentation of factor inputs and opportunities to improve market structures. Economic integration, then, tends to yield unequal costs and benefits for different member-states. F. Foroutan (1992) describes economic differences among sub-Saharan African countries as the major obstacle to achieving trade and factor market integration. These economic differences, he argues, cause concern that the benefits of integration will gravitate toward those countries whose manufacturing sectors are relatively more developed: e.g. Kenya, Mauritius and Zimbabwe in COMESA; South Africa and Zimbabwe in SADC; Côte d'Ivoire, Ghana and Senegal in ECOWAS; and Cameroon in ECCAS. These concerns have given rise to two phenomena: compensation schemes and selective liberalization schemes.

It is necessary to emphasize, because it is often overlooked, that one of the major causes of polarization in the defunct East African Community was the disproportionate sharing of benefits from the cooperation project. It will be important to ensure that during the process of strengthening RECs, deliberate and corrective policies and mechanisms are designed to promote equitable and balanced development. A number of devices to check and redress significant unequal access to benefits are available in the regional integration literature.[34] The choice may be between income transfers and instruments that seek to effect a change in the emergent patterns of trade, and development which income transfers may not address. Under the latter option, there is a choice between instruments that principally rely on the market, and instruments that rely on deliberate, planned rationalization of industrial development. In each case, the chief objective is to bring about profitable specialization, subject to the requirements of balanced development (Robson, 1983:20-21). Once again, the role of sub-regional leaders comes to the fore. They would be expected to shoulder a heavier burden of the cooperation and integration enterprise.

To be successful, African sub-regional and regional integration arrangements need to embrace a knowledge-based development strategy. In a knowledge-based economy, the prevailing cultural, social, economic, political and institutional conditions favor the generation and dissemination of knowledge and its systematic interaction with technological innovation. Together, these linked factors would provide the foundations for economic growth in a highly competitive global economy (Thomas, 1994; Mytelka, 1994; 1999). In the first place, both Clive Thomas and Lynn Mytelka recognize the fact that, if what is nationally and regionally produced is not only to satisfy local demand but also to serve as a basis for exports, then the continuous technological upgrading of the production and quality of export services is mandatory. Enhanced productivity, particularly in agriculture, would be the only means of raising economy-wide income and welfare levels.

This new development thinking breaks with traditional theory and practice of the promotion of South-South cooperation. It moves away from trade as the mechanism whereby specialization and economies of scale can develop, towards a more dynamic perspective, one in which knowledge, linkage, and flexible structures are fundamental building blocks. In short, the model postulates the active involvement of the state, the private sector and other non-governmental economic actors, in the design and launching of new forms of South-South cooperation. It also advocates policies that foster networking for technological adaptation and innovation among such actors across national boundaries in the South. Such arrangements, it is argued, would give rise to denser networks of user-producer linkages, than existed in the past.within and across national and regional markets. The strategy will first seek to satisfy user demands, and adjust to continuous changes in tastes, prices, and competitive conditions nationally and regionally, and to move on to an international level only much later. This version of regional cooperation and integration would not only create economic benefits for member countries, but would also serve as a credible instrument for enhancing peace and security in the region by multiplying points of interaction among people and groups with similar interests (Rugumamu, 1997:283).

In order to achieve the above objectives, the innovation-driven model of regional cooperation and integration proposes the establishment of a strategic regional partnership in research and development. The model also promotes the sharing and spreading of the costs and risks of technological acquisition, adaptation, innovation and commercialization. It further proposes that, by using national and regional resources, research and development institutions would gradually develop and introduce knowledge-intensive products and processes in all national and regional economic sectors and markets. The model further proposes a dynamic scientific and technological springboard for Africa's future insertion at a competitive point in the world economy. As pointed out earlier, for Africa to make any breakthroughs in this important endeavor, an international campaign must be mounted to ensure that there is fair use of intellectual property rights and fair implementation of TRIPs. This will require that the TRIPs agreement be implemented in a way that enables developing countries to use safeguard provisions that secure access to technologies of overriding national importance. It will also require that commitments under TRIPs, and under other multilateral agreements that seek to promote technology transfer to developing countries in the South, must be enforced by a new and rigorous international regime.

Africa will need to engage the multilateral financial, trade and development institutions as well as regional organizations more proactively than has previously been the case. The continental leadership must not only seek to maintain a strong physical presence in Brussels, Geneva, New York and and Washington D.C., but, equally importantly, must quickly learn how to negotiate and actively lobby for its pressing interests and concerns in the global economy. Recent experience in negotiations on bio-safety, the TRIPs agreement, and the ACP-E.U. agreements show that only a handful of developing countries have the resources and skills to negotiate positions that reflect their vital national interests. Most of them, particularly those from Africa, either do not participate at all or are under-prepared and stretched among too many negotiations. As would be expected, most major global negotiations continue to be driven by a few countries from the North. Their superior economic and institutional resources are abundantly reflected in their overwhelming ability to set the negotiations agenda, as well as to define broad parameters for implementation that are perceived to be favorable from their own point of view (Oxfam, 2002).

Unlike the previous Lomé Conventions, the new partnership agreement signed in the city of Cotonou, Benin, in June, 2000, is flexible and can be reviewed and amended regularly. In this agreement, both parties agree to implement measures for protecting patented products, including those owned by corporations in the E.U. that effectively patent plant and animal extracts. In contrast to the provisions of TRIPs, the references to protecting biodiversity are general in nature and particularly unclear with regard to implementation. This is a clear manifestation of weak negotiating capacity on the part of the South. The ACP should have bargained in such a way as to ensure that it was categorically clear how biodiversity would be protected, with a firm commitment on protection from commercial interests. Moreover, they should have pushed for reforms of the TRIPs agreements to reduce the length and scope of patent protection and to demand the creation of patent-free zones in the least developed countries. Attendant concessionary measures, such as parallel imports, compulsory licensing, and price controls for important drugs would have enhanced access by poor people in the South. National and regional capacities will have to be developed and nurtured in order to undertake more effective and credible negotiations with the North in future.

Regional alliances for researching and disseminating technologies are likely to be effective if they address common regional concerns and pool their expertise and resources. The Association for Strengthening Agricultural Research in Eastern and Central Africa (ASARECA) is an excellent example in this regard. Founded in 1994, the Association seeks to improve the management of national agricultural research systems, increase effective use of scarce resources, utilize economies of scale, and make research more accountable to farmers' needs and market demands. ASARECA also provides a way of channeling support from institutional agricultural research centers, advanced research institutes, the private sector and donors. Pooling expertise has created a critical mass equivalent to 22 scientists working full-time on potatoes, and another 15 scientists working full-time on sweet potatoes. By 1998, this network had released fourteen new varieties of potatoes and sixteen varieties of sweet potatoes that were disease-resistant and tolerant to acidic and marginal soils, with yields three times those of local varieties, and with better post-harvest qualities (Mrema, 2001).

Other analysts earlier advanced similarly compelling arguments in favor of dynamic South-South cooperation and integration arrangements. Amsden (1980) stressed the transfer of appropriate technology through trade between countries at similar levels of development. He also emphasized the economies of scale that permit higher x-efficiency and more innovation. Michael Webb and J. Fackler underscored the argument that countries in the South are more likely to be successful in export markets in which they have lower entry costs. The markets in the South are more similar in business customs, laws and culture than those in the North. Moreover, the quality standards in neighboring markets may be lower than in the markets of industrialized countries. In the final analysis, there may be learning by doing in production, as well as learning to export by doing (Webb and Fackler, 1993).

It is now widely recognized in Africa that, without internal security and domestic stability, it is virtually impossible to guarantee national economic development or sustained inter-state cooperation and integration. The causes of conflict, particularly the intra-state ones, are many and varied. The key causes include: attempts at monopolizing the state and its resources; disputes over territory; lack of openness in the political space; conflicts over unfulfilled expectations in the aftermath of political transitions; fundamentalist religious opposition to secular authority; warfare arising from state degeneration or state collapse; protracted conflict within politicized military forces; and conflict linked to one-party dominance. These conflicts have periodically assumed horrendous proportions, spawning population displacement, refugees and migration. In his 1998 report to the Security Council, the current U.N. Secretary General Kofi Annan lamented Africa's insecurity:

> Since 1970 more than 30 wars have been fought in Africa, the vast majority of them intra-state in origin. In 1996 alone, 14 out of 53 countries in Africa were afflicted by armed conflicts, accounting for more than half of all war-related deaths worldwide and resulting in more than 8 million returnees and displaced persons. The consequences of these conflicts have seriously undermined Africa's efforts to ensure long-term stability, prosperity, and peace for its people…. Preventing such wars is no longer a matter of defending states or protecting allies. It is a matter of defending humanity itself (Annan, 1998).

The challenges facing the A.U. in its current efforts to establish an early warning capability are almost the same as those facing all international organizations. The knowledge of an impending conflict does not always translate into the political will to act. The decision to intervene is more often based on the political calculations of member-states regarding where their greatest national self-interest lies. Thus, the A.U. and the U.N. were unable to mobilize international forces to de-escalate conflicts in Congo Brazzaville and the Comoros even when they had reliable warning signs. In order for early warning to translate into early action, African politics will have to evolve gradually from petty rivalries and divisions to unity on critical matters of regional security (Rugumamu, 2001).

Although most African sub-regional organizations were born out of the need for economic cooperation and integration, in recent times they have assumed the role of security cooperation and conflict management. Thus, through the learning process, more controversial areas have been brought into the field of cooperation and integration. This is what some neo-functionalists have referred to as 'spillover effects' (Caporaso, 1970). The move toward security regionalism is consistent with the post-Cold War concept of shared responsibility between the United Nations and regional organizations. However, as noted earlier, the major powers have been the least prepared to intervene directly in the areas of little security interest to themselves.

The concept of shared responsibility is based on the idea that regional organizations are better able to provide the necessary focus to security crises in their respective regions than is the United Nations. The underlying assumptions are that regional and sub-regional organizations are closer to conflicts, and therefore more familiar with the local political and social conditions. In addition, they have a comparative advantage in playing a leading role in the management of such conflicts.[35] Regional economic integration arrangements, such as ECOWAS, SADC and IGAD, have increasingly assumed the role of security cooperation and conflict management. ECOWAS has a Community Standing Mediation Committee that created the ECOWAS Monitoring Group (ECOMOG). ECOWAS peacekeeping initiatives are well known on the continent. The Community gained a good measure of international recognition through its massive peacekeeping efforts in Liberia, Sierra Leone, and Guinea-Bissau (Aning, 1999). Likewise, SADC efforts in peacekeeping and conflict management were deployed in the Democratic Republic of Congo and Lesotho. Emphasizing the need for coordination between the U.N., the then O.A.U. and the various sub-regional organizations, the current U.N. Secretary-General has had occasion to note:

> Peacekeeping efforts need to be well coordinated and well prepared...the newly established United Nations liaison office at the OAU headquarters in Addis Ababa will consolidate cooperation between the two organizations and facilitate the coordinated deployment of political efforts to prevent, contain and resolve conflicts in Africa.... Cooperation between the United Nations and the sub-regional organizations such as the Economic Community of West African States, the Southern African Development Community, and the Intergovernmental Authority on Development, which are working actively to address peace and security in their sub-regions, is also being strengthened (Annan, 1998: Para 20).

Both SADC and ECOWAS sub-regional conflict management initiatives have been roundly criticized as hollow structures for conflict resolution in Africa. They have been accused of lacking properly institutionalized crisis prevention and management structures, as well as integrated systems, processes and methods to deal with the broader issues of democracy and human rights. More specifically, the initiatives are criticized for being predominantly military in nature, lacking neutrality, and for virtually failing to involve non-state actors. Above all, sub-regional military interventions are faulted for being essentially *ad hoc* and not in compliance with specific operating rules and procedures (Malan, 1999; Aning, 1999; Hutchful, 1999). Despite these and other glaring practical shortcomings, such initiatives are the new mode of regionally-based peacekeeping operations. They should be strongly supported because organizations take time to grow and mature and they need all the political support that can be mustered if they are to endure. In order to properly restructure, strengthen and equip these organizations, broadly based debates should be initiated in each sub-region to define its security threats and propose strategies for how best to manage them. A consensus on the types and nature of the national and regional threats to peace and security should be sought in order to arrive at the right mix of policies, strategies and institutional mechanisms for confronting them. It would be prudent for a realistic collective security program to start from a modest agenda that would be enlarged and strengthened over time. Such a strategy could prevent over-zealous politicians from chasing inappropriate and largely illusory goals.

It should be emphasized that, as important as regional and sub-regional collective security is, nation-states remain the basic building blocks and decision-making *loci* for multinational economic and security regimes. International cooperation requires that individual member countries command a critical minimum of institutional, economic and social coherence. Indeed, as Barry Buzan argues, without strong, efficient and responsive states, there will be no security, national or otherwise (Buzan, 1991). This apocalyptic view is consonant with Leslie Brown's often quoted assertion that "aggregating weakness does not lead to collective strength" (Brown, 1986). Africa's security arrangements are, to say the least, an aggregation of weakness. As noted earlier, state formation and state building in Africa have not, on the whole, produced robust foundations on which to construct larger security and economic arrangements. This important observation speaks eloquently to the urgency of mobilizing efforts toward 'bringing the state back in' in order to preside over national policy management as well as democratic renewal and consolidation.

Finally, for durable and sustainable peace, stability and development to flourish in Africa, state building and democratic governance should be brought to the center stage of continental politics and international relations. Africa's national and sub-regional politics should begin to be rooted in a process of pluralism and popular participation. This basic yet cardinal democratic prerequisite demands that governments not only be legitimate, but also have the authority and capacity to rule. Most importantly, such governments can be expected to promote respect for all basic freedoms and to create the necessary conditions for durable and sustainable peace and security. As Eboe Hutchful (1999:81) has insightfully concluded, "without acceptable standards of governance in the region...a regional security mechanism is liable to degenerate into a protection racket for autocrats." In this very sense, therefore, the ongoing debates about economic, social and political restructuring at all levels in Africa deserve everyone's strong support.

Viability of the Scenario

Under the current circumstances, this is a preferred scenario for Africa, yet it is the least likely to come about in the short or medium term. This is precisely because the objective conditions necessary for the implementation and realization of a genuine cooperation and integration project are largely non-existent. It is one thing for African leaders to agree on the virtues of implementing continental economic cooperation and integration and quite another to live by those commitments. First, the requisite national and regional forces to propel Africa's social transformation in a sustained way are evidently lacking. As Scenario One has projected, in the short and medium term, grandiose visions of Africa's future will seem to be far-fetched at best, and diversionary at worst. As long as peace, security and democratic governance continue to elude most countries on the continent, the visions of economic transformation and political renaissance will remain empty slogans. The persistence of violent national civil strife will continue to systematically divert scarce national resources and political goodwill away from real human development efforts to senseless wars and destruction. The ambitious visions and programs of the Abuja Treaty, the African Union, or NEPAD will soon be dropped from popular discourse. Democratically functioning and dynamic national economies are a necessary condition for any effective integration schemes. In the foreseeable future, instead of coordinating and harmonizing national and regional development and security policies and programs, most African states and societies will be embroiled in the politics and economics of survival. Thus, a common and shared vision and ideology for mutually beneficial regional development will fail to evolve and take root.

Second, the new visions of development from Africa are, to say the least, a prescription for disaster. In fact, they sound very much like 'home-grown' collective structural adjustment programs. They continue to be trapped in the same neo-liberal development policies, which, as this study has demonstrated, are largely responsible for the continent's underdevelopment, poverty, eco-destruction and powerlessness. The new visions essentially fail to interrogate the systemic logic of the world economy, asymmetrical power relations, and rules and institutions that are rigged in favor of the strong. Viewed retrospectively and strategically, in the short and medium term, these new development visions should have proposed, among critical issues, the democratization of global governance and removal of the powers of veto of the Bretton Woods institutions over microeconomic policy. They should also have endorsed the principle of full debt cancellation; the right for Africa to develop its ability to trade by protecting key sectors, promoting diversification and regulating predatory business practices of TNCs; termination of tariff escalation that prevents Africa from processing its raw materials; an agreement on a timetable to phase out subsidies that result in dumping of agricultural products; and an agreement to support development with substantially more and untied resources.

In the long run, as capitalism continues to generate injustice and instability, grassroots movements will seek a series of structural reforms whose cumulative effect would be to transform radically, not to simply reform global capitalism. This will be the basis for articulating truely new visions for Africa or radically improving on the visions discussed earlier. Once again, the African leadership has squandered a golden opportunity to engage the people and the international community in programmatic visions that seek to decisively break with the exploitative, repressive, and oppressive past, and to embrace rights-based, democratic, and equitable development (Callinicos, 2001:124-125; Bond and Manyanya, 2002:187). Not surprisingly, Scenario One, which predicts doom and gloom, immediately comes to mind.

Third, as Terry Boswell and Christopher Chase-Dunn (2000:1999) have counseled, the central question for any strategy of transformation is one of agency. Who are the actors who will most vigorously and effectively lead and defend the struggle for emancipation? The assumption that there is sufficient political will and committed leadership to undertake an ambitious rebirth of the continent, political renewal and economic regeneration in Africa has, for too long, been inadequately problematized. If the experience of the last 40 years of independence is any guide, the predatory and undemocratic ruling elite in most of Africa is ill-positioned to provide the requisite political leadership. They have amply demonstrated that they lack the capacity to establish legitimacy, democratic or economic governance, and have failed to secure security and peace for their citizens. Can the ruling class commit political suicide? Is there any possibility that it can reinvent itself? It is also highly doubtful that the proposed NEPAD's Political Peer Review Mechanism will have sufficient teeth to tame the undemocratic and predatory character of the majority of states in Africa.

The challenges of reviving and transforming African political economies are not only about getting the local, national and regional socio-economic policies and institutions right, but, most significantly, seeking to radically change its relations with the industrialized economies of the North. To be sure, the current uncritical preoccupation with multilateral institutions is unlikely to alter asymmetrical North-South relations or to structure productive and enlightened development cooperation. The present and past blueprints for cooperation, namely, the United Nations New Agenda for the Development of Africa, the Millennium Summit Goals, the Afro-Euro Summit's Cairo Plan of Action, the World Bank's Strategic Partnership, the Monterrey Consensus on Financing for Development, and the IMF's Poverty Reduction Strategy Papers, have had negligible impact on the structure of North-South relations. Unless both the North and South collectively negotiate and implement realistic but radical changes in the global economic and political governance framework, Africa will not stand any significant chance of achieving structural stability, economic growth or sustainable development. Ultimately, the fundamental challenge of development squarely remains in the hands of the entire global community.

CHAPTER 5

CONCLUSION: STRUCTURAL STABILITY, INTEGRATION AND SUSTAINABLE DEVELOPMENT

Introduction: In Search of an Alternative Development Strategy

... For all its advances, it [globalization] still reflects a haughty disregard for the rest of the world. There is no talk about negotiation with the poorer countries, no talk about finding a fairer voice for those countries in the new international system. The rest of the world is called on to support the G-7 declarations, but not to meet for joint problem-solving...Until the poor are brought into the international financial system with real power, the global economy cannot be stable for long (Sachs, 1998).

The foregoing discussion of three projections of Africa's future has important implications for the continent's policy choices, institutional arrangements and development strategies. While there are a few notable exceptions, both states and markets in most of Africa have failed to provide jobs, basic social services or personal security for their citizens. Such deprivation has had social consequences as some of the marginalized and excluded have turned to crime, drugs or violence. In this regard, whichever development scenario is selected, the continent's position in the world system in the short and medium term is likely to deteriorate further from its present precarious state. The initial prospects for economic growth and political stability will be slow, unstable, and at times regressive; international trade will exhibit both product and partner concentration and the terms of trade are likely to worsen. The debt situation will deteriorate and the incidence and depth of poverty will rise, largely due to HIV/AIDS; and, in the absence of affordable medicine and healthcare, other deadly diseases will spread.

Africa's policy challenges are considerably more complex than the simple question as to whether to open up its economies or not. It has been argued repeatedly that innovative policy and institutional responses to Africa's continuing marginalization, exclusion and alienation need to be sought. The off-the-shelf 'best practices, policies or institutions' from the Bretton Woods institutions will have limited import. To be sure, the African people have always proved their adaptability and creativity and there are some promising signs as well as much hope for a better future. Contrary to Francis Fukuyama's widely publicized contention that liberal capitalism represents the end of history, we argue that the struggles by the marginalized and excluded from below are providing the fundamental motor to challenge the obscene patterns of world poverty and inequality amidst the ostentatious wealth within each bloc of the triad. Neo-liberalism has increasingly become a target of anti-establishment wrath for every popular social movement around the world pursuing democracy, social justice and equity.

Democratic and popular grassroots social movements have begun setting the stage for a new world order. Efforts are being made to weaken, challenge and roll back the conceptual framework that informs the fundamentalist neo-liberal philosophy. There is greater recognition that most of the poorest countries are trapped in a vicious cycle of stagnation and poverty, and are unable to benefit from globalization. Macroeconomic stabilization, together with the opening of the economies of the poorest countries to the rest of the world and freeing markets from government interference, has not resulted in economic growth or sustainable development. These movements are not only expressing dissent, but they are also providing some basis for developmental and democratic alternatives to the system that is currently in place. They are struggling to establish a world order that seeks to promote a value system that places people above profits in the development process, and where capital is a means rather than the end. It is also a world order that seeks to promote the principle of the right of peoples to self-determination in all its dimensions, internal as well as external, political as well as economic, social and cultural, and based on the principles of democracy, justice and equality.

In short, this is a people-centered development strategy. It seeks major modifications in the social, political and economic rationale that drives the current pattern of economic and political development. Such a strategy should be based primarily on the needs and demands of the people, fulfilled through participatory approaches to development. It encompasses the democratization of control, ownership and management of productive assets and resources, so that these processes are directed and driven by truly democratic people's institutions both nationally and internationally (Khotari, 1984).

As pointed out earlier, there are various anti-systemic world movements against globalization. The opposition is uneven among countries and within countries. What distinguishes the level and intensity of these struggles are different degrees of political consciousness and traditions of struggle, and the nature and character of the leadership. In the industrial countries of the North, workers have been mobilized against plant relocations, cuts in pensions and health plans, and increases in job insecurity. In the South, workers and peasants are being mobilized against low prices for primary commodities and services, low wages, harsh working conditions, exorbitant prices for imports and retrenchment from civil service jobs. Free trade policies and subsidies to agricultural producers in the North have led to the devastation of peasant producers in the South and have radicalized peasants and landless rural workers. Peasants in Africa are withdrawing from traditional cash crop production for export, to the production of food for domestic use and exchange (Hyden, 1980; Cheru, 1989; 2002).

Already, there are emerging trends toward increased cooperation, networking, knowledge and information sharing among national, regional and global NGOs, think-tanks and social movements in important issue areas. These include economic justice, debt, the environment and human rights, to mention only a few. The rise in transnational civil society campaigns has accompanied the emergence of new multi-stakeholder processes as an important feature of global power and decision-making. The openings for progressive politics have widened worldwide and their cumulative effects are weighing heavily on every state and on the capitalist world system as a whole. In April 1998, for example, the Organization for Economic Cooperation and Development (OECD) was forced by the global coalition of civil society movements to abandon negotiations on the Multilateral Agreement on Investment (MAI). This stillborn agreement was a system of rules worked out between the industrial countries, using their own grouping, the OECD. The proposed rules would have allowed investing corporations to sue a host government if they were discriminated against. The proposed rules also outlawed requirements that corporations use local suppliers, restricted the practice of hiring a minimum number of local employees, combated any local rules restricting foreign ownership of media or utility companies, and removed restrictions on investors' ability to move money across borders. In short, MAI would have gone a long way toward eroding the capacity and autonomy of states, particularly those in Africa.[36]

It has been emphasized that, at a strategic level, the alliances among social movements will coalesce around the specific issue areas that would facilitate institution building, such as the environment, a global living wage, debt, gender equality and global good governance. In order for anti-systemic movements and forces against capitalist polarization to develop and succeed, various institutional arrangements, norms and processes should be put in place and strengthened. Strategically, it was pointed out that major actors would have to have a full and informed grasp of the complexity of the objective conditions, both internal and external, that determine the context of any policy, strategy or institutional choices. It is to these prerequisites that we now turn.

The Imperative of National and Regional Integration

It is important to define the elements of an alternative development vision that is capable of uniting the struggles on a national level, where competing political choices and strategies are on the table. Chapter Four has demonstrated that the process of globalization and liberalization poses multifarious challenges, while also offering various opportunities. Globalization is forcing countries to liberalize, deregulate and privatize their economies, while at the same time promoting organization of production across national borders. Both tendencies have the effect of vertically integrating weak economies into the dominant structures of the global economy, thus making it doubly difficult to integrate nationally or regionally. The ability to successfully manage the challenges posed by globalization will be a critical aspect of national and regional policy-making in the years ahead. It was also noted that, given Africa's economic realities, a single-minded pursuit of World Bank/IMF structural adjustment policies and export-oriented development strategies has doubtful potential for economic transformation during the time of declining rates of investment, negative terms of trade and aid, and of debt overhang. The low or declining demand for traditional commodities means that such policies cannot serve as the engine for Africa's development in the coming years. Nor can the emerging non-traditional exports, such as flowers, fruit and vegetables generate sustainable economic development. Marginal and disjointed incremental changes in the skewed national and global economic and political power structures are not likely to make any dent in the poverty, underdevelopment, powerlessness, or marginalization that haunts much of Africa.

The challenges posed to African economies and societies by globalization and liberalization require more than reactive, short-term adjustments to the consequences of capitalist marginalization. New and imaginative visions, long-term policies and predictable institutions in Africa will have to be developed and nurtured. It is our hope that as vibrant cross-sectional debates on alternative futures become generalized, we will see democratic, emancipatory, and broad-based development policies, institutions and strategies emerge and take root.

Debates about possible futures for Africa will unleash a genuine struggle for popular democracy. The process of reconstituting the new African state will, of necessity, require a new and more committed leadership to preside over a genuine democratic agenda for development. At its core, the new agenda will seek to deconstruct the repressive and inefficient neo-colonial state, since as it will seek to open up national and regional political systems and create popular and democratic structures and processes that will guarantee basic freedoms and empower the people and their communities. In this regard, the people themselves will be forced to take difficult and deliberate strategic decisions on how best to promote rapid, equitable and sustainable development. The struggle should seek to totally reject foreign-crafted and imposed development policies. One of the fundamental imperatives of an alternative development strategy for Africa is to reclaim the state as well as ownership and autonomy in policy management. In this regard, therefore, national ownership essentially means that development policies, institutions and strategies are democratically negotiated, formulated and collectively implemented, rather than being driven by donor governments or imposed by the IMF, World Bank, or WTO.

In the process of executing people-centered development, sovereign peoples have an inalienable right to make mistaken policy decisions and to be accountable for such decisions. It is their right to debate and articulate national development perspectives based on their own history, experience and goals. It is this right that consolidates the culture of internal policy debates that is essential for building popular consent. Ultimately, policy ownership will be essential for reorienting national and regional policies in order to deal with the concrete structural conditions that characterize Africa's underdevelopment, marginalization and poverty. As K.Y. Amoako (the Executive Secretary of the Economic Commission for Africa) has observed, "the lessons of the failure of past initiatives point to an experience which shows that Africans must lead Africa out of poverty, and that the most effective policies and programs are those based on domestic processes of consultation and decision-making" (Amoako, 2001:4). For this to happen, a new and enlightened leadership will have to emerge at every level and take over the struggle for a new agenda. These observations have been borne out by recent findings showing a significant positive correlation between ownership of policy reforms and development outcomes in Africa. It was found that ownership does matter, because it directly affects a development program's acceptance and implementation at national and local level. Domestic ownership generates political support and buy-in by relevant stakeholders, who are more likely to view the initiative as a worthy indigenous one, rather than dismissing it as a foreign imposition (Gray and McPherson, 2001; Tsikata, 2001). The basic way in which national ownership could be strengthened and consolidated is by imploring international financial institutions and donor agencies to step back from policy formulation processes and not impose what they consider to be the 'right policy choices' for Africa.

In order to correct national fragmentation, underdevelopment and marginalization, people-centered and people-driven development seeks to place the general population at the core of its national, regional and global accumulation strategy. This agenda places the general satisfaction of human needs before the pursuit of profit, and the extension of democratic control of governing institutions ahead of the extension of private power that is central to neo-liberal global governance. It also seeks to strike a balance between personal initiative and the pursuit of collective goals. In this vein, Clive Thomas (1974) advances two famous 'iron laws of transformation.' One of the laws refers to the necessity of planning for a convergence of consumption patterns with the social needs of the majority of the population. The other is the planned convergence of consumption patterns with domestic output, based principally on the use of domestic resources. Under this strategy, which Samir Amin (1990) aptly refers to as 'autocentric development,' social needs replace external demand structures as the primary engine of the national accumulation process. The ultimate objective of development becomes the enhancement of the material and spiritual well-being and dignity of each and every member of society.

If the strategy of socio-economic transformation is a planned convergence of domestic resource use and demand, then the first point of investigation of a long-term sustainable development strategy must be to carefully establish what constitutes the major resource content of demand, and what scope there is for matching this demand to the economy's resource configuration. In this sense, since agriculture is the backbone of most African economies, and since food and food security is at the core of their basic daily livelihood, then, logically, the national development policy should concentrate its attention and resources on this critical sector in order to encourage and promote technical innovation, protect it from cheap imports, and provide infrastructure, education and an institutional framework to regulate transparent economic transactions. Samir Amin (1992) writes that, because Africa has not experienced an agricultural revolution characterized by sustained agricultural growth and an increase in food production per capita, economic transformation has remained elusive. The basic precondition for effective development is the modernization and intensification of agriculture. It is also a necessary condition for industrialization, urbanization, and social development. Therefore, the progressive expansion of opportunities to the rural poor and their dynamic integration into the national economy should go side by side with the imperative of diversifying the production structure of national economies. There should be a gradual and systematic shift from dependence on traditional primary commodity exports toward a competitive manufacturing sector geared to domestic and regional markets, with a view to achieving industrialization and a sustainable balance of payments status. As pointed out earlier, the objective of this strategy is first to satisfy the basic needs of the majority of the people. Unlike the orthodox thinking on industrialization, the role of the state in this endeavor will be paramount. Some protection and subsidization of the infant industries will be required initially before exposing them to international competition. As S. Dell counsels:

> There is no single industrial country that did not employ vigorous protection at some stage in its history. Among the much-applauded newly industrializing countries...the most important have highly regulated economies. Even so highly an industrialized country as Japan, the miracle economy of the century, continues to this day to protect its industrial development in a variety of ways. While Japan is under great pressure to dismantle this protection, the important lesson of Japan to developing countries and for the Fund is that properly managed protection, so far from being an obstacle to growth, is an indispensable instrument in protecting growth (Dell, 1982:602).

In Scenario Two, we emphasized the need to create economic spaces in which states can play an active and leading role. As emphasized earlier, the role of the state figures prominently in historical and contemporary explanations of European, American and Japanese development experiences, and more recently in the economic success stories of the NICs of South East Asia. States have historically provided not only political but also economic leadership. They have played the role of the great public entrepreneur, educator, and creator and supporter of private business. Alexander Gerchenkron's (1962) classic work on the late industrializing European states established the proposition that the more economically backward a country, the more its economy needed strong state intervention to overcome structural obstacles. The most cited obstacles include mobilization of domestic and foreign resources, identifying potential niches within the global economy, protecting vulnerable sectors from external competition, orchestrating incentives to ensure that domestic firms play their assigned roles, ensuring that entrepreneurs have access to the requisite factors of production, fostering local mastery of foreign and indigenous technologies as well as participating directly in strategic investment where high risks discourage private investors. Contrary to popular assumption and official rhetoric, orthodox liberalism has never been the dominant form of political economy in the North. With the qualified exceptions of the Netherlands and Switzerland, all other major European and American economies made aggressive use of various forms of protectionism and subsidies (Koponen, 2003:211).

Equally importantly, the new and emerging development challenges in Africa urgently call for a reconstituted state. Gone are the days when predatory, repressive and inefficient states could be tolerated. The new development imperatives require not only markedly enhanced institutional, technical and managerial capacities of the state, but also completely reconstituted social and economic institutions with solid democratic credentials. Such institutions should seek to promote human development and safeguard the freedom and dignity of all the people. In Chapter Four, we referred to the evolution and nurturing of developmental states in Africa. This is a democratic state that is devoted to the public interest, including economic security and society's development. It is a state that will muster the will and capacity to mobilize domestic social alliances in order to make and execute difficult egalitarian policy choices, facilitate the development of indigenous production clusters, encourage regional cooperation and integration, and facilitate strategic production links and developmental partnerships with transnational actors – all aimed at building a dynamic investment-export nexus and expanding the pool of national skills.

We have also emphasized the argument that the days of regional integration on a voluntary or casual basis are also long gone. As was noted in Chapter Four, regional cooperation and integration should now be perceived as a continental imperative. Africa's response to the current development crisis calls for the re-conceptualization and revamping of regional economic cooperation and integration within the broader context of a coordinated sub-regional and regional security plan. Not only should the ongoing debates about how best to operationalize and integrate a few useful insights found in the Abuja Treaty, the African Union, and the New Partnership for Africa's Development be supported and debated extensively, but, most importantly, such debates should seek to evolve emancipatory development policy alternatives. As has been pointed out repeatedly, if developed and relatively strong economies like those of the United States, Germany, France and Japan find it necessary to engage in regional economic cooperation and integration and collective security, then the case for African unity must be theoretically and strategically compelling. Economic arguments aside, a united and integrated Africa stands a better chance of responding proactively to the multifaceted challenges posed by globalization than if each individual country goes it alone. A united continental posture is likely to maximize Africa's collective bargaining power *vis-à-vis* other external actors, as well as to minimize the current duplication, divisions and wasteful competition. Arguably, a united Africa will have the capacity, willingness and international acceptance to negotiate smart political and economic bargains with, or to resist unfavorable policy impositions from other regional blocs or multilateral institutions and major countries. It was posited that, under the current inauspicious circumstances, it would be almost impossible to resolve Africa's nagging development problems on an individual basis--problems posed by structural powerlessness, growing poverty, pervasive human insecurity, external debt, unfavorable international trade and environmental degradation.

More than ever before, political and economic solidarity among regional blocs in the South will be critical in the era of economic cooperation and policy coordination. Economic cooperation should include an increase in integrated production and trade, investment, technological transfer and communications links at the bilateral level and between regions. On the issue of policy coordination, countries in the South should emulate the North by spearheading initiatives aimed at creating and strengthening public and private centers of policy research that will provide timely strategic thinking and long-term planning. By the same token, greater collaboration and networking among sub-regional policy research institutions of Africa should be encouraged, especially in information sharing and the coordination of policies and positions.

The Peace and Security Imperative
In Africa, major conflict has visited virtually every country or its immediate neighbor since the mid-1960s. It is worth noting that, in addition to destroying lives and property, violent conflict also assaults social capital, undermining trust and networks. More ominously, violent social conflicts accentuate an environment of uncertainty and direct the energies of states and civil society to the primary task of survival rather than to long-term development

challenges. Prevention, reconciliation, and reconstruction must be the first order of business. As the African Leadership Forum (1991) correctly observes Africa's shattered economies will not be able to recover in the absence of durable and sustainable peace, democracy and political stability. One need not be reminded that sustainable development may be impossible under the conditions currently reigning in Somalia, the Democratic Republic of Congo, Rwanda, Sierra Leone, the Sudan, Rwanda, Burundi, or Liberia. Similarly, Africa's star performing economies – Botswana and Mauritius – both score highly in terms of economic growth, poverty reduction and political freedoms.[37] In Scenario One, we argued that cycles of political violence and instability, as well as economic mismanagement, are inimical to the development of any large-scale regional cooperation and integration, effective participation in international and global affairs, foreign investment, or entrepreneurial dynamism.

The study has noted that underlying most of the contemporary violent conflicts in Africa is the reality that the security threats to the state and the population are less and less external to the continent. If sustainable peace and security in Africa have to be secured and nurtured, then the root causes of conflict must be studied and addressed. At the most fundamental level, the absence of democracy and justice are almost always the principle cause for the absence of peace and security. Systematic discrimination and exclusion, denial of access to public assets and services, extreme poverty concentrated in one group – distinct by ethnicity, religion or region – facilitate conflict by providing more readily available domestic combatants.

Since the beginning of the 1990s, the continent has acquired the dubious honor of being number one in hosting the largest number of armed conflicts and complex emergencies. In fact, intra-state conflicts in Africa can no longer be considered as temporary deviations from a stable national or regional security pattern. They have become a permanent feature. Africa is increasingly becoming a continent of refugees and displaced persons. We saw that while more armed conflicts occurred in Africa than in any other major region of the world, the continent's institutional and organizational capacity to manage them did not develop at a commensurate pace. The various mechanisms and institutions that strengthen the citizens' voice and transparency, such as a free press, elections and participation in politics and in civil society organizations, have been extremely slow to include the disenfranchised, build mandates and generate consensus. Without instituting effective mechanisms for preventing and resolving social conflicts and nurturing democratic practices, Africa cannot hope to realize any of the promises of globalization, however broadly defined.

What can Africa do for itself? Can the African Union and the United Nations achieve a shared vision of mutual partnership, cooperation and coordination in responding to the continent's need for peace, security, emergency relief, reconstruction and development? What complementary role can sub-regional organizations play in the maintenance of peace and stability in their respective regions, and how can they enhance their internal capacity to respond vigorously and pre-emptively to armed conflict? There are no easy and straightforward answers to these questions. Suffice it to say that the ultimate and most effective approach to conflict prevention is the creation and nurturing of fair and democratic societies, where competition over land, resources, and political access and control would become relatively less explosive issues. Resource distribution, for example, is one of the defining features of power relations in any society. Gross inequalities in resource distribution, use, management and development can result in conflict either nationally or internationally. Governments, rebels and even peacekeepers have fought over the control and exploitation of diamonds, gold and timber in several African countries.

The genocide in Rwanda has been largely explained as a resource war between the Hutus and Tutsis. Resources and resource installations, such as rivers or dams, have been used as targets of violence, conflict and war. Moreover, the practice of secret deals between transnational companies and unaccountable governments has been a source of social conflict. To be sure, rich natural resources provide opportunities, but they do not ensure results. They frequently contribute to the opposite, as has been tragically demonstrated by the recent experience in several African countries. If imprudently managed, valuable natural resources may not only trigger wars, but may also sustain them. During the 1980s and 1990s, economically driven conflicts in Angola, Liberia, Sierra Leone, the DRC and the Sudan turned low-intensity conflicts into full-scale war and prolonged terror and violence. Furthermore, as experience has amply demonstrated, if there are no clear political goals, wars over resources are particularly hard to end (Reno, 1995; 2000).

Democratic politics in Africa will require collectively agreed-upon constitutions that provide the broad rules for the political game. It needs to be emphasized that democratically crafted constitutions will be effective only when civil society organizations, together with political parties, are promoted and strengthened critical actors. The emergence of an increasingly vibrant civil society and the incorporation of more women and youth into positions of economic and political power will significantly increase not only the chances for improved resource management and promotion of confidence-building measures, but will also promote the establishment of trust through cooperation. Indeed, such developments would be tangible evidence of an African renaissance. Incidentally, the practice of authoritarian states in Africa to strip citizens of their right to security of life, without receiving condemnation from fellow African states, often condoned under the thin veneer of non-interference in the internal affairs of the state, is increasingly challenged on a global scale. Repressive and predatory regimes worldwide, as well as other human rights violators, are being exposed and held accountable for their actions. In fact, the traditional norms of sovereignty, consent and non-interference in internal affairs are no longer defined in absolute terms. They are being postulated as 'normative concepts of responsibility'. Consequently, national sovereignty now requires a system of governance that is based on democratic citizens' participation, constructive management of social diversity, respect for fundamental human rights, and the equitable distribution of national wealth and opportunities for development (Falk, 1995; Hyden, 1993).

With a broadened conceptualization of sovereignty and the U.N.'s proactive stance on security, African people should put pressure on the international community, particularly the United Nations, to respond immediately to the endless plight of its war-ridden societies without hiding under the cover of national sovereignty. Although the U.N. Charter, Article 2(7) stipulates that it will not intervene in matters that are essentially within the domestic jurisdiction of any state, under Chapter VII of the U.N. Charter, the Security Council has the power to determine what constitutes a "threat to the peace, breach of the peace, and act of aggression; and shall make recommendations, or decide what measures shall be taken…to maintain or restore international peace and security." Such measures, according to Article 42 of the same Charter, may include "…such action by air, sea, or land forces as may be necessary to maintain or restore international peace and security." The decision for any U.N. intervention in conflict ridden countries should be driven by humanitarian considerations, particularly those pertaining to refugees and internally displaced persons – people who can be seen not only as civilian victims of war deserving protection, but also as people who could potentially destabilize neighboring countries and regions. In this regard, the narrowly defined sovereignty behind which predatory states traditionally hid in order to abuse their citizens is no longer internationally tenable (Rugumamu, 2001c).

The Constitutive Act of the African Union has gone a long way toward defining why and when to intervene in the internal affairs of member-states. It allows for intervention without the consent of the target state. Article 4 (h) provides for "the right to intervene in a member state pursuant to a decision of the Assembly in respect of grave circumstances, namely: war crimes, genocide and crimes against humanity." Moreover, Article 4 (j) provides for "the right of member states to request intervention from the Union in order to restore peace and security". Finally, Article 23 (2) provides that "any member-state that fails to comply with the decisions and policies of the Union may be subjected to other sanctions, such as the denial of transport and communications links with other member-states and other measures of a political and economic nature to be determined by the Assembly." Indeed, unlike the O.A.U. Charter, the A.U's Constitutive Act provides for unprecedented powers of intervention. What is critically important is for enlightened African states to rise to the challenge and use the Act to protect their own citizens and their fellow Africans in any part of the continent.

Although a legitimate nostalgia for exclusive sovereignty still lingers in Africa, a new global consensus appears to be crystallizing rapidly (not infrequently motived for the case of the U.S.A. by less than noble reasons) toward a much more broad redefinition of sovereignty. Substantively and institutionally, new ground has been broken. The African continent is under pressure to perform the task of state and nation building democratically. In this regard, the continent needs to marshal all available national, regional and international support in order to facilitate the building and nurturing of politically responsive and administratively effective states. The norms of democratic governance, human rights and nation building should be integrated into all development cooperation arrangements and, most importantly, they should be provided with the requisite political and material support. Of course, simplistic quick fixes would serve little practical purpose.

As noted earlier, the current Security Council's willingness to intervene in inter-communal and civil conflicts has called into question the absolute nature of sovereignty. While almost all states value their sovereignty highly, many others (as well as multilateral agencies) are beginning to adopt a more qualified position toward the sovereignty of others, particularly those states that behave poorly toward their own citizens or neighboring communities. As Richard Falk observes:

There is a clear trend away from the idea of unconditional sovereignty and toward a concept of responsible sovereignty. Governmental legitimacy that validates the exercise of sovereignty involves adherence to minimum humanitarian norms and a capacity to act effectively to protect citizens from acute threats to their security and wellbeing that derive from adverse conditions within a country (Falk, 1993:8).

Since the end of the Cold War, the role of the United Nations in the governance of post-conflict societies has expanded significantly. Prior to and during the Cold War, the U.N. was mainly involved in monitoring borders and cease-fires and in the conduct and monitoring of elections. However, this involved little actual governance of territories (Strohmeyer, 2001). From the early 1990s, however, the United Nations has intervened directly in various internal conflicts to restore peace and security. The first major U.N. exercise in governance came in the 1991 Agreement on a Comprehensive Political Settlement of the Cambodian Conflict. The Agreement created the Supreme National Council, composed of representatives of the various Cambodian factions, which delegated governmental functions to the U.N., to be exercised by the U.N. Transitional Authority for Cambodia (UNTAC). In 1994, the UN intervened in Iraq to protect the Kurds from President Saddam Hussein's alleged genocidal attacks. It was the first time since the Congo crisis that the U.N. had taken sides and defined a country's domestic problem as both an international security issue and an international responsibility. In 1999, the U.N. Security Council authorized virtual trusteeships or protectorates in Kosovo and East Timor, and assumed the responsibility for protecting and providing for the local population. However, as noted in Chapters Three and Four, Africa seems to have been shortchanged by the United Nations and the continent's security needs have not been a significant Security Council priority. Its various responses to Africa's security crises have been not only slow, but also hesitant. It is time the African Union demanded and received equal treatment by this world body.

The Security Council has a mandate to secure peace and security for all its member countries. But in the view of Africans, the Security Council is notorious for double standards when it comes to African peace and security concerns and it is not uncommon for the continent to get a raw deal. As pointed out earlier, the Security Council demonstrated slow and sometimes feeble initial approaches in the 1990s to the internal conflicts in Burundi, Rwanda, Sierra Leone and the Democratic Republic of Congo. This foot-dragging and indifference contrasts sharply with the recent cases of Security Council involvement in Kosovo and the U.N. intervention in post-conflict reconstruction in Afghanistan. After the end of a combined NATO military campaign, the Security Council mandated the World Bank and the European Commission to coordinate the international effort to support Kosovo's reconstruction and recovery. Under this mandate, the two institutions were responsible for "coordination of matters related to economic recovery, reform and reconstruction of the Southeast European region, including mobilizing donor support, providing economic analysis, developing appropriate conditions and implementing projects and programs." To implement this joint mandate, a EC-World Bank joint office was opened in Brussels and a website providing information on the Balkans was launched. As the initial assessment report concluded, "the international community's immediate response to the crisis in the region has been swift" (World Bank, 1999).[38]

The experience of post-conflict reconstruction in Africa compares unfavorably with those in Kosovo and Afghanistan. Much-needed assistance has not been forthcoming and, when pledges are made, the disbursement process has often been too slow to mitigate the effect of conflict on victims and to facilitate a smooth shift from emergency to reconstruction and development (Rugumamu, 2001:28). Africa should demand treatment equal to others in all aspects of international security management.

The Imperative of Democratization

This study has also underscored the urgent need to address questions of democratic governance at all levels. It was argued that, as we rethink visions of development, collective measures should be taken to respond to the idea of economic and political marginalization that the neo-liberal global governance entails. It was also emphasized that global governance cannot override the importance of democratic governance in different nations' settings. In fact, if they are ruled by authoritarian elites who allocate special privileges to their supporters and neglect to meet the basic needs of the vast majority of the people, there is little hope that the international system would be cooperative and peaceful. In the absence of democratic local governance, global and regional arrangements are bound to fail or will simply have limited effectiveness. Democratic global governance has to be built from the ground up and then be linked back to the local conditions.

Democracy traditions come in many shapes and sizes and there is no single model. Democracy is a terrain of struggle for the legitimization of power, both historically and spatially. One of the primary concerns is the extent to which the adopted forms of organization provide for the widest possible space for the representation of the interests of the majority of society and protect the minority. This means, therefore, that the building of popular democracy begins by creating and/or reforming national institutions, policies and values based on unique historical experiences, and not on agendas set elsewhere. Our point of departure would be how to contend with the character of the post-colonial state in Africa. As observed earlier, for well over four decades of independence, most post-colonial states in Africa demonstrated gross incapacity and lack of legitimacy. They were, at different moments, instruments for class, ethnic and religious intimidation, corruption, and suffocation of civil society. They presided over growing poverty, deep social and economic deformities, and rigidly controlled power structures that disadvantaged the masses. People-based development strategies call for a different kind of state and for different modes of political management.

One of the many challenges of the new Africa will be to broaden and deepen the democratic space by strengthening democratic public institutions, activating civil society and consolidating the advance of human freedom. The starting point should be to wage a war against the greatest fallacies that underpin popular notions of democracy in Africa. These include notions such as that majority rule is democratic, that elections alone can guarantee a democracy, and that the holding of elections is equivalent of securing democracy. Indeed, periodic and regular elections are a necessary condition for democracy. They are not, however, a sufficient condition for democracy, nor for political, civic, and economic freedom. Democracy is a complex process, which includes strengthening institutions of representation based on the law.

Integral to the concept of democracy is the concept of freedom. Democracy is seen as the only political system that can guarantee all types of freedom, including civic, political, economic, social and cultural freedom, which are guaranteed on the basis of the equality of men and women, of members of all ethnic and religious groups, and to freedom by all these to advocate diverse political views, without any distinction. In conceptualizing the state-society nexus, democracy need not be taken as simply formal democracy, i.e. the existence of a multiparty system and regular elections. It has to include questions of promotion of social justice, equity and equality rather than just setting up 'democratic institutions' and promoting 'good governance' as prescribed by aid agencies. It has to involve the restructuring of relations and redressing imbalances (both historical and contemporary) among the people in all their manifestations, with respect to gender, ethnicity, class, race and religion. Above all, democracy must be redefined to include access and control of productive resources that enable citizens to reproduce as well ensure more equitable social development.

Africa's record on this score leaves a lot to be desired. For most of the 1990s, some African states, most notably Zimbabwe, Malawi, Cameroon and Kenya responded to the pressures for democratization by promulgating a variety of political reforms including rewriting constitutions, legalizing opposition parties, and holding regular elections. Yet in all these cases, the systems that were put in place, and the timing, rules and procedures for elections were carefully calculated to produce 'victory' for the incumbents. Upon winning, the incumbents tended to resist pressures for further political openings based on their claim of having received a popular and democratic mandate.

Worse still, the euphoria and optimism of the transition to democracy in Africa has slowly but inexorably been replaced by disillusionment and discontent, as democracy's promise of economic and social prosperity has failed to materialize. In fact, the promotion of democracy and economic liberalism would appear to be two sides of the same coin. Some genuine efforts by a number of African states to consolidate democratic institutions, culture and procedures were variously constrained by the heartless economics of structural adjustments. Structural adjustment policies imposed heavy hardships on the general public that had eagerly looked to democratic leaders to bring a reprieve from poverty and deprivation. It is not at all surprising that the democratization process in Africa has tended to degenerate into 'exclusionary democracies,' which allow for political competition but cannot adequately and effectively respond to the demands of the majority of the citizens in any meaningful way. The new Africa will be required to interrogate not only the economics of growth and distribution, but equally importantly, how to reform various social and state institutions through which critical development policies of vital national interest are made.

Ordinarily, social and institutional reforms tend to be gradual and do not occur easily. However, as a matter of urgent continental interest, democratizing Africa should seek to quickly change the internal balance of social forces so that it privileges the popular masses and consolidates their leadership position - as the ultimate social power that drives every institution and the process of development. Arguably, enlightened leadership will invest the popular masses with a considerable agenda-setting power, which will affect not just which issues are brought to the table but, critically, when. The institutions for reform and transformation include legislative, judicial and investigative bodies within the state, plus interest groups, the mass media, civic associations and political parties within society. It is these institutions and processes that make it possible for political leaders to be accountable to their citizens after making public choices and allocating resources. Such a renewed environment will provide the right opportunity to develop economic and social policies, which will be conceived as genuinely people-owned and which will focus squarely on the real needs of the majority of the citizens. We particularly emphasized that involving non-state actors in the entire policy management process will be one of the major features of the new development vision.

Moreover, we stressed that the participation of civil society organizations in the local, national and regional policy managment process is only conceivable within specific, socially engineered institutional frameworks. These comprise both permissive policies and positive support for underprivileged civil society actors. Such a framework would also include the establishment of legal and policy instruments that would institutionalize the nature and character of the participatory process itself. These collectively devised frameworks would help to put in place mechanisms to provide an adequate infrastructure for independent thinking, active participation, and unrestricted dialogue. It is just such a complex set of institutions that would clarify the objectives and modalities of the dialogue in the policy management process. Such institutions would also influence, locally and nationally, specific mechanisms for selecting representatives and competent dialogue partners, as well as the boundaries of their involvement, taking into account the legitimate roles of governments and parliaments. Finally, these institutions would be expected to define the desired output of the dialogue process, as well as the ways and means of institutionalizing the process itself. Then, and only then, would the development process be perceived as 'people-owned' and genuinely democratic.

We also cautioned that introducing the principles of participation and dialogue between government, civil society and other international development partners means more than just setting up consultation mechanisms. It would take ample political resources to institutionalize this. There is little tradition, culture or experience to go by, with respect to effective participation of these stakeholders in policy management. In most African countries, structured dialogue and participation mechanisms driven by African actors are few and the role of different actors in a dialogue process remains largely unqualified. Initially, genuine forms of participation may be resisted or blocked by non-democratic regimes in Africa. The lack of a dialogue culture, appropriate mechanisms and capacity, might lead to poorly prepared and managed processes and turn the whole concept into simply a ritual with little or no substance. It will, therefore, require time, experimentation, and stocktaking of best practices, as well as flexibility and institutional innovations, in order to build trust, dialogue mechanisms and working relations between different actors.

As a starting point, the national and regional policy management dialogue could consider making use of existing structures and institutions. National and regional trade union organizations and Chambers of Agriculture and Commerce would be the first candidates to be considered for informed participation in the national, regional and international policy management dialogue. These, for example, have the organizational capacity, skills and willingness to participate in structured and institutionalized dialogue. They are not only the most organized and structured element of civil society but, most importantly, trade unions possess a rich tradition of effective bargaining with governments and private sector organizations. They are eminently qualified organizations to participate in any national or regional forum for policy formulation, implementation, or evaluation.

The Imperative of Global Restructuring and Mutual Cooperation

Africa's future depends not only on the radical transformation of its internal national and regional policies and institutions, but also significantly on the transformation of its international relations with the wealthy and industrialized economies and institutions of the North. There is a common understanding that the principles of democracy are poorly established in international relations. So far, most efforts at global governance have been too top-heavy, steered by the strongest players and their vested interests in the sphere of international economy and politics. The rules, norms and institutions have largely been imposed from above and intended to be binding on the rest of the international community. It has to be realized that global governance is not simply a system of control and subordination, but a vehicle to develop commonly accepted norms, rules, policies and guidelines for a more just, democratic and open worldwide development. The NEPAD vision calls on the development of a more productive and enlightened partnership between Africa and the key international and multilateral actors of the North. Only a realistic transnational dialogue between various stakeholders, including national governments, international organizations, civil society groups and business actors, can collectively agree on key international institutions and covenants that will be needed to provide a legal framework, organizational structure and funding sources without which effective action is impossible. Above all, it will be important to appreciate the fact that the application of the new global governance norms takes into account the diverse conditions in which particular regions, individual countries, or a set of actors find themselves.

Africa cannot be expected to build a strong competitive economy as the world moves toward greater liberalization and competition without a deliberate and fundamental global change in value preference and institutional reforms. As a matter of fact, more than ever before, Africa needs every possible institutional support and protection from the most predatory aspects of globalization.[39] It urgently requires a democratically engineered multilateral system that works for a fair, equitable and balanced world system. The endless debate on stability and growth versus democracy and equity is essentially a meaningless dialogue of the deaf. As weaker players in the world political economy, individual African states lack the economic and political strength to pursue their interests through bilateral action or threat of sanctions. But they also lack the retaliatory capacity to defend themselves against such actions or threats. In other words, individual African states have no effective means to coerce the North into taking actions that, by definition, threaten their own power, privilege, and wealth. As noted earlier, it is naïve to expect those states, corporations and social forces that benefit from the present liberal world order to consent easily and speedily to effective reform, let alone its transformation. One of the critical conditions for a meaningful and productive dialogue on global governance is the inclusiveness of the participants.

It was also noted that global power and wealth structures are skewed in favor of the countries of the North. By the same token, the post-World War Two governance institutions reflect the power relations and modes of thinking that prevailed during the time of their establishment. Both dominate the international agenda, ideology, institutions and processes, which have a direct bearing on present and future trends in economic and political affairs. What is required for Africa is to strategize on how to maximize both the voice and power of the South in general, and of Africa in particular, in the emerging dialogue on global governance. New thinking about global ethics that recognizes a 'duty of care' beyond borders, as well as within them, and a global deal between rich and poor states is gradually gaining intellectual prominence. It advocates extending social democracy beyond borders, and seeks to strengthen solidarity between those social forces in different regions of the world that are contesting globalization and are seeking a more just and humane world order. Such a world order would think seriously about creating international public goods that would be available to all members of the international society.[40] African countries as a collective, together with other countries in the South, should actively work with progressive forces in the North in order to place their development agenda at center stage in international economic and political negotiations. For this to happen, the struggle should be directed at the democratization of international relations, institutions and processes, so that the South can play an active role in major decision-making institutions (Held, 1997; Falk, 1995; 1999).

As pointed out earlier, unbridled neo-liberal global governance can neither contain nor control new threats, nor responsibly address development concerns. The need for practical action in global governance arises from several sources, most of them connected with the fact that the nation-state is often too small and ineffective a unit to cope with the consequences of globalization. In this regard, the collective South should reassert the belief in the central role of the U.N. in global security and development and intensify the struggle against its decline or manipulation by a few big powers and the WTO. The call for greater inclusion and democracy at the United Nations has revolved around three main proposals. The first involves expanding representation in the U.N. system – increasing the plurality of voices so that the institution is not seen as being solely for governments and bureaucrats. The demand for greater representation arises from the compelling argument that the contemporary international agenda is shaped largely in response to multiple forces of global interconnectedness, and by the emergence of a global civil society and of global market forces that often manage to elude the regulatory mechanisms of the state system. The overriding concern is that the will of the international community should be based on procedures that make the United Nations institutions more representative, accountable and democratic. There have been proposals for a 'People's Assembly,' with citizens around the world electing representatives. In addition, proposals have been made to allow civil society organizations to participate in the discussions of the General Assembly, the Economic and Social Council and the Security Council. Both proposals are likely to go a long way toward making the world body more inclusive and accountable. We should hasten to reiterate our earlier observation that if such reforms fail to progress, the growing militarization of the management of the global system will be dangerously abetted, erasing any significant hope of a system of governance that is both credible and legitimate.

The second set of reforms focus on shifting power in the U.N. system toward those institutions with more democratic decision-making procedures. Some reforms would redress the imbalance in power, weighted toward organizations, like the IMF, World Bank and the Security Council in which a few powerful countries dominate decision-making. The third set of reforms seeks to remove or reduce those U.N. procedures that are seen as fundamentally undemocratic. Among these, the use of the veto at the Security Council has attracted much attention. In the post-Cold War period, countries from both North and South are calling for more accountability and openness of, as well as representation on, the Security Council. In this regard, several proposals have been suggested, ranging from enlarging the Council by increasing both the permanent and non-permanent seats, to limiting the issues that can be vetoed. Several countries, particularly the five permanent members, oppose increasing the number of permanent seats. The basic argument being advanced is that greater participation and representation is not only likely to render decision-making clumsy and unworkable but, also make progress unattainable. Many other countries support increasing membership, but on a rotational basis through periodic elections, and with a quota of seats assigned to every region (Global Governance, 1995; UNDP, 1995; ILO 2004; Annan 2004).

On the development front, the South should struggle to reform the global trade and finance institutions, and the rules and policies that have historically marginalized the poor. As proposed by Global Governance (1995), the reform agenda should seek to establish the U.N. Economic Security Council, a forum that would provide collective and enlightened leadership in economic, social and environmental fields. Such a high profile forum would spotlight the increasing importance of the economic dimensions of the emerging world order, as well as the insufficiency of the institutional arrangements of the Bretton Woods system. It would also ensure that the U.N. possesses an arena suitable for the formulation of global economic policy and capable of providing credible regulatory authority as needed. The proposed Economic Security Council would be more broadly based and more representative than the G-7 or the Bretton Woods institutions, and would be more effective and proactive than the U.N. system as presently constituted. The proposed Council would genuinely search for alternative development models and policy strategies that would integrate economic, environmental and security concerns for humanity, with an eye to social justice. Understandably, this broad-based Council would also seek gradual institutional change and policy reforms that could radically alter the prevailing levels of inequality and poverty, without destroying the global economy.

This brings us to the economic norms, policies and practices of multilateral financial and trade institutions. As previously noted, although countries in the South are deeply affected by the decisions of institutions such as the IMF, World Bank, and WTO, they have little power or influence over these institutions' mode of decision-making. Votes are weighted largely in accordance with the economic power of member countries. Nearly half of the voting power in the World Bank and the IMF is in the hands of a few industrialized countries. Yet more profoundly, the heads of the World Bank and the IMF are chosen according to a political convention, whereby the United States and Europe nominate their candidates for each institution respectively. Not surprisingly, the economic advice to their borrowers is often based on a narrow world-view that reflects the interests of their most powerful members. The standard mechanism to date has been the seal of approval of the World Bank and IMF on macroeconomic policy, dictated from the top down, justified by Washington's need to rebuild the confidence of international investors. It was observed that, for well over two decades, most African economies were in virtual receivership and it was those financial institutions that dictated economic policies and key decisions as well as procedures of government. This practice deprived national and continental actors of the autonomy to make independent decisions on behalf of their respective constituencies. It also resulted in the adoption of one-size-fits-all economic policies, which were often poorly adapted to a country's specific needs, lacked broad popular support, and failed to make economic transformation and poverty reduction a priority. This skewed governance system, favoring only the rich and powerful, has to be stopped and reversed.

Peoples of the South in general, and Africans in particular, should struggle to be subjects of their own policies for change and transformation, instead of being the objects of decisions made by others. It needs hardly be stressed that substantive reforms of decision-making structures and processes of the Bretton Woods institutions be promptly negotiated, to give the majority of humanity the right to adequate participation, and the right to review policies and rules in order to reflect their interests. More specifically, the democratic character of these institutions also needs to be enhanced by increasing the proportion of votes allocated to each member country, and by making them more accountable for their actions not just to their board members, but also to the people affected by their decisions.

Unlike the IMF and the World Bank, which are governed by 'one dollar one vote,' the WTO system is based on 'one country one vote.' Its formal voting structure and dispute settlement system both allow, in principle, for greater input from its smaller and poorer member states, and create the impression of a more equitable outcome. However, the unmistakable structural power of the North in the WTO is demonstrated by the sheer size of their representation in Geneva. Over and above the official representatives, the U.S.A., European and Japanese delegations are supported by huge numbers of commercial staff, lawyers, academic consultants and special advisors monitoring every fine detail of the WTO agreements. Moreover, the WTO is said to be a member-driven organization in the sense that, since it has no permanent executive board, delegates from member countries are actively involved in its day-to-day activities. If they are not, their interests are simply ignored. As pointed out earlier, sub-Saharan African countries, by contrast, suffer from severe under-representation, with nineteen countries having one delegate each or no delegate at all. It is not surprising that, until the Seattle demonstrations, trade negotiations at the WTO tended to weigh heavily against the interests of the poorly represented South (Blackhurst, 1998; Oxfam, 2002). The South needs to consider not only the nature of their representation at the WTO but, equally importantly, to re-examine the economic philosophy and norms that govern the activities of this institution. The basic social principles of equity, fairness and justice should form the core foundations of the reformed WTO.

It was further noted that the rules and regulations that make up the world trading system are biased against the very economies and societies that most need a fair system for sustainable development. We have argued earlier on that export growth in the South would seem to be chiefly dependent on factors beyond its control. The terms of trade of non-fuel commodities *vis-à-vis* manufactures have continued to fall and many African economies have suffered tremendous losses. These losses adversely affect the sustainable development prospects of such countries, since they contribute to the debt problem and to persistent poverty in many communities. A deliberate reform in the South's terms of trade *vis-à-vis* the North through some institutional mechanisms would be required in order to stem or reverse the current South-to-North flow of economic resources. Seriously affected countries have a special need for compensatory and contingency financing without IMF-related conditions or compromised ODA flows. The World Bank (2000) recommendation of considering the provision of a global commodity price insurance instrument to address the key price volatility problems of developing countries, should be aggressively pursued. Such a multilateral instrument would also help to create conditions for a more equitable trading system, reduce resource wastage and unsustainable consumption patterns, and expand financial resources in the South for the transition to sustainable development.

The WTO system claims to apply universal rules that seek to restrict the scope for bilateral power politics. Unfortunately, the universality principle easily obscures the power imbalance among the signatory states. Weak states need special and differential trade rules that allow them to generate growth and poverty reduction. Under the GATT regime, the 'Trade and Development' chapter acknowledged that trade liberalization has different implications for developing countries than for developed economies. What is presently disturbing is the fact that the implementation of the TRIMs and TRIPs agreements will markedly reduce Africa's development options. As noted above, foreign investment regulation measures, such as local content requirements and foreign exchange balancing, were instituted by early-industrializing economies in order to protect their balance of payments, promote local firms and enable more linkages to the local economy. The TRIPs regime will hinder Africa's indigenous technological development by inflating royalty and license fees paid to transnational corporations. The prohibition of investment measures and patent laws will make elusive the attainment of development goals in general, and the rapid industrialization objectives in particular. These agreements should be re-evaluated with a view to assessing their development impact on African economies, and for actions to be taken in order to broaden the provisions for the special and differential treatment of disadvantaged sectors of the world economy. What is observed about TRIMs and TRIPs could also be said about the implications for Africa of a wholesale adaption of the provisions of the General Agreement on Trade in Services (GATS).

Finally, and in a similar vein, unsustainable debt remains a central ingredient in the cycle of stagnation and generalized poverty in Africa. Yet the debt relief provided within the framework of the HIPC initiative opens little extra fiscal space to enable a durable exit from debt bondage. In this regard, comprehensive debt relief, indeed debt cancellation, should be one of the important ways of compensating African people for centuries of brutalization, exploitation, domination and underdevelopment. However, debt forgiveness will be no solution as long as the international and structural obstacles to genuine sustainable development remain in place. In short, the debt crisis is a systemic and structural problem and its solution requires profound institutional and policy reforms at all levels as argued above, beginning with internal socio-political and economic reforms in Africa to global democratic governance and equity. Gone are the days when Africa's development woes were either entirely blamed on internal forces or singularly on global imperialism. Collective responsibility is one of the primary keys to equitable, just, and sustainable development for all.[41]

Endnotes

Chapter 1

1. Unless otherwise specified, the words Africa and sub-Saharan Africa are used interchangeably in this book. The later, however, refers to all countries in Africa other than those in North Africa, namely Algeria, Egypt, Libya, Morocco and Tunisia.

2. In the Gramcian sense, two types of hegemony may be identified: on the one hand, the hegemonic power exercises a function of political and moral direction in the international system. In this sense, the hegemon takes into account the interests and aspirations of allied countries and renounces part of the narrow economic corporate benefits which its position might enable it to acquire. On the other hand, hegemony may be an imperialistic domination based on force and fraud, and not on the consensus of other countries or a group of countries. Under the second type of self-serving hegemony, the international system is unlikely to be stable for long.

3. A recent classification gives a five-level grouping of countries of the South. They include the newly industrialized countries of South and East Asia; the oil-dependent South; the newly impoverished countries from the former second world of Eastern Europe (Romania, Bulgaria, Poland, most of Russia, Albania, and parts of the former Yugoslavia); the countries that are trying to restructure their economies and development policies with a view to accelerating their integration into the North (Mexico, Argentina, Brazil, India and China); and the very poor South (Africa and parts of Latin America and Asia). For details see The Group of Lisbon (1995).

4. Military power is largely unipolar, with the United States the only country possessing both intercontinental nuclear weapons and large modern air, naval, and ground forces capable of projecting its power around the globe. But economic power is tripolar, with the United States, Japan and Europe representing two-thirds of the world. See Nye (2000:218).

5. The most important transformation underlying the emergence of the world economy concerns not only the management of production and distribution, but also the production itself. According to Gary Gereffi (1994) these networks operate under two main configurations: producer-driven commodity chains (in industries such as automobiles, computers and aircraft), and buyer-driven commodity chains (in industries such as garments, footwear, toys and housewares).

6. Immanuel Wallerstein argues that earlier tendencies were for inter-state systems to be turned into world empires through conquest e.g. the Macedonian, Roman, or Mongol Empires. Capitalism was transformed into an inter-state system in which hegemonic core states rise and fall but do not form core-wide empires. Wallerstein (1975; 1983).

7. Charles Kindleberger (1981:247) argues "for the world economy to be stable, it needs a stabilizer, some country that would undertake to provide a market for distress goods, a steady if not counter-cyclical flow of capital, and a rediscount mechanism for providing liquidity when the monetary system is frozen in panic."

8.   The theoretical tendency by some world system analysts to highlight the unequal exchange between the core and periphery countries has received scathing criticism from other Marxists. They are accused of being circulationists at the expense of studying social classes and class relations, and examining the relations of exploitation of labor rooted in specific social relations. See Brenner (1977) and Petras (1978).

Chapter 2

9.   Earlier on in the *Communist Manifesto* Karl Marx and Frederick Engels tersely captured the historical roots of capitalism as a world system in the following words "... the discovery of America and the rounding of the Cape, opened up fresh ground for the rising bourgeoisie. The East Indian and Chinese markets, the colonization of Africa, trade with the colonies, the increase in the means of exchange, and in the commodities generally, gave to commerce, to navigation, to industry, an impulse never before known, and thereby to the revolutionary element in the tottering feudal society, a rapid development (Marx and Engels, 1970:59).

10. As Lenin emphasized in *Imperialism: The Highest Stage of Capitalism* "...Since we are speaking of colonial policy, in the epoch of capitalist imperialism, it must be observed that finance capital and its foreign policy, which is the struggle of the great powers for economic and political division of the world, give rise to a number of transitional forms of state dependence. Not only are the two main groups of countries, those owning colonies, and the colonies themselves, but also diverse forms of dependent countries which politically are formally independent but, in fact are enmeshed in a net of financial and diplomatic dependence, typical of this epoch" (Lenin, 1970:263).

11. In her work, *Dictators and Double Standards,* former US ambassador to the United Nations Jeane Kirkpatrick (1982:51-52) justifies the US government support for dictators in the South by claiming that "right authoritarian regimes, whatever their faults, were natural allies, and potentially reformable. Left totalitarian regimes and movements, however, were irredeemable."

12. The critical turning point of the Soviet Union's relations with Africa was marked in 1981 when it rejected Mozambique's application for membership in the Council for Mutual Economic Assistance (COMECON).

Chapter 3

13. In 1993, exports as a share of the GDP of 17 core economies accounted for 12.9 percent, as opposed to 14.5 percent in 1913. Similarly, capital transfers as a share of their GDP were still smaller than in 1890. See UNDP (1997:83).

14. By 1995, NAFTA covered a population of about 385 million and a combined economic production exceeding $8 trillion per year. It represents the biggest economic powerhouse in the world.

15. The U.S-UK coalition against Iraq in 2003 defied the basic principles of both the U.N. Security Council and of NATO.

16. Africa's cooperation and integration performance contrasts sharply with that of Asia, Latin America and the Caribbean. Intra-ASEAN trade, for example, rose from 15 percent in 1970

to 24.7 percent in 1997. Intra-CARICOM trade rose from 4.3 percent in 1980 to 17.2 percent in 1996. Intra-MERCOSUR trade grew from 9 percent in 1990 to 22.7 percent in 1996. In the case of CACM, intra-group exports as a percentage of total exports within the area rose from 7.5 percent in 1960 to 21.6 percent in 1996 (ECA, 1996:3-4).

17. The Monterrey Consensus is the official document adopted by the International Conference on Financing for Development, held in March, 2002, in Monterrey, Mexico.

18. Sir W. Arthur Lewis, one of the leading economists of the time, was blunt about the motive of giving aid: "when you look at the table showing how much each of the one-hundred countries receive in foreign aid, it is a distribution which cannot be defended on any principle of need, size of population, absorptive capacity or any economic test.... politics was the chief determinant of aid" (Lewis, 1971:12).

19. In terms of magnitude, both trade and investment are dwarfed by finance. However, due to data lacunae, we have decided to exclude global finance from this study.

20. Multilateral rule-making in the area of investment, and especially FDI, has a troubled history. It proved impossible to reach an agreement on the U.N. Code of Conduct in Transnational Cooperations in the late 1970s and 1980s.

21. This characterization is not entirely persuasive. As noted earlier, whereas controls and regulations governing capital flows remain strong in China, it receives more FDI than any other country, thanks to its large and rapidly growing market and cheap labor.

22. As pointed out earlier, migration involving the movement of people from countries where there is a labor surplus to countries where there is a labor shortage started almost five centuries ago with slavery, from Africa to the New World. This was later followed by the movement of indentured labor, another form of servitude, of Indians and Chinese to the New World, Southern Africa and Southeast Asia.

Chapter 4

23. The extent of this impoverishment is evident in the fact that the 50 poorest countries, which together have 20 percent of the world's population, control only 2 percent of the world income (UNDP, 1997).

24. According to Noam Chomsky, " a rogue state is a threat to its neighbors and to the entire world, an 'outlaw nation' led by a reincarnation of Hitler who must be contained by the guardians of the world order" (Chomsky, 2000:12).

25. Lawrence Summers, former World Bank Chief Economist, was quoted rationalizing the dumping of waste in poor countries "I think the economic logic behind dumping a load of toxic waste in the lowest-wage country is impeccable and we should face up to it" (*The Economist* 8 February 1998).

26. In another study, Christopher Layne (1993:245) notes that the Pentagon's Defense Planning Guidance for fiscal year 1994-1999 indicated the vision of a unipolar world order and proposed that four measures be taken:

    i)   Ensure that no rival superpower arises anywhere in the world.
    ii) Discourage advanced industrial nations from challenging American leadership.

iii) Use military force, if necessary, to prevent the proliferation of nuclear weapons.

iv) Form coalitions with other nations where possible, but act indepenaently where such coalitions are not forthcoming.

27. The double standards of governments in the North and multilateral financial institutions should be exposed. First, during the 1920s, 13-15 percent of exports as reparations payment by Germany was perceived as too high and was considered as one of the factors that brought about the rise of the Nazis. Second, in the 1953 London Agreement, the allies agreed to a substantial cancellation of the German debt. Initially, they had asked for a debt-service ratio of 10 percent, but German negotiators argued that this was much too high. The creditors settled for 3.5 percent. Third, Britain reached a debt settlement with the United States in 1944, which called for a debt service ratio of 4 percent. In short, the World Bank and the IMF debt sustainability thresholds are historically unjustifiable. For details, see Halon (1998).

28. The United Nations Millennium Declaration adopted several specific, quantified and monitorable goals for development and poverty reduction by 2015. They included seven targets:

♦ Halve the proportion of the world's people living on less than $1 a day.
♦ Halve the proportion of the world's people suffering from hunger.
♦ Halve the proportion of the world's people without access to safe drinking water.
♦ Achieve universal completion of primary schooling.
♦ Reduce maternal mortality rates by three-quarters.
♦ Reduce under-five mortality rates by two-thirds.
♦ Halt and begin to reverse the spread of HIV/AIDS, malaria, and other major diseases.

29. The concentration and centralization of capital have tended to consolidate under the new wave of globalization. The 2002 Human Development Report, for example, notes that the richest 1 percent of the world's people receive as much income each year as the poorest 57 percent. See UNDP (2002:2).

30. These include, among others: free movements of persons, rights of residence and establishment; transport and communications; rules of origin; customs cooperation within the community; industry; trade promotion; solidarity, development and a compensation fund; food and agriculture; science and technology; a pan-African parliament; and human resource development.

31. Going by the EU example, the Maastricht Treaty put in place strict convergence criteria to be fulfilled by member-states before being accepted into the monetary union. Africa would be well advised to take a leaf out of the book of the E.U.'s convergence instruments.

32. The theory posits that there are two important capabilities necessary for regime leadership, namely, its capacity to act given its size, power, economic strength, administrative efficiency and its responsiveness. It is the ability of its political system to control its own behavior and redirect its own attention. For more details on this, see Deutsch et al., 1957:40.

33. The African Development Bank Group has attributed the inability of countries to access the Bank's resources mainly to the pervasive weaknesses of sub-regional organizations and

national governments in identifying and promoting multinational projects, and to widely differing perceptions among participating countries regarding the costs and benefits of regional projects. For details on the role of the ADB in regional cooperation, see Otieno (1990), Ndiaye (1990), and the African Development Bank (1999).

34. Theoretically, these imbalances could be resolved through one of the following: (i) proportional distribution of benefits according to the differential growth rates of respective economies; (ii) the 'uncontrolled' sharing of benefits, with more accruals to the strongest and fastest growing economies; (iii) distribution of benefits in favor of the poorer and slower growing economies; or (iv) equal distribution of benefits. For more discussion on compensatory schemes see Mshomba (1999).

35. However, what this argument fundamentally misses is the fact that sub-regional organizations in Africa do not have the comparative advantage to act. They lack most of the basic resources to deploy troops, and to finance economic reconstruction and rehabilitation in complex conflict situations. For informed discussion on the subject, see Hutchful (1999).

Chapter 5

36. One of the significant features of these new movements is the pressure they exert on governments and corporations to respond to the needs of the South. Most prominently, through aggressive global campaigns, the International Campaign to Ban Landmines succeeded in 1997 in getting the Mine Ban Treaty prohibiting the use, production, trade and stockpiling of antipersonnel landmines. For details see the International Campaign to Ban Landmines (2002).

37. Botswana enjoyed average annual growth of 14.5 percent from 1970 to 1980, and 9.6 percent from 1980 to 1995. Over the same quarter century, Mauritius maintained a steady growth rate of over 6 percent. Moreover, Mauritius has succeeded in doubling its per capita gross domestic product since the mid-1980s, which now exceeds $3,000 (ADB, 2000).

38. The program for Reconstruction and Recovery for Kosovo, whch was drawn up by the European Commission and the World Bank in support of the United Nations Mission in Kosovo, had three main objectives:

a) To develop a thriving, open and transparent market economy, which can provide jobs to Kosovars. This involves restarting the rural economy, encouraging the development of the private sector, and addressing the issues of public enterprise.

b) To support the restart of public administration and to establish transparent, effective and sustainable institutions. Focus to be placed on setting up the central institutions that are key to economic recovery, developing municipal governance, and restoring peace and order through an effective police and judiciary.

c) To mitigate the impact of the conflict and to start addressing the legacy of the 1990s, with a focus on restoring adequate living conditions, such as housing and landmine clearance, rehabilitating the infrastructure networks needed for economic development and social sectors such as education and health (European Commission/World Bank. November, 1999).

39. Under the GATT arrangements, poor countries from the South were accorded special and differential treatment. This arose from the recognition that countries at different levels of economic, financial and technological development had different capacities and needs. Many of the rules enshrined in the WTO threaten to further marginalize the South. They are inconsistent with the internationally accepted objectives and policies of poverty reduction.

40. Such collective goods include, for example, global ecological balance, biodiversity, financial stability, international peace and security, and global disease control.

41. The 1992 Rio Conference adopted the principle of common but differentiated responsibilities between the North and South in ensuring equitable and sustainable development for all.

References

Abrahamsen, R. (2000): *Disciplining Democracy: Democracy Discourse and Good Governance in Africa.* London: Zed Press.

Adedeji, A. (1989): "Africa in the 1990s: A Decade for Socio-Economic Recovery and Transformation or Another Lost Decade." *1989 Founder's Day Lecture of the Nigerian Institute for International Affairs.* Lagos, Nigeria.

Adepojou, K. (1995): "Migration in Africa: An Overview," in J. Baker and T. Aina (Eds). *The Migration Experience in Africa.* Uppsala: Nordiska Afrikainstitutet.

Andreas, P. (2000): *Border Games: Policing the US-Mexico Divide.* Ithaca: Cornell University Press.

Africa Confidential (1995): Vol. 36 (6).

ACP. (1998): *Technical Notes on Economic and Trade Cooperation.* ACP/00/001/98 Rev. 2 Brussels.

African Development Bank (2000): *Annual Report 1999.* Abidjan: ADB.

African Leadership Forum (1991): *The Kampala Document: Toward a Conference on Security, Stability, Development and Cooperation in Africa.* Kampala, ALF.

Aina, T. (1996): "Globalization and Social Policy in Africa," *CODESRIA Working Paper* No. 6.

Ake, C. (1996): *Democracy and Development in Africa.* Washington D.C: Brookings Institution.

Ake, C. (1991): "Rethinking African Democracy," *Journal of Democracy* 2 (1).

Ake, C. (1973): "Explaining Political Instability in New States," *Journal of Modern African Studies* 11(3).

Aluko, M. (2000): "Debt Relief, Loot, Recovery and Constitutional Reform in Nigeria." *http://www.africapolicy.org/docs00/nig0006*.htm.

Aly, A. (1994): *Economic Cooperation in Africa: In Search of Direction.* Boulder, CO: Lynne Rienner.

Amin, S. (1998): *Africa in the Age of Globalization.* London: Zed Press.

Amin, S. (1992): *Empire of Chaos.* New York: Monthly Review Press.

Amin, S. (1990): *Maldevelopment: Anatomy of the Global Future.* Tokyo: United Nations University Press.

Amin, S. (1974): *Accumulation on a World Scale.* New York: Monthly Review Press.

Amsden, A. (1980): "The Industry Characteristics of Intra-Third World Trade in Manufactures," *Economic Development and Cultural Change* 29.

Amoako, K. (2001): "Fulfilling Africa's Promise," *Millennium Lecture at 10 Downing Street,* London.

Amsden, A. (1980): "Industry Characteristics of Intra-Third World Trade in Manufactures," *Economic Development and Cultural Change* 29.

Aning, K. (1999): "Peacekeeping Under ECOMOG: A Sub-Regional Approach," in Cilliers, J. and G. Mills (Eds). *From Peacekeeping to Complex Emergencies: Peace Support Missions in Africa.* Johannesburg and Pretoria: SAIIA and ISS.

Annan, K. (1998): *Report on the Causes of Conflict and the Promotion of Durable Peace and Sustainable Development in Africa.* UN.A/52/871-S/1998/318. UN: New York.

Anyang' Nyong'o, P. (2002): *The Study of African Politics: A Critical Appreciation of A Heritage.* Nairobi: Heinrich Boll Foundation.

Anyang' Nyong'o, P. (1990): "Regional Integration in Africa: An Unfinished Agenda" in P. Anyang' Nyong'o (Ed). *Regional Integration in Africa: An Unfinished Agenda.* Nairobi: Academy Science Publishers.

Arrighi, G. (1999): "Globalization, State Sovereignty, and the 'Endless' Accumulation of Capital," in D. Smith *et. al.* (Eds). *States and Sovereignty in the Global Economy.* London: Routledge.

Arrighi, G. (1994): *The Long Twentieth Century: Money, Power and the Origins of Our Time*. London: Verso.

Armstrong, J. (1985): *Long-Range Forecasting: From Crystal Ball to Computer*. New York: John Wiley.

Arndt, S. (1998): "Super-specialization in the Gains from Trade," *Contemporary Economic Policy*.

Arnold, W. (2001): "Japan's Electronic Ship Takes a Toll on Southeast Asia," *New York Times* 1.

Asante, S. (1990): "Regional Economic Cooperation and Integration: the Experience of ECOWAS" in P. Anyang' Nyong'o (Ed). *Regional Integration in Africa: Unfinished Agenda*. Nairobi: Academy Science Publishers.

Asante, S. (1981): "Lomé II: Another Machinery for Updating Dependency," *Development and Cooperation* 3.

Baldwin, D. (1985): *Economic Statecraft*. Princeton, NJ: Princeton University Press.

Bayart, J. *et. al.* (1999): *The Criminalization of the State in Africa*. Oxford: James Currey.

Bello, W. (1994): *Dark Victory*. London: Pluto Press.

Bhattachrya, O., P. Montiel, and S. Sharma (1997): "Can sub-Saharan Africa Attract Private Capital Flows?" *Finance and Development*.

Blackburn, R. (1998): *Making of New World Slavery: From the Baroque to the Modern 1492-1800*. London: Verso.

Blackhurst, R. (1998): "The Capacity of the WTO to fulfil its Mandate" in Krueger, A (Ed). *The WTO as an International Organization*. Chicago: University of Chicago Press.

Bloom, D. and M. Murshed (2001). "Globalization, Global Public Bad Rising Criminal Activity and Growth." *WIDER Paper*. WIDER, Helsinki.

Bond, P. and S. Manyanya (2002): *Zimbabwe's Plunge: Exhausted Nationalism, Neoliberalism and the Search for Justice*. Trenton, NJ: Africa World Press.

Boswell, T. and C. Chase-Dunn (2000): *The Spiral of Capitalism and Socialism*. Boulder, CO: Lynne Rienner.

Boutros-Ghali, B. (1992): *An Agenda for Peace: Preventive Diplomacy, Peacemaking and Peacekeeping*. New York: UN.

Boyer, R. (1987): *Technical Change and the Theory of Regulation*. Paris: CEPREMAP.

Brenner, R. "The Origins of Capitalist Development: A Critique of Neo-Smithian Marxism," *New Left Review* 104:25-92.

Brett, E. (1973): *Colonialism and Underdevelopment in East Africa*. New York: Nok Publishers.

Brown, L. (1999): *State of the World 1999*. New York: WW Norton Company.

Brown, L. (1986): "Regional Collaboration in Resolving Third World Conflicts," *Survival* 28(3)

Burbach, R. *et. al.* (1997): *Globalization and its Discontents*. London: Pluto Press.

Buzan, B. (1991): "New Patterns of Global Security in the Twenty-first Century," *International Affairs* 67(3).

Callaghy, T. (2000): "Africa and the World Economy: More Caught Between a Rock and A Hard Place" in J. Harberson and D. Rothchild (Eds). *Africa in World Politics: The African State System in Flux*. Boulder CO: Westview Press.

Callaghy, T. (1993): "Vision and Politics in the Transformation of the Global Political Economy: Lessons from the Second and Third World" in R. Slater and S. Dorr (Eds). *Global Transformation and the Third World*. Boulder, CO: Lynne Rienner.

Callinicos, A. (2001): *Against the Third Way*. Cambridge: Polity Press.

Commission on Global Governance (1995): *Our Global Neighborhood*. Oxford: Oxford University Press.

Caporaso, J. (1970): "Encapsulated Integrative Patterns versus Spillovers: The Case of Agricultural and Transport Integration in the EEC," *International Studies Quarterly* 14 (4).

Cardoso, F. (1993): "The North-South Relations in the Present Context: A New Dependence" in M. Carnoy (Ed). *The New Global Economy in the Information Age*. University Park PA: Pennsylvania State University Press.

Castells, M. (1998): *Information Age: Economy, Society and Culture*. London: Blackwell Publishers.

Castells, M and L. Tyson (1989): "High Technology and the Changing International Division of Production: Implications for the US Economy" in J. Purcell (Ed). *The Newly Industrializing Countries in World Economy: Challenges for US Policy*. Boulder CO: Lynne Rienner.

Castells, M. (1993): "Information Economy and the New International Division of Labor" in M. Carnoy, *et. al.* (Eds). *The New Global Economy*. University Park PA: Pennsylvania State University Press.

Chabal, P. and J. Daloz (1999): *Africa Works: Disorder as Political Institution*. Oxford: James Currey.

Chafer, T. (2002): "Franco-African Relations: No longer Special," *African Affairs* 101(404).

Chase-Dunn, C. (1998): *Global Formation: Structure of the World Economy*. Updated edition. Lanham, MD: Littlefield Publishers.

Chase-Dunn, C. "Technology and the Logic of World System" in Palan, R. and B. Gills (Eds). (1994): *Transcending State-Global Divide: Neo-Structural Agenda of International Relations*. Boulder, CO: Lynne Rienner.

Chase-Dunn, C. (1984): "Interstate System and Capitalist World Economy," *International Studies Quarterly* 25(1).

Chege, M. (2002): "Sierra Leone: The State that Came Back from the Dead," *The Washington Quarterly* 25(3).

Chege, M. (1994): "What's Right with Africa?" *Current History* 93(583).

Cheru, F. (2002): *Africa Renaissance: A Roadmap to the Challenge of Globalization*. London: Zed Books.

Cheru, F. (1989): *The Silent Revolution in Africa: Debt, Development and Democracy*. London: Zed Books.

Chomsky, N. (2000): *Rogue States: The Role of Force in World Affairs*. London: Pluto Press.

Clark, N. (1990): "Development Policy, Technology Assessment and the New Technologies," *Futures* 22(9).

Clark, N. and C. Juma (1991): *Biotechnology for Sustainable Development*. Nairobi: ACTS Press.

Clever, G. and R. May (1995): "Peacekeeping: The African Dimension," *Review of African Political Economy* 22 (66).

Collier, P. and C. Pattillo (2000): "Investment and Risks in Africa" in Collier, P. and C. Pattillo (Eds). *Investment and Risk in Africa*. London: Macmillan Press.

Collier, P. (1998): "Globalization: Implications for Africa" in Z. Iqbal and M. Khan (Eds). *Trade Reform and Regional Integration in Africa*. Washington DC: IMF Institute.

Commission for Global Governance (1995): *Our Global Neighborhood*. New York: Oxford University Press.

Cox, R. (1987): *Production, Power, and World Order: Social Forces in the Making of History*. New York: Columbia University Press.

Davidson, B. (1992): *The Black Man's Burden: Africa and the Curse of the Nation-State*. London: James Curry.

Davidson, B. (1991): "What Development Model?" *Africa Forum* 1(1).

Dearden, S. (1999): "Immigration Policy in the European Union" in M. Lister (Ed). *New Perspectives on European Union Development Cooperation.* Boulder CO: Westview Press.

Dell, S. (1982): "Stabilization: Political Economy of Overkill," *World Development* 10 (8).

Deng, F. and T. Lyons (1993): "Introduction: Promoting Responsible Sovereignty in Africa" in F. Deng and T. Lyons (Eds). *African Reckoning: A Quest for Good Governance.* Washington DC: Brookings Institution.

Deutsch, K. (1957): *Political Community and the North Atlantic Area.* Princeton NJ: Princeton University Press.

Diop, C. (1974): *The African Origins of Civilization: Myth or Reality.* New York: L. Hill,.

Duffield, M. (1994): "The Political Economy of Internal Wars: Asset Transfer, Complex Emergencies and International Aid" in J. Macrae and A. Zwi (Eds). *War and Hunger: Rethinking International Responses to Complex Emergencies.* London: Zed Books.

EC. (1997): *Green Paper on the Relations between the European Union and the ACP Countries on the Eve of the 21ˢᵗ Century: Challenges and Options for a New Partnership.* EU: Luxembourg.

ECA (1990): *African Charter for Popular Participation in Development and Transformation.* E/ECA/CM.14/11. Arusha, Tanzania.

ECA (1999): *African Integration: Lessons from EU and NAFTA.* Addis Ababa: EAC/RCID/078/99.

ECA (1989): *African Alternative Framework to Structural Adjustment Program for Socio-Economic Recovery and Transformation.* UNECA: Addis Ababa.

ECLA (1998): "Trade and Industrial Policies: Past Performance and Future Prospects," Santiago: Economic Commission for Latin America.

Ecology Editor (1987): "Tropical Forests: A Plan for Action," *The Ecologist* 17 (4&5).

Enloe, C. (1989): *Bananas, Beaches and Bases: Making Feminist Sense of International Politics.* Berkeley: University of California Press.

Elbadawi, I. and F. Mwega (1998): "Regional Integration, Trade and Direct Foreign Investment in sub-Saharan Africa" in Z. Iqbal and M. Khan (Eds). *Trade Reform and Regional Integration in Africa.* Washington DC: World Bank.

Elmandjra, M.(1983): "South-South Cooperation: A Peaceful Decolonization of the Future," *IFDA Dossier* 38.

Emmanuel, A. (1972): *Unequal Exchange: A Study of the Imperialism of Trade.* New York: Monthly Review Press.

Falk, R. (2000): *Human Rights Horizons: The Pursuit of Justice in a Globalizing World.* New York: Routledge.

Falk, R. (1999): *Predatory Globalization: A Critique.* Cambridge: Polity Press.

Falk, R. (1995): *On Humane Governance.* Cambridge: Polity Press.

Falk, R. (1993): "Sovereignty and Human Dignity: The Search for Reconciliation" in Deng, F. and T. Lyons (Eds). *African Reckoning: A Quest for Good Governance.* Washington, DC: Brookings Institution.

Falk, R. (1992): *Explorations at the Edge of Time: The Prospects for World Order.* Philadelphia PA: Temple University Press.

Falk, R. (1975): *A Study of Future Worlds.* New York: Free Press.

Fanon, F. (1974): *The Wretched of the Earth.* Harmondsworth: Penguin.

Feldstein, M. and C. Horioka (1980): "Domestic Savings and International Capital Flows," *Economic Journal* 90.

Fernandez, A. (1993): "Stabilization, Exports and Regional Development: The Northeast in the 1980s." *Research Paper # 8* Brighton: University of Sussex.

Finger, M. and P. Schuler (2000): "Implementation of the Uruguay Round Commitment: The Development Challenge." *The World Economy*, 23(4).

Fluvian, C. (1997): "The Legacy of Rio," *The State of the World*. New York: Norton and Company.

Foroutan, F. (1992): "Regional Integration in sub-Saharan Africa: Past Experience and Future Prospects" in J. de Melo and A. Panagariya (Eds). *New Dimensions in Regional Integration*. Cambridge: Cambridge University Press.

Franda, M. (2002): *Launching into Cyberspace: Internet Development and Politics in Five World Regions*. Boulder CO: Lynne Rienner.

Frank, G. (1991): "No Escape from the Laws of World Economics," *Review of African Political Economy* 50.

Frank, G. (1979): *Mexican Agriculture 1592-1630: Transformation of the Mode of Production*. Cambridge: Cambridge University Press..

Frank, G. (1978): *Dependent Accumulation and Underdevelopment*. London: Macmillan.

Frank, G. (1966): "The Development of Underdevelopment," *Monthly Review* 18(4).

Frazer, J. (1997): "The African Crisis Response Initiative: Self-Interested Humanitarianism," *The Brown Journal of World Affairs* 4(2).

French, H. (1997): "Coping with Ecological Globalization" in Worldwatch Institute. *State of the World 1997*. New York: W.W. Norton and Company.

Fukuyama, F. (1992): *The End of History and the Last Man*. New York: Free Press.

Fukuyama, F. (1989): "End of History," *The National Interest* 16.

Gereffi, G. (1994): "The Organization of Buyer-Driven Global Commodity Chains: How U.S. Retailers Shape Overseas Production Networks" in G. Gereffi and M. Korzeniewicz (Eds). *Commodity Chains and Global Capitalism*. Westport CT: Greenwood Press.

Gewald, J. (1999): *Herero Heroes: Socio-Political History of the Herero of Namibia 1890-1923*. Oxford: James Curry.

Gilpin, R. (2001): *Global Political Economy*. Princeton NJ: Princeton University Press.

Gilpin, R. (1981): *War and Change in World Politics*. Cambridge: Cambridge University Press.

Graham, C. (1994): *Safety Nets, Politics, and the Poor: Transitions to Market Economics*. Washington, DC: The Brookings Institution.

Gray, C. and M. McPherson 2000): "The Leadership Factor in African Policy Reform and Growth," *Economic Development and Cultural Change* 49(4).

Gershenkron, A. (1962): *Economic Backwardness in Historical Perspective: A Book of Essays*. Cambridge: Harvard University Press.

Gilpin, R. (1987): *The Political Economy of International Relations*. Princeton NJ: Princeton University Press.

Griffin, K. (1991): "Foreign Aid after the Cold War," *Development and Change* 22(4).

Group of Lisbon (1995): *Limits of Competition*. Cambridge: MIT Press.

Gulvin, C. (1996): "The French Economy and the End of the Cold War" in Chafer, T. and B. Jenkin (Eds). *France: From Cold War to the New Order*. Basingstoke: Macmillan.

Guy, M. (1995): "Continuity and Change in Franco-Africa Relations," *Journal of Modern African Studies* 33(1).

Haggard, S. (1995): *Developing Nations and the Politics of Global Integration*. Washington DC: Brookings Institution.

Hanlon, J. (1998): "African Debt Hoax," *Review of African Political Economy* 25(77).

Hamilton, A. (1904): "Report on Manufacturers" in Lodge, H. (Ed). *The Works of Alexander Hamilton*, Vol. 4, New York: Putman.

Hardin, G. (1968): "The Tragedy of the Commons," *Science* Vol 162 (3859).

Harrison, G. *et. al.* (1999): "Quantifying the Outcome of the Round," *Finance and Development* 32 (4).

Held, D. *et. al.* (1999): *Global Transformations: Politics, Economics and Culture*. Stanford CA: Stanford University Press.

Held, D. (1997): "Democracy and Globalization," *Governance* 3 (3).

Helleiner, G. (1993): "External Resource Flows, Debt Relief and Economic Development" in G. Cornia and G. Helleiner (Eds). *From Adjustment to Development in Sub-Saharan Africa*. London: Macmillan.

Henson, S. (2000): *Impact of Sanitary and Phytosanitary Measures on Developing Countries*. Reading: University of Reading, Center for Food Economics Research.

Hettne, B. and A. Inotai (1994): *The New Regionalism: Implications for Global Development and International Security*. Helsinki: UNU/WIDER.

Herbst, J. (1989): "The Creation and Maintenance of National Boundaries in Africa," *International Organization* 43(4).

Hine, R. (1992): "Regionalism and Integration of the World Economy," *Journal of Common Market Studies* 30(2).

Hirst, P. and G. Thompson (1999): *Globalization in Question*. 2nd Edition. Oxford: Polity Press.

Hobsbawm, E. (1994): *The Age of the Extremes: A History of the World 1914-1990*. New York: Pantheon Books.

Hobsbawm, E. (1992): *Nations and Nationalism Since 1780: Program, Myth and Reality*. 2nd Edition. Cambridge: Cambridge University Press.

Hobsbawm, E. (1979): "The Development of the World Economy," *Cambridge Journal of Economics* 3(3).

Hobson, J. (1905): *Imperialism: A Study*. Ann Arbor: University of Michigan Press.

Holsti, K. (1996): *The State, War, and the State of War*. New York: Cambridge University Press.

Hoogvelt, A. (1997): *Globalization and the Post-Colonial World: The New Political Economy of Development*. Baltimore MD: Johns Hopkins University Press.

Hook, S. (1996): "Introduction: Foreign Aid in a Transformed World" in S. Hook (Ed). *Foreign Aid Toward the Millennium*. Boulder CO: Lynne Rienner.

Hopkins, T. (1982): *World Systems Analysis: Theory and Methodology*. Beverly Hills CA: Sage Publications.

Huntington, S. (1996): *The Clash of Civilizations and the Remaking of the World Order*. New York: Simon and Schuster.

Hurrell, A. (1995): "Regionalism in Theoretical Perspective" in L. Fawcett and A. Hurrell (Eds). *Regionalism in World Politics: Regional Organizations and International Order*. Oxford: Oxford University Press.

Hutchful, E. (1991): "Eastern Europe: Consequences for Africa," *Review of African Political Economy* 50.

Hutchful, E. (1999): "The ECOMOG Experience with Peacekeeping in West Africa" in M. Malan (Ed). *Whither Peacekeeping in Africa?* ISS Monograph Series 36. Pretoria: ISS.

Hyden, G. (1987): "Debt: The Development Trap," *Africa Report* 32 (6).

Hyden, G. (1980): *Beyond Ujamaa in Tanzania: Underdevelopment and Uncaptured Peasantry.* Berkeley and Los Angeles: University of California Press.

Ibingira, G. (1973): *The Forging of an African Nation.* New York: The Viking Press.

ICBL (2002) *Landmine Monitor Report 2001: Toward a Mine-Free World.* HTTP://www.icbl.org

Ihonvebere, J. (1992): "Surviving at the Margins: Africa and the New Global Order," *Current World Leaders* 35(6).

Ihonvebere, J. (2000): *Africa and the New Order.* New York: Peter Lang.

Inayatullah, S. (1990): "Deconstructing and Reconstructing the Future," *Futures* 22(2) .

International Institute for Strategic Studies (2002): *Strategic Survey 2001/2002.* Oxford: Oxford University Press.

Isenberg, D. (1997): *Soldiers and Fortunes Ltd: A Profile of Today's Private Sector Corporate Mercenary Firms.* Washington, DC: Center for Defense Information.

Jackson, R. and C. Rosberg (1982): *Personal Rule in Black Africa.* Berkeley and Los Angeles CA: University of California Press.

Jensen, M. (1999): "Policy Strategies for Africa: Information and Communications Infrastructure," Paper Presented at Africa Development Forum 1999. http:// www.un.org/depts/eca/adf.

Jubilee (2000): *An Emerging Scandal: Debt Cancellation and the Broken Promise of Cologne.* http://www.jubilee2000uk.org/reports/scandal.html.

Kaplan, R. (1994): "The Coming Anarchy," *The Atlantic Monthly, May.*

Koechlin, T. (1995): "The Globalization of Investment," *Contemporary Economic Policy* 13.

Kennedy, P. (1987): *The Rise and Fall of Great Empires: Economic Change and Military Conflict from 1500 to 2000.* New York: Random House.

Keohane, R. (1980): "The Theory of Hegemonic Stability and Changes in International Economic Regimes" in Holisti, O. and A. George (Eds). *Change in the International System.* Boulder CO: Westview Press.

Khotari, R. (1993): *Poverty: Human Consciousness and the Amnesia of Development.* London: Zed Books.

Khotari, R. (1984): "Communications for Alternative Development: Toward a Paradigm," *Development Dialogue* 1-2.

Khor, M. (2001): *Rethinking Globalization.* London: Zed Press.

Kindleberger, C. (1981): "Dominance and Leadership in the International Economy," *International Studies Quarterly* 5(2).

Kirkpatrick, J. (1982): *Dictators and Double Standards.* New York: Simon and Schuster.

Klak, T. (1998): "13 Theses on Globalization and Neo-liberalism" in T. Klak (Ed). *Globalization and Neo-liberalism: The Caribbean Context.* Lanham, MD: Rowman and Littlefield.

Koponen, J. (2003): "Introduction: The faces of Globalization" in Koponen, J (Ed). *Between Integration and Exclusion: Impacts of Globalization in Mozambique, Nepal, Tanzania and Vietnam.* Helsinki: Institute of Development Studies.

Krasner, S. (1985): *Structural Conflict: The Third World Against Global Liberalism.* Los Angeles: University of California Press.

Krasner, S. (1984): "Approaches to the State: Alternative Conceptions and Historical Dynamics," *Comparative Politics* 16(2).

Krause, J. (1996): "Gender Inequalities and Feminist Politics in Global Perspective" in E. Kofman and G. Young (Eds). *Globalization: Theory and Practice.* London: Pinter.

Kumar, N. (2001): *Developing Countries in the International Division of Labor in the Software and Service Industry: Lessons from the Indian Experience.* Geneva: ILO Report.

Kuhne, W. (2001): *The Security Council and G8 in the New Millennium: Who is in Charge of International Peace and Security?* Ebenhausen Germany: Stiftung Wissenschaft and Politik.

Lall, S. (2002): "Transnational Corporations and Technology Transfer" in Nayyar, D. (Ed). *Governing Globalization: Issues and Institutions.* Oxford: University of Oxford.

Lake, A. (1995): "U.S. Support for Democracy in Africa," US Department of State, *Dispatch.*

Lenin, V. (1970): "Imperialism: The Highest Stage of Capitalism" in Lenin, V. *Collected Works Vol. 22.* Moscow: Progress Publishers.

Leys, C. (1996): "The Crisis in Development Theory," *New Political Economy* 1(1).

Liftwich, A. (1993): "Governance, Democracy and Development in the Third World," *Third World Quarterly* 14 (3).

List, F. (1904): *The National System of Political Economy.* London: Longman's Green.

Lister, M. (1998): "Europe's New Development Policy" in M. Lister (Ed). *European Union Development Policy.* New York: St Martin's Press.

Lister, M. (1999): "The European Union's Relations with African, Caribbean, and Pacific Countries" in M. Lister (Ed). *New Perspectives on the European Union Development Cooperation.* Boulder CO: Westview Press.

Maasdorp, G. (1992): "Economic Cooperation in Southern Africa: Prospects for Regional Integration," *Conflict Studies* 253.

Maizels, A. (1992): *Commodities in Crisis: The Commodity Crisis of the 1980s and the Political Economy of International Commodity Prices.* Oxford: Clarendon Press.

Malan, M. (1999): "Debunking Some Myths about Peacekeeping in Africa" in J. Cilliers and G. Mills (Eds). *From Peacekeeping to Complex Emergencies.* Johannesburg and Pretoria: South African Institute for International Affairs and Institute for Policy Studies.

Mandaza, I. (1990): "SADCC: Problems of Regional, Political and Economic Cooperation in Southern Africa: An Overview" in P. Anyang' Nyong'o (Ed). *Regional Integration in Africa: Unfinished Agenda.* Nairobi: Academy Science Publishers.

Maniruzzaman, T. (1982): *The Security of Small States in the Third World.* Canberra: The Australian National University.

Marx, K. (1976): *Capital: A Critique of Political Economy. Vol. 1* London: Penguin Books.

Marx, K and F. Engels (1970): "Manifesto of the Communist Party" in Marx, K. and F. Engels. *Selected Works Vol. 1.* Moscow: Progress Publishers.

Mazrui, A. (1999): "African Security: The Erosion of the State and the Decline of Race as a Basis for Human Relations" in Thomas C. and P. Wilkin (Eds). *Globalization, Human Security and the African Experience.* Boulder CO: Lynne Rienner.

Mazrui, A. (1994): "Decaying Parts of Africa Need Benign Colonialism," *International Herald Tribune.*

Mbembe, A. (1995): "Complex Transformations in the Late Twentieth Century," *Africa Demos* 3.

McCarthy, C. (1999): "Regional Integration in sub-Saharan Africa: Past, Present, and Future" in A. Oyejide et al. (Eds). *Regional Integration and Trade Liberalization in sub-Saharan Africa.* London: McMillan Press.

McCarthy, C. (1995): "Regional Integration: Part of the Problem or Part of the Answer?" in S. Ellis (Ed). *Africa Now: People, Policies and Institutions.* London: James Currey.

McNeill, J. et. al. (1991): *Beyond Interdependence: Meshing of the World's Economy and the Earth's Ecology.* New York: Oxford University Press.

McQueen, M. (1998): "ACP-EU Trade Cooperation after 2000: An Assessment of Reciprocal Trade Preferences," *Journal of Modern African Studies* 38.

Meadows, D. *et. al.* (1972): *The Limits to Growth.* New York: Basic Books.

Mengisteab, K. (1996): *Globalization and Autocentricity in Africa's Development in the 21ˢᵗ Century.* Trenton NJ: Africa World Press.

Mikesell, R. (1988): "The Changing Demand for Raw Materials," in J. Sowell and S. Tucker (Eds). *Growth, Exports and Jobs in a Changing World Economy.* New Brunswick: Transaction Books.

Mistry, P. (1995): "Open Regionalism: Stepping Stone or Milestone Towards an Improved Multilateral System" in J. Teunissen (Ed). *Regionalism and the Global Economy: The Case of Latin America and the Caribbean.* The Hague: FONDAD.

Mitrany, D. (1966): *A Working Peace System.* Chicago: Quadrango Books.

Mittelman, J. (1999): "Rethinking the New Regionalism in the Context of Globalization" in B. Hettne, A. Inotai and O. Sunkel (Eds). *Comparing Regionalism: Implications for Global Development.* London: Macmillan.

Mkandawire T. and C. Soludo (1999): *Our Continent our Future.* Trenton NJ: Africa World Press.

Modelski, G. (1978): "The Long Cycle of Global Politics and the Nation-State," *Comparative Studies in Society and History* 20(2).

Mortimore, M. (1998): "Getting a Lift: Modernizing Industry by Way of Latin American Integration," *Transnational Corporation* 7(2).

Mrema, G. (2001): *Correspondence on the Association for Strengthening Agricultural Research in Eastern and Central Africa.* Entebbe: Kampala Press.

Mshomba, R. (1999): *Africa in the Global Economy.* Boulder CO: Lynne Rienner.

Mudenda, G. *et. al.* (1994): *Joint PTA/SADC Study on Harmonization, Rationalization, and Coordination of the Activities of the Preferential Trade Area for Eastern and Southern Africa (PTA) and SADC.* Harare: SAPES.

Mulat, T. (1998): "Multilaterialism and Africa's Regional Economic Communities," *Journal of World Trade* 32 (4).

Mulat, T. (1998): "The AEC Treaty, Trade Liberalization and Regional Integration" in OAU (Ed). *Trade Liberalization and Regional Integration: Proceedings of the Workshop on Trade Liberalization and Regional Integration.* OAU: Addis Ababa.

Munro, W. (1996): "Power, Peasants and Political Development: Reconsidering State Reconstruction in Africa," *Comparative Studies in Societies and History* 38 (1).

Myers, N. (1984): *The Primary Source: Tropical Forests and Our Future.* New York: Norton.

Mytelka, L. (1999): *Competition, Innovation and Competitiveness in Developing Countries.* Paris: OECD Development Center.

Mytelka, L. (1994): "Regional Cooperation and the New Logic of International Cooperation" in L. Mytelka (Ed). *South-South Cooperation in a Global Perspective.* Paris: OECD.

Mytelka, L. and S. Langdon (1979): "Africa in the Changing World Economy" in C. Legum (Ed). *Africa in the 1980s: A Continent in Crisis.* New York: McGraw-Hill.

Nayyar, D. (2002): "Cross-border Movements of People" in Nayyar, D. (Ed). *Governing Globalization: Issues and Institutions.* Oxford: Oxford University Press.

Ndiaye, B. (1990): "Prospects for Economic Integration in Africa" in P. Anyang' Nyong'o (Ed). *Regional Integration in Africa: Unfinished Agenda.* Nairobi: Academy Science Publishers.

NEPAD (2001): "The New Partnership for Africa's Development." OAU: Abuja.

Nkrumah, K. (1974): *Kwame Nkrumah.* London: Panaf.

Nkrumah, K. (1965): *Neo-Colonialism: The Last Stage of Imperialism.* London: Thomas Nelson and Sons.

Nyang'oro, J. (1999): "Hemmed in? The State in Africa and Global Liberalization" in D. Smith *et. al. State and Sovereignty in the Global Economy*. New York: Routledge.

Nyang'oro, J. (2000): "The African Growth and Opportunity Act of the United States," *Cooperation South* 2.

Nye, J. (2000): *Understanding International Conflicts: An Introduction to Theory and History.* 3rd Edition. Longman: Addison Wesley.

Nyerere, J. (1977): "The Process of Liberation," *New Outlook*. Dar es Salaam 5.

OAU (1981): *Lagos Plan of Action for the Economic Development of Africa 1980-2000.* Geneva: Institute of Labor Studies.

O'Brian, D. (1991): "The Show of State in a Neo-Colonial Twilight: Francophone Africa" in J. Manor (Ed). *Rethinking Third World Politics*. London: Longman.

O'Brian, K. (2000): "Private Military Companies and African Security" in A. Musah and J. Feyami (Eds). *Mercenaries: An African Security Dilemma*. London: Pluto Press.

Ohmae, K. (1985): *Triad Power: The Coming Shape of Global Competition*. New York: Free Press.

Ohmae, K. (1990): *The Borderless World: Power and Strategy in the International Economy*. London: Collins Press.

OECD (2001): *The DAC Journal: Development Cooperation Report*. Paris: OECD.

OECD (1998):. *Development Cooperation Reports*. Paris: OECD,.

OECD (1996a): *Globalization and Industry*. Paris: OECD.

OECD (1996b): *Shaping the 21st Century*. Paris: OECD.

Ohlson, T. and S. Stedman (1994): *The New is Not Yet Born: Conflict Resolution in Southern Africa*. Washington DC: Brookings Institution.

Olson, M. (1995): "Multilateral and Bilateral Trade Policies" in J. de Melo and A. Panagariya (Eds). *New Dimensions in Regional Integration*. New York: Cambridge University Press.

Olukoshi, A. and L. Laakso (Eds) (1996): *Challenges to the Nation States in Africa*. Uppsala: Nordiska Afrikainstitutet.

Omach, P. (2000): "The African Crisis Response Initiative: Domestic Politics and Convergence of National Interests," *African Affairs* 99 (394).

Onimode, B. (2000): *Africa in the World of the 21st Century*. Ibadan: Ibadan University.

Onimode, B. (1992): "African Cooperation and Regional Security" in O. Obasanjo and F. Moshi (Eds). *Africa: Rise to Challenge*. Abeukuta: Africa Leadership Forum.

Otieno, J. (1990): "The Experience of the African Development Bank in Financing Regional Integration Projects in Africa" in P. Anyang' Nyong'o (Ed). *Regional Integration in Africa: Unfinished Agenda*. Nairobi: Academy Science Publishers.

Otsuki, T. *et. al.* (2001): *A Race to the Top?: A Case Study of Food Safety Standards and African Exports*: The World Bank Policy Research Working Paper 2563. Washington DC: World Bank.

Ottaway, M. (1999): *Africa's New Leaders: Democracy or State Reconstruction?* Washington, D.C: Carnegie Endowment for International Peace.

Overbeek, H. (2000): "Globalization, Sovereignty, and International Regulation: Reshaping the Governance of International Migration" in B. Ghosh (Ed). *Managing Migration: Time for a New International Regime?* Oxford: Oxford University Press.

Oxfam International (2002): *Rigged Rules and Double Standards: Trade, Globalization, and the Fight against Poverty*. Oxfam: London.

Oxfam International (2000): "Globalization: Submission to the UK Government's White Paper on Globalization." http://oxfam.org.uk/policy/papers/global1a.htm,

Oxfam International (1998): *Making Debt Relief Work: A Test of Political Will*. Oxfam: London.

Parfitt, T. (1996): "The Decline of Eurafrica? Lomé Mid-term Review," *Review of African Political Economy* 67.

Petras, J. and H. Veltmeyer (2001): *Globalization Unmasked: Imperialism in the 21ˢᵗ Century*. London: Zed Books.

Petras, J. (1978): *Critical Perspectives on Imperialism and Social Class in the Third* World. New York: Monthly Review.

Pieterse, J. (2000): "Shaping Globalization" in Pieterse J. (ed). *Global Futures: Shaping Globalization*. London: Zed Press.

Pijl, K. (1998): *Transnational Classes and International Relations*. New York: Routledge.

Price-Smith, A. (2001): *The Health of Nations: Infectious Disease, Environmental Change and Their Effects on National Security and Development*. Cambridge: MIT Press.

Pfaff, W. (1995): "A New Colonialism? Europe Must Go Back to Africa," *Foreign Affairs* 74 (1).

Raffer, K. (1999): "Lomé or Not Lomé: The Future of European-ACP Cooperation" in M. Lister (Ed). *New Perspectives on the European Union Development Cooperation*. Boulder CO: Westview Press.

Ravenhill, J. (1993): "When Weakness is Strength: The Lomé IV Negotiations" in I. Zartman (Ed). *Europe and Africa: The New Phase*. Boulder CO: Lynne Rienner.

Ravenhill, J. (1985): "The Future of Eurafrica" in T. Shaw and O. Aluko (Eds). *Africa Projected: From Recession to Renaissance*. New York: St. Martin's Press.

Reed, D. (Ed) (1996): *Structural Adjustment, the Environment, and Sustainable Development*. London: Earthscan.

Reno, W. (2000): "Clandestine Economies, Violence and States in Africa," *Journal of International Affairs* 53 (2).

Reno, W. (1995): *Corruption and State Politics in Sierra Leone*. Cambridge: Cambridge University Press.

Riddell, R. (1999): "The End of Foreign Aid to Africa? Consensus about Donor Policies," *African Affairs* 98.

Robinson, C. (1981): *Dark Victory*. Madison: University of Wisconsin Press.

Robson, P. (1983): *Integration, Development and Equity: Economic Integration in West Africa*. London: George Allen and Unwin.

Rodney, W. (1972): *How Europe Underdeveloped Africa*. London: Bogle-L'Ouverture.

Rodrik, D. (2000): "Participatory Politics, Social Cooperation and Economic Stability," *Mimeo:* Harvard University.

Rodrik, D. (1999): *The New Global Economy and Developing Countries: Making Openness Work*. Washington DC: Overseas Development Council.

Rosen, E. (2002): *Making Sweatshops: The Globalization of the U.S. Apparel Industry*. Los Angeles: University of California Press.

Rotberg, R. (2002): "The Nature of Nation-States Failure," *The Washington Quarterly*.

Rugumamu, S. (2002): "Globalization and Marginalization in EU-African Relations in the Twenty-first Century" in Ikubolajeh Logan, B. (Ed). *Globalization, the Third World State and Poverty Alleviation in the Twenty-first Century*. Aldershot: Ashgate.

Rugumamu, S. (2001a): "Conflict Management in Africa : Diagnosis and Prescriptions" in Assefa, T et al. (Eds). *Globalization, Democracy and Development in Africa: Challenges and Prospects*. Addis Ababa: OSSREA.

Rugumamu, S. (2001b): "Globalization and Africa's Future: Towards Structural Stability, Integration and Sustainable Development," *AAPS Occasional Paper* 5(2) Harare, AAPS.

Rugumamu, S. (2001c): "State Sovereignty and Intervention in Africa," *Conflict Trends* No. 4.

Rugumamu, S. (2001d): "Africa's Debt Bondage: A Case for Total Cancellation" *Eastern and Southern Africa Research Review* 17(1).

Rugumamu, S. (2000): "New Partnership Agreement between ACP and EU: Unresolved Issues," *Cooperation South*, 2.

Rugumamu, S. (1999a) "Globalization, Liberalization and Africa's Marginalization," *AAPS Occasional Paper* 4 (1) Harare: AAPS.

Rugumamu, S. (1999b): "EU-ACP Partnership: An Appraisal," *Cooperation South* No. 2 December.

Rugumamu, S. (1997): Lethal Aid: The Illusion of Socialism and Self-Reliance in Tanzania. Trenton NJ: Africa World Press.

Ruigrok, W. and R. van Tulder. (1995): The Logic of International Restructuring. London: Routledge.

Rwegasira, D. (1996): "Economic Cooperation and Integration in Africa: Experiences, Challenges and Opportunities," *ADB Research Paper* No. 26.

Rweyemamu, J. (1973): Underdevelopment and Industrialization in Tanzania. Nairobi: Oxford University Press.

Sachs, J. (1998): "Stop Preaching" *Financial Times.*

Salim, A. (1992): OAU Report of the Secretary General on Conflicts in Africa. Addis Ababa: OAU.

Sandbrook, R. (1985): *The Politics of Africa's Economic Stagnation.* Cambridge: Cambridge University Press.

Sander, H. (1996): "Multilateralism, Regionalism and Globalization: The Challenge to the World Trading System" in Sander, H. and A. Inotai (Eds). *World Trade After the Uruguay Road.* London: Routledge.

Saul, J. and C. Leys (1999): "Sub-Saharan Africa in Global Capitalism," *Monthly Review* 51(3).

Scholte, J. (1999): "Security and Community in a Globalizing World" in C. Thomas and P Wilkin (Eds). *Globalization, Human Security and the African Experience.* Boulder, CO: Lynne Rienner.

Schwartz, P. (1991): *The Art of the Long View: Planning for the Future in an Uncertain World.* New York: Doubleday.

Senghaas, D. (1985): *The European Experience: A Historical Critique of Development Theory.* Dover NH: Berg Publishers.

Seton-Watson, H. (1977): *Nations and States: An Enquiry into the Origins of Nations and the Politics of Nationalism.* Boulder CO: Westview Press.

Shaw, T. (1995): "African Development in a Changing World Order" in B. Onimode and R. Synge (Eds). *Issues in African Development.* Ibadan: Heinemann Books.

Shaw, T. (1994): "The South in the New World (dis) Order: Towards a Political Economy of Third World Foreign Policy in the 1990s," *Third World Quarterly* 15(1).

Shaw, T. (1985): "Introduction: Are the 1980s Characterized by Crisis and/or Conjecture?" in T. Shaw. and O. Aluko (Eds). *Africa Projected.* New York: St. Martin's Press.

Shaw, T. (1982): "Introduction: The Political Economy of Africa's Futures" in T. Shaw (Ed). *Alternative Futures for Africa.* Boulder CO: Westview Press.

Shaw, T. (1982): "Africa's Futures: A Comparison of Forecasts" in T. Shaw. (Ed). Alternative Futures for Africa. Boulder CO: Westview Press.

Shaw, T. (1975): "Discontinuities and Inequalities in African International Politics," *International Journal* 30(3).

Sisk, T. (1995): "Institutional Capacity-Building for African Conflict Management" in D. Smoke and C. Crocker (Eds). Africa: *Conflict Resolution: The U.S. Role in Peacemaking.* Washington, DC: US Institute of Peace Press.

Smith, D. (1997): "Creative Destruction: Capitalist Development and China's Environment.", *New Left Review.*

Sonko, K. (1990): "Debt in the Eye of the Storm: The African Crisis in a Global Context," Africa Today 37(4).

Soresen, G. (1991): Democracy, Dictatorship and Development. London: Macmillan.

Soubra, Y. (1993): "Information Technology and International Competition in Construction Services: Opportunities and Challenges" in UNCTAD. *Information Technology and International Competitiveness: The Case of the Construction Service Industry.* New York: UNCTAD.

South Commission (1990): *The Challenge to the South.* Oxford: Oxford University Press.

Srinivasan, T.N. (1998): "Regionalism and the WTO: Is Non-Discrimination Passe?" in A. Krueger (Ed). *The WTO as an International Organization.* Chicago: Chicago University Press.

Stalker, P. (2000): *Workers Without Frontiers: The Impact of Globalization on International Migration.* Boulder, CO: Lynne Rienner.

Stein, H. (1992): "Iindustrialization, Adjustment, the World Bank and IMF in Africa," *World Development* 20(1).

Stonier, T. (1983): *The Wealth of Information: A Profile of Post-Industrial Economy.* London: Thames Methuen.

Takeyh, R. and Nicolas, G. (2002): "Do Terrorist Networks Need a Home?" *The Washington Quarterly* 25 (3.

Taylor, P. *et. al.* (1997): *Documents on Reform of the United Nations.* Brookfield VT: Dartmouth Publishing House.

Tandon, Y. (2000): "Globalization and Africa's Options" in D. Nabudere (Ed). *Globalization and the Post-Colonial African State.* Harare: AAPS Books.

Tandon, Y. (1982): "Who is the Ruling Class in the Semi-Colonies?" in Y. Tandon (Ed). *University of Dar es Salaam Debate on Class, State and Imperialism.* Dar es Salaam: Tanzania Publishing House.

Therborn, G. (1980): *The Power of Ideology and the Ideology of Power.* London: Verso.

Thomas, C. (1999): "Introduction" in Thomas C. and P. Wilkin (Eds). *Globalization, Human Security, and the African Experience.* Boulder CO: Lynne Rienner.

Thomas, C. (1994): "An Innovation-driven Model of Regional Cooperation" in L. Mytelka (Ed). *South-South Cooperation in a Global Perspective.* Paris: OECD.

Thomas, C. (1974): *Dependence and Transformation: The Economics of Transition to Socialism.* New York: Monthly Review Press.

Thompson, W. (1988): *On Global Wars: Historical-Structural Approaches to World Politics.* Columbia, SC: University of South Carolina Press.

Thorp, W. (1971): *The Reality of Foreign Aid.* New York: Praeger Publishers.

Thucydides (1951): *The Peloponnesian Wars: Book V* (Melian Dialogues). Translated by R. Crawley. New York: Random House.

Todaro, M. (1981): *Economic Development in the Third World.* 2nd Edition. New York: Longman.

Tordoff, W. (1998): *Government and Politics in Africa.* London: Macmillan Press.

Toye, J. and C. Jackson (1996): "Public Expenditure Policy and Poverty Reduction: Has The World Bank Got It Right?" *IDS Bulletin* 27 (1).

Toynebee, A. (1948): *Civilization on Trial.* New York: Oxford University Press.

Tsikata, Y. (2001): "Owning Economic Reform: A Comparative Study of Ghana and Tanzania," *Discussion Paper 2001/53.* Helsinki: UN University/WIDER.

Twitchett, C. (1978): "Toward a New ACP-EEC Convention," *The World Today* 34 (2).

UNAIDS and World Bank (2001): *Aids, Poverty Reduction and Debt Relief: Implications for Debt Reduction*. Washington DC: World Bank.

UNCTAD (2001): *Economic Development in Africa: Performance, Prospects and Policy Analysis*. New York and Geneva: UN.

UNCTAD (2000): *The Least Developed Countries 2000 Report*. Geneva: UN.

UNCTAD (2000): *Foreign Direct Investment in Africa: Performance and Potential*. New York: UNCTAD.

UNCTAD (1992): *Transnational Corporations as Engines of Growth*. New York: UNCTAD.

UNCTAD (1997): *World Investment Reports*. Geneva: UNCTAD.

UNDP (2001): *Human Development Reports*. New York: Oxford University Press.

UNHCR (1997): *State of the World Refugees: A Humanitarian Agenda*. New York: Oxford University Press.

UNRISD (1995): *States of Disarray: The Social Effects of Globalization*. Geneva: UNRISD.

U.S. Government (2002): *U.S. Homeland Security*. US Government: Department of Home Security.

Van de Walle, N. (2000): "Africa and the World Economy: Continued Marginalization or Re-engagement" in J. Harbeson and D. Rothchild (Eds). *Africa in World Politics: The African State System in Flux*. Boulder CO: Lynne Rienner.

Viner, J. (1937): *Studies in the Theory of International Trade*. London: Harper and Brothers.

Villalon, L. (1998): "The African State at the End of the 20th Century: Parameters of the Critical Conjucture" in L. Villalon and P. Huxtable (eds). *The African State at a Critical Conjucture*. Boulder CO: Lynne Rienner.

Walle, N.V. (1999): "Aid's Crisis of Legitimacy: Current Proposals and Future Prospects," *African Affairs*, 98.

Wallerstein, I. (1983): "The Three Instances of Hegemony in the History of the Capitalist World Economy," *International Journal of Comparative Sociology* 24 (1-2).

Wallerstein, I. (1979): *The Capitalist World Economy*. Cambridge: Cambridge University Press.

Wallerstein, I. (1974): *The Modern World System*, Vol. 1. New York: Academic Press.

Walters, M. (1995): *Globalization*. London: Routledge.

Wannacott, P. and M. Lutz. (1989): "Is there a Case for Free Trade Areas?," *Economic Impact* 69.

Watson, R. (Eds) (1996): *Climatic Change 1995: Impacts, Adaptations and Mitigations of Climatic Change: Scientific-Technical Analyses in Contributions of Working Group 11 to the Second Assessment Report of the Intergovernmental Panel of Climatic Change*. New York: Cambridge University Press.

Webb, M. and J. Fackler (1993): "Learning and the Time Interdependence of Costa Rican Exports," *Journal of Development Economics* 40.

Wienner, M. (1995): *Global Migration Crisis: Challenges to States and to Human Rights*. New York: Harper Collins.

Wertheim, W. (1992): "State and the Dialectics of Emancipation", *Development and Change* 23 (3).

Wilkin, P. (1999): "Human Security and Class in the Global Economy" in Thomas, C. and P. Wilkin (Eds). *Globalization, Human Security, and the African Experience*. Boulder, CO: Lynne Rienner.

World Bank (2002): *Globalization, Growth, and Poverty: Building an Inclusive World Economy*. World Bank Policy Research Report. World Bank: Oxford University Press.

World Bank (2001): *Africa Development Indicators*. Washington DC: World Bank.

World Bank (2000): *World Development Reports*. New York: Oxford University Press.

World Bank (2000): *Can Africa Claim the 21ˢᵗ Century?* Washington DC: The World Bank.

World Bank (1996a): *Social Dimensions of Structural Adjustment: World Bank Experience 1980-1993*. Washington DC: World Bank.

World Bank (1994): *Adjustment Africa: Reforms, Results and the Road Ahead*. New York: Oxford University Press.

World Bank (1989): *Sub-Saharan Africa: From Crisis to Sustainable Growth*. Washington DC: World Bank.

World Bank (1981): *An Accelerated Development in sub-Saharan Africa: Agenda for Action*. Washington D.C: World Bank.

World Watch Institute (1991): *The State of the World*. New York, WW Norton and Company.

Yeats, A. (1995): "What are OECD Trade Preferences Worth to sub-Saharan Africa?" *African Studies Review* 38(1).

Yeats, A. (1996): "What Caused sub-Saharan Africa's Marginalization in World Trade," *Finance and Development* 33(4).

Young, C. (1999): "The Third Wave of Democratization in Africa: Ambiguities and Contradictions" in R. Joseph (Ed). *State, Conflict, and Democracy in Africa*. Boulder CO: Lynne Rienner.

Young, C. (1994): "Democratization in Africa: Contradictions of Political Imperatives" in Widner, J. (Ed). *Economic Change and Political Liberalization in Africa*. Baltimore MD: The Johns Hopkins University.

Young, C. (1994): *The African Colonial State in Comparative Perspective*. New Haven: Yale University Press.

Subject Index

Printed in the United Kingdom
by Lightning Source UK Ltd.
115602UKS00001B/87